Second Edition

Essays

Thought and Style

Brian
Kellow

John
Krisak

Prentice Hall Ginn Canada
Scarborough, Ontario

Canadian Cataloguing in Publication Data
Main entry under title:

Essays : thought and style

2nd ed.
ISBN 0-13-378225-5

1. Readers—Essays. 2. Readers (Secondary).
3. English essays—20th century.
I. Kellow, Brian. II. Krisak, John.

PE1421.E77 1995   808.84   C95-932154-3

Prentice-Hall, Inc., Englewood Cliffs, New Jersey
Prentice-Hall International, Inc., London
Prentice-Hall of Australia, Pty., Ltd., Sydney
Prentice-Hall of India Pvt., Ltd., New Delhi
Prentice-Hall of Japan, Inc., Tokyo
Prentice-Hall of Southeast Asia (PTE) Ltd., Singapore
Editora Prentice-Hall do Brasil Ltda., Rio de Janeiro
Prentice-Hall Hispanoamericana, S.A., Mexico

ISBN 0-13-378225-5

Publisher: Donna MacCallum
Managing Editor: Linda McGuire
Editor: Karen Alliston
Production Co-ordinators: Stephanie Cox and Rose Marie Walsh
Art Director: Alex Li
Cover and Interior Design: Anne Goodes
Cover and Interior Photos: Ron Fehling
Permissions: Angelika Baur
Composition and Typesetting: Arlene Edgar

Printed and bound in Canada by Transcontinental Printing Inc.
  3 4 5 BG 2000

Policy Statement
Prentice Hall Ginn Canada and the authors of *Essays: Thought and Style,*
Second Edition are committed to the publication of instructional materials
that are as bias-free as possible. This anthology was evaluated for bias
prior to publication.

Contents

Writing to Observe   1

Labour Day is a Dreaded Bell in the
  Schoolyard of the Mind   *Harry Bruce*   3

Blasting Music to Drown Out Reality   *Sydney J. Harris*   7

You Can't Always Get Done What
  You Want   *Marjorie Kelly*   10

Living Like Weasels   *Annie Dillard*   15

Writing to Describe   21

Where the World Began   *Margaret Laurence*   23

Shyly Slipping a Poem from the Purse   *Bronwen Wallace*   30

Seven Wonders   *Lewis Thomas*   36

The Monster   *Deems Taylor*   43

Writing to Define   49

Faces of the Enemy   *Sam Keen*   51

Arks Can't Save Aardvarks   *Stan Rowe*   57

Marginal Men   *Barbara Ehrenreich*   63

In Bed   *Joan Didion*   68

Writing to Explain   75

The Leering That Has to Stop   *Ann Fuller*   77

Unreasonable Facsimile   *Frederick Allen*   81

The Same Ticking Clock   *Carol Shields*   87

"On a Field, Sable, the Letter A, Gules":
  Signs, Symbols, and Possession
  of Thought   *Neil McDonald*   92

Writing to Analyze a Process   103

Why Leaves Turn Color in the Fall   *Diane Ackerman*   105

Life as We Know It   *Michael Bérubé*   110

Deficits   *Michael Ignatieff*   122

Thunderstrokes and Firebolts   *Janice McEwan*   130

Imelda   *Richard Selzer*   138

Writing to Persuade   153

A Poet's Advice to Students   *e.e. cummings*   155
Pandora Was a Feminist   *Mary Meigs*   158
The Character of Hamlet's Mother   *Carolyn G. Heilbrun*   163
My Home Is Not Broken, It Works   *Carol Kleiman*   173
Individual Liberty and Public Control   *Bertrand Russell*   177
Institutionalized Racism and
    Canadian History   *Adrienne Shadd*   183

Writing to Reflect   191

In Selfish Pursuit   *Anthony Brandt*   193
Listening to Boredom   *Joseph Brodsky*   200
On Hating Piano Lessons   *Phyllis Theroux*   205
Welfare was a Life Raft, but Now
    We Can Swim   *Barbara Hager*   209
The Suit   *Norman Doidge*   213
Are There Any Questions?   *Robert Fulghum*   220

Writing to Inspire   227

Reply to the U.S. Government   *Chief Seattle*   229
Naked to Laughter when Leaves Fall   *Ray Guy*   234
Shakespeare, Prince of Light   *Pablo Neruda*   238
Tiananmen   *Maggie Helwig*   243
The Almond Trees   *Albert Camus*   247

On Writing an Essay   252
Exemplar Essay
The Time Factor   *Gloria Steinem*   259

Contents by Theme   262

Acknowledgments

This project has been enriched by the support of many people—colleagues, friends, and family whose help we would now like to acknowledge formally. Special thanks are also extended to the following people at Prentice Hall Ginn Canada, whose contributions to this book have been extensive and with whom we have worked so closely—Karen Alliston, Linda McGuire, and Donna MacCallum.

Brian Kellow
John Krisak

For Rebecca, Rachel, Leah, Tessa, Sarah, Geoffrey, Brian, and David

Prentice Hall Ginn Canada wishes to express its sincere appreciation to the following Canadian educators for contributing their time and expertise in reviewing this anthology.

Stephen D. Bailey, English Department Chair, Burnaby North Secondary School, Burnaby School District #41, British Columbia

Lynne Beckett, English Teacher, Lester B. Pearson Catholic High School, Carleton Roman Catholic School Board, Ontario

Jill Brindle, Assistant Head of English, Governor Simcoe Secondary School, Lincoln County Board of Education, Ontario

Carol E. Chandler, Supervisor of English/Language Arts, Halifax District School Board, Nova Scotia

Adrian Graham, Head of English and Drama, York Humber High School, Board of Education for the City of York, Ontario

A. Hodgins, English Teacher, Matthew McNair Senior Secondary School, Richmond School District #38, British Columbia

Helen Ible, English Teacher, W.P. Wagner School, Edmonton Public Schools, Alberta

Carol Mayne, English Teacher, St. Francis Xavier High School, Edmonton Catholic Schools, Alberta

Carl J. McLuhan, Assistant Head of English, John Fraser Secondary School, Peel Board of Education, Ontario

Robin Pearson, English Department Head, Bluevale Collegiate Institute, Waterloo County Board of Education, Ontario

Thelfa Yee-Toi, English Department Head, Campbell Collegiate, Regina Public School Board, Saskatchewan

Inclusion of a person in this list does not necessarily indicate endorsement of the text.

Preface

A fine essay expresses interesting thought in an engaging style. The thought can be on any subject; the style can be daring or restrained. In the excellent essay the reader hears the authentic voice of the practised and confident writer.

The essays in this collection deal with subjects ranging from weasels to poetry; from Shakespearean characters to AIDS posters; from Newfoundland to Tiananmen Square. Essays written with lyric intensity are balanced by those expressed in straightforward, concrete prose. This range of subjects and diversity of approaches will give the reader some indication of the adaptability of the essay genre.

The essays are grouped according to purposes for writing. Some essays define an issue or problem, while others describe, explain, or rhapsodize. The alternative listing of contents at the back of the book arranges the essays by theme.

The study questions and assignments are designed to illuminate both the thought and style of each essay. Thought questions help students develop their abilities to describe, summarize, analyze, and evaluate the ideas in the essays. Style and Structure questions direct students to scrutinize the language, sentence structure, and organization of the essays, and to identify their purpose, audience, and point of view. Response and Extension activities encourage students to respond personally, critically, and creatively to the essays. Unit Synthesis activities at the end of each unit ask students to make connections among the essays in the unit and to consider some of the broader issues that they address. Suggestions for comprehensive independent study projects and lists of further readings are also included.

Some of our favourite writers are here. We are envious of you who are discovering them for the first time.

Brian Kellow
John Krisak

Writing to Observe

I've been noticing lately how inept most of us are at judging time . . . . If we were as bad at estimating space as we are at estimating time, we'd be crashing into the furniture and dropping coffee cups off our desks.

Marjorie Kelly

Labour Day is a Dreaded Bell in the Schoolyard of the Mind

Harry Bruce

Labour Day was like a sniff of the woods or a glimpse of the sea before they led you down to the dungeon. All other statutory holidays were an escape from school. Labour Day was its entrance, the stairway to an aeon of misery, a last meal, a last drag on a cigarette. At a cabin on a widening of the dark Magnetawan River, I'd sometimes smell Labour Day's deadly gloom as early as mid-August. While birch crackled in the kitchen stove and pancakes sizzled at breakfast, while I played rummy by coal-oil lantern or knocked about in a leaky punt under singing trees, while I routed the evil sheriff in my own Sherwood Forest, and even as I lifted a forkful of home-made raspberry pie to my mouth, a cold bell might ring in the far schoolyard of my mind. It was a signal. Now, Labour Day was yawning, getting to its feet, slouching toward me. It would take me back. All this would end.

I hated school. If Tom Hansen, 24, of Boulder, Colorado, wins his $350,000-suit against his mother and father for ruining his life with "psychological malparenting," I'm going to hit the Toronto education authorities for the psychological malteaching they put me through. School was hot, degrading, boring and occasionally terrifying, a house of despair in which big tyrants tormented small victims. The teachers, like prison guards, knew society wanted their institutions to be unpleasant for us inmates; and the worst punishment they could inflict, next to The Strap, was a "detention." It was an order to do extra time in the hole (school).

The vocabulary of discipline and insult, the smell of chalk and ink and old chewing gum, the feel of the hardwood bench under your haunches, the sickening realization that things would be this way till the end of an inconceivably distant June . . . all these awaited us on the morning after going to bed on Labour Day. After Christmas, kids asked one another, "Wud ya get?" After Labour Day, they asked, "*Who'd* ya get?" I'd say, "Mr. Such-and-such" or "Miss So-and-so." In a cruel flash, I'd learned the name and scowl of the adult who would dominate my daylight hours for ten months to come; and the other kid always replied, "You poor sucker."

Good morning, Miss Authoritarian. Good-bye, bonfires on the beach. Hello there, line-ups, marching in columns of two, standing stiffly at attention, sitting with your hands folded on your desk, keeping your trap shut. Good-bye picnics on the flat, sun-baked stone of deserted islands, good-bye blackberry bushes in bee-loud glades. Hello, scribbler and ruler. Good-bye, cry of the loon, depredations of the racoon, sunburn at noon, and hide-and-seek by the light of the moon. Good morning, *sir*.

There's another side to the Labour Day story, of course. Sadly, slowly, as though he were savouring the last moments of our crashing shore in Nova Scotia, an old friend from Toronto folded his tent, loaded his van. The Labour Day weekend had started, and he had 1,300 miles to drive. "Why not stick around a few days?" I said. "Can't," he grunted. "Got to be in class Tuesday morning." My friend is a high-school teacher. "Jeez, I hate Labour Day," he said, and rumbled out of my life for a few more seasons.

Labour Day is the prelude to work, and the death of play. Down at the Canadian National Exhibition, the unions are on parade. Out around the country, traffic fatalities mount. Thousands of family cars mournfully crawl away from wilderness retreats to city duties. Thousands of guitars, hibachis, sleeping bags, bathing suits, car-top boats, golf clubs and fishing poles are city-bound. Thousands of young lovers wonder if, ever again in another summer, they'll see the golden partners with whom they've recently lost their virginity. Will he, or she, really write? Can a fair-weather romance survive the killer winter? Camps close, and board up the season. Hotels cut their rates, and banish staff. Is that tree dead, or is it just that its leaves have already begun to turn? The chestnuts ripen. The days are shorter, and the nights cooler. Labour Day is a bummer.

Earlier than I needed to know, it taught me that no summer ever repeats itself, friendships must die, good times must always end, and the years melt people and beloved places. Of all holidays, Labour Day is the one that makes you grow up. And feel old. Nowadays, I dislike it more than ever.

Thought

1. In small groups, compare your feelings about Labour Day with those of Harry Bruce. How relevant to your own experience are the metaphors he uses for school?

2. Did the author's anecdote about his friend the teacher surprise you? Explain.

3. "Of all holidays, Labour Day is the one that makes you grow up." Explain in your own words what this statement means to you.

Style and Structure

4. a) How does the opening sentence establish the tone of the essay?
   b) Show how the author's point of view effectively creates this tone.

5. How does Bruce make effective use of contrast in the fourth paragraph?

6. Choose three of the author's observations and show how they lead directly to his final comments.

7. In what ways does the tone of the concluding paragraph contrast with that of the introduction? Explain this shift by tracing the development of the essay.

8. "Slouching toward me" and "bee-loud glades" are both allusions to poems by W. B. Yeats. List other instances of figurative language in this essay, and describe their effectiveness in conveying Bruce's thought.

Response and Extension

9. Write a letter to yourself explaining how this school year will be different from all previous years. Seal the letter in an envelope and do not open it until the last day of class.

10. Using Bruce's essay as your model, write about a time when you've dreaded an imminent change in your life. What did the experience teach you?

11. Write a personal essay for your school newspaper in which you explain what represents the end of summer for you. Try to use some of Bruce's writing techniques (e.g. contrast, parallel structure, rhetorical questions, short sentences for special effect) to develop your own thought.

12. In groups, devise a different calendar for the school year. Present it to the class, justifying the changes you have made.

13. Choose a line or image from the essay with which you most strongly identify. Write a personal response that describes your connection to this thought.

Blasting Music to Drown Out Reality

Sydney J. Harris

The contractor sent around two sullen, slack-jawed young assistants to do some repair work on the tennis court across the road. They brought with them, inevitably, as standard equipment for the job, a powerful portable radio which kept blasting away for a full afternoon.

Call me any ugly word you will, such as snobbish or elitist, it remains my firm and unshakeable opinion that such people are as close to the moronic line as it is possible to get and still function in a social order. The tolerance for a high decibel rate, masquerading as "music," is in my opinion inversely proportional to the level of intelligence.

I can understand the need for what my children call elevator music in some factories or even restaurants, to keep the help from falling asleep or brooding on the essential monotony of their jobs. It is less pardonable in dentists' offices and such, but there it is at least relatively soft and easily ignored.

But these young men are working in August among grass and flowers and birds and birch trees, with a lovely view of the water and the cliffs and everything you might want to feast your senses on; instead, they anesthetized themselves with the junkiest of junk music throughout this God-given afternoon in a serenely sylvan setting.

My own theory is that people such as that turn on the radio not to bring something in, but to shut something out. It is not in order to hear the music, but in order that the vacuum in their minds may be soothed by sound, so that silence does not force them into thinking about themselves or experiencing the real world of perception and sensation. And basically, what they want to shut out is the reality of their existence. This urge, almost a compulsion, to keep reality at arm's length is nearly pandemic in our society. It accounts not only for the incessant, frenetic music, but also for the drugs, the booze, the sports mania, the television addiction, the intense preoccupation with trivia—all of which act as opiates, dulling any sense of reality.

Marx's harsh dictum of the last century can almost be turned upside down today to read: "Opium is the religion of the people." And nowhere—not even in drugs or booze—can this be more clearly seen than in the kind of music spewing forth from portables and automobile radios and most hi-fi sets.

Music began as a celebration of nature and an exploration of the human spirit. Bach elevates us, Mozart delights us, Beethoven deepens us; all bring us closer to the wellsprings of life. Now this great gift has been turned against itself, blasting forth a cacophony to dull and deaden and dehumanize the soul.

Thought

1. Why do you think some people feel the need to dull their sense of reality?
2. a) What is the thesis of this essay?
   b) Do you think the author supports his thesis convincingly? Explain.
3. Does the author's conclusion proceed logically from his argument? Explain.

Style and Structure

4. For whom (to what audience) is the author writing? How do you know?
5. Show how the author's diction reveals his bias.
6. Quote two sentences from the essay that you think are judgmental, and explain why.
7. What does Harris's "appeal to authority" reveal about his taste in music?

Response and Extension

8. In groups discuss the importance that you attach to: music, silence, thought, boredom. You may wish to read Joseph Brodsky's essay, "Listening to Boredom" (p. 200), for broader perspective. Develop a short audio or audio-visual presentation as a summary of the observations and comments from your discussion.

9. **a)** Develop a thesis based on your observations of the relation of
    i) portable radios and tape players with headphones
    ii) radios and tape players used in public places without headphones

    to issues of

    iii) personal space
    iv) public space
    v) individual rights
    vi) collective rights.

    b) Write a personal essay that develops this thesis.

10. Present a short biography of one of the composers Harris mentions. As part of your presentation, play selections from the composer's music.

11. Write a personal essay that rebuts Harris's argument. Include your own specific observations about what significance music has for you.

12. For discussion: Loud music can be considered an enhancement of the imagination, rather than a suppression of the real.

You Can't Always Get Done What You Want

Marjorie Kelly

I've been noticing lately how inept most of us are at judging time. A project expected to take a half day takes two full days. The meeting scheduled for two hours needs three. I mean, really: If my colleagues and I were as bad at estimating space as we are at estimating time, we'd be crashing into the furniture and dropping coffee cups off our desks.

When it comes to time, we always seem to be on the side of optimism: Like infants reaching for the moon, we imagine something is within our grasp when in reality it is far beyond reach. And we go crashing about as a result. "I'll write these three letters this morning," I tell myself. Crash. I get one done. "I'll have those two articles edited by the end of the day," a fellow editor tells me. Crash. It takes him into next week. Yet each day we go on making our plans (promises, predictions) with little awareness of how inaccurate they so often prove to be. We seem to believe each day anew that *this* time we'll get it all done, *this* time we'll make the hours conform to our wishes. Our faith in our ability to control the future might be touching if it weren't so absurd.

And lately I've begun asking myself: What on earth is going on here? Since so many of us make the same errors so routinely, I've begun to think there's something at work beyond our own personal mistakes—something deeper, or more basic. I suspect it has something to do with the way we conceptualize time.

In a curious way, our awkwardness at "moving" through time makes sense, if we think of ourselves as new to the dimension of time, as infants are new to spatial reality. For it's only since Einstein that we have come to speak of time as a fourth dimension added to the three dimensions of space. And the four-dimensional reality, as break-throughs in the new physics and other fields of science show, is vastly different from our old view of the world, in ways that we have barely begun to assimilate.

When we think of time, most of us function unconsciously in the linear way of thinking that has dominated Western thought since the time of Isaac Newton and René Descartes: imagining time to be a forward movement of orderly and unchanging cadence—hours, days, months, years—laid out like a grid upon our lives. Trusting this to be a valid picture of time, we naturally approach time management as the task of inserting appropriate tasks into appropriate slots. And when our days fail to follow such orderly paths, unfolding instead in chaotic and unpredictable ways, we think ourselves undisciplined. We blame ourselves, rarely thinking that our worldview might be askew.

But it may be that the discomfort we feel, trying to operate in a linear view of time, isn't a mistake but a clue. Instead of seeing our unpredictable days as aberrations, we might examine them for the information we need to conceptualize time more accurately—much as the unpredictable behavior of subatomic particles led physicists into the new world of quantum reality. Instead of feeling guilty about our personal chaos, we might learn from it, looking to find the larger patterns that science now tells us govern even the unpredictability of chaos.

In examining my own experience of time, I've made a number of observations. The first is that time is not uniform, as the old clockwork worldview tells us, but instead unfolds in its own way—unpredictable in a daily sense, but ordered in some larger way. Time has its own topography, with all sorts of different terrain that is not marked on the temporal maps of our calendars and schedule books. I've come to recognize, for example, that there are days that carry me forward like a stream downhill: On these days every call I make connects, all my conversations are wonderful, and projects I've been working on click together effortlessly. I try to get a lot done these days, because I know that what I start is likely to be finished successfully. Such days, you might say, are like valleys in which time flows smoothly.

But there are also rocky and mountainous days: the days when I can't get anyone on the phone, bad news comes in the mail, and deals that were 99 percent done evaporate before my eyes. I consciously avoid making important calls or decisions on these days, and when I leave the office I drive with special caution—because I know these are times I'm more likely to have an accident or get a ticket.

Why time operates like this I don't know, but I've seen it often enough in my own life and the lives of others to recognize it. Yet our culture is ill-equipped to see such patterns in any systematic way. And this inability to recognize the differences in "identical" slots of time may be, I suspect, one reason our schedules so often fail.

A second observation about time struck me one afternoon a few months back, when a fellow editor and I were facing a stack of manuscripts that needed to be edited that day. We had used up more than half our time on just one article, and we stared glumly at the remaining pile—believing, instinctively, that the best way to get through them was to plow ahead without stopping. After all, as our watches told us, we had a fixed amount of time, and a fixed amount of work to fit into that slot, so taking a break would *subtract* from the time available. Time is a matter of mathematics, right? But it didn't work that way. Exhausted and stiff, we decided to take a walk along a nearby creek—and though we came back feeling slightly naughty, we also felt refreshed and clear. Much to our astonishment, we flew through the rest of the editing in an hour. The moral of the story, you might say, is that when you're traveling the terrain of time, the shortest distance between two points may be a detour.

All this is not to say, of course, that linear time is no longer a useful concept—only that it is a less than complete description of how we experience time. Physicist Fred Alan Wolf, in *The Eagle's Quest*, refers to linear time as "chronos"—the clock time that rules the world of thinking. But he points also to another kind of time, which he terms "mythos"—the seamless sense of events flowing together into the larger story of our lives, which we experience through our intuitive feelings.

We might think of mythos as the pattern in which chronos is imbedded. And when we misjudge time, it may not be that we're misjudging chronos ("I didn't allow enough time for that task"), but that we're somehow misreading the human mythos. For while chronos has to do with hours on a clock face, mythos has to do with relationships: to each other, to our bodies, to the world.

Through observations like these, we might see time not as a linear path moving toward the future, but as the unfolding motion of a whole system. We might conceptualize time as the medium in which we can see the motion of the larger whole—the movement that demonstrates to us, over and over again, that nothing really is separate from anything else. This might serve as a reminder that beneath the urgency of our machinelike days—filled with to-do lists and rigid schedules with which we "manage" time—there is something else at work: a rhythm, a movement carrying us along, and we move with it, whether we realize it or not.

As difficult as it is for us Westerners to accept, managing our time may not be possible in any total sense. Just as in any day there is both dark and light, in time there must be both order and disorder. Perhaps our real task is to find balance between acceptance and control: to learn to read the topography of time and accept what it holds in store—even unwelcome chaos—but at the same time to find ways within the larger order to exercise our own will.

Perhaps the chaos so many of us feel isn't a problem but an opening, a door into a new relationship to time, where only half our task is getting life to do what we want it to do. The other half is discovering where life itself wants us to go.

Thought

1. In groups, discuss the ways in which you conceptualize time. Do Kelly's observations correspond to your own experiences?

2. Do you agree with Kelly's assertion that "when we think of time, most of us function unconsciously in the linear way of thinking"? Explain.

3. Evaluate the accuracy of Kelly's observation that "time is not uniform."

4. According to Fred Alan Wolf, what is the difference between "chronos" and "mythos"?

Style and Structure

5. Construct an outline of Kelly's essay, then identify the various parts of her argument using the following terms: thesis, support, development, and conclusion.

6. a) Select two anecdotes from Kelly's essay and explain how she uses them to develop her thesis.

   b) What impact do her anecdotes have upon the tone of the essay?

7. How does Kelly's analogy in the second paragraph work to underscore her thesis?

8. Consider Kelly's "appeal to authority." In small groups, assess what this strategy contributes to the essay.

9. Comment on the effectiveness of Kelly's use of transitional words and phrases in the first sentence of each paragraph.

Response and Extension

10. Discuss in groups whether or not one can "move" through time.

11. Examine the author's diction for indications that time has a spatial dimension. Make a list, then explain the idea of space contained in three of these references.

12. Based on your observations, compose some of your own similes and metaphors describing time.

13. Place an analog wristwatch on your desk beside a digital chronometer. Discuss the various assumptions about the nature of time conveyed by each of these measurement tools.

14. If watches, clocks, calendars, and daybooks distinguish patterns in "chronos," what instruments have humans devised to measure "mythos"?

15. Write a narrative account of your experience of "mythos," with particular reference to photographs and other memorabilia.

Living Like Weasels

Annie Dillard

A **weasel** is wild. Who knows what he thinks? He sleeps in his underground den, his tail draped over his nose. Sometimes he lives in his den for two days without leaving. Outside, he stalks rabbits, mice, muskrats, and birds, killing more bodies than he can eat warm, and often dragging the carcasses home. Obedient to instinct, he bites his prey at the neck, either splitting the jugular vein at the throat or crunching the brain at the base of the skull, and he does not let go. One naturalist refused to kill a weasel who was socketed into his hand deeply as a rattlesnake. The man could in no way pry the tiny weasel off, and he had to walk half a mile to water, the weasel dangling from his palm, and soak him off like a stubborn label.

And once, says Ernest Thompson Seton—once, a man shot an eagle out of the sky. He examined the eagle and found the dry skull of a weasel fixed by the jaws to his throat. The supposition is that the eagle had pounced on the weasel and the weasel swiveled and bit as instinct taught him, tooth to neck, and nearly won. I would like to have seen that eagle from the air a few weeks or months before he was shot: was the whole weasel still attached to his feathered throat, a fur pendant? Or did the eagle eat what he could reach, gutting the living weasel with his talons before his breast, bending his beak, cleaning the beautiful airborne bones?

I have been reading about weasels because I saw one last week. I startled a weasel who startled me, and we exchanged a long glance.

Twenty minutes from my house, through the woods by the quarry and across the highway, is Hollins Pond, a remarkable piece of shallowness, where I like to go at sunset and sit on a tree trunk. Hollins Pond is also called Murray's Pond; it covers two acres of bottomland near Tinker Creek with six inches of water and six thousand lily pads. In winter, brown-and-white steers stand in the middle of it, merely dampening their hooves; from the distant shore they look like miracle itself, complete with miracle's nonchalance. Now, in summer, the steers are gone. The water lilies have blossomed and spread to a green horizontal plane that is terra firma to plodding blackbirds, and tremulous ceiling to black leeches, crayfish, and carp.

This is, mind you, suburbia. It is a five-minute walk in three directions to rows of houses, though none is visible here. There's a 55 mph highway at one end of the pond, and a nesting pair of wood ducks at the other. Under every bush is a muskrat hole or a beer can. The far end is an alternating series of fields and woods, fields and woods, threaded everywhere with motorcycle tracks—in whose bare clay wild turtles lay eggs.

So. I had crossed the highway, stepped over two low barbed-wire fences, and traced the motorcycle path in all gratitude through the wild rose and poison ivy of the pond's shoreline up into high grassy fields. Then I cut down through the woods to the mossy fallen tree where I sit. This tree is excellent. It makes a dry, upholstered bench at the upper, marshy end of the pond, a plush jetty raised from the thorny shore between a shallow blue body of water and a deep blue body of sky.

The sun had just set. I was relaxed on the tree trunk, ensconced in the lap of lichen, watching the lily pads at my feet tremble and part dreamily over the thrusting path of a carp. A yellow bird appeared to my right and flew behind me. It caught my eye; I swiveled around— and the next instant, inexplicably, I was looking down at a weasel, who was looking up at me.

Weasel! I'd never seen one wild before. He was ten inches long, thin as a curve, a muscled ribbon, brown as fruitwood, soft-furred, alert. His face was fierce, small and pointed as a lizard's; he would have made a good arrowhead. There was just a dot of chin, maybe two brown hairs' worth, and then the pure white fur began that spread down his underside. He had two black eyes I didn't see, any more than you see a window.

The weasel was stunned into stillness as he was emerging from beneath an enormous shaggy wild rose bush four feet away. I was stunned into stillness twisted backward on the tree trunk. Our eyes locked, and someone threw away the key.

Our look was as if two lovers, or deadly enemies, met unexpectedly on an overgrown path when each had been thinking of something else: a clearing blow to the gut. It was also a bright blow to the brain, or a sudden beating of brains, with all the charge and intimate grate of rubbed balloons. It emptied our lungs. It felled the forest, moved the fields, and drained the pond; the world dismantled and tumbled into that black hole of eyes. If you and I looked at each other that way, our skulls would split and drop to our shoulders. But we don't. We keep our skulls. So.

He disappeared. This was only last week, and already I don't remember what shattered the enchantment. I think I blinked, I think I retrieved my brain from the weasel's brain, and tried to memorize what I was seeing, and the weasel felt the yank of separation, the careening splashdown into real life and the urgent current of instinct. He vanished under the wild rose. I waited motionless, my mind suddenly full of data and my spirit with pleadings, but he didn't return.

Please do not tell me about "approach-avoidance conflicts." I tell you I've been in that weasel's brain for sixty seconds, and he was in mine. Brains are private places, muttering through unique and secret tapes—but the weasel and I both plugged into another tape simultaneously, for a sweet and shocking time. Can I help it if it was a blank?

What goes on in his brain the rest of the time? What does a weasel think about? He won't say. His journal is tracks in clay, a spray of feathers, mouse blood and bone: uncollected, unconnected, loose-leaf, and blown.

I would like to learn, or remember, how to live. I come to Hollins Pond not so much to learn how to live as, frankly, to forget about it. That is, I don't think I can learn from a wild animal how to live in particular—shall I suck warm blood, hold my tail high, walk with my footprints precisely over the prints of my hands?—but I might learn something of mindlessness, something of the purity of living in the physical senses and the dignity of living without bias or motive. The weasel lives in necessity and we live in choice, hating necessity and dying at the last ignobly in its talons. I would like to live as I should, as the weasel lives as he should. And I suspect that for me the way is like the weasel's: open to time and death painlessly, noticing everything, remembering nothing, choosing the given with a fierce and pointed will.

I missed my chance. I should have gone for the throat. I should have lunged for that streak of white under the weasel's chin and held on, held on through mud and into the wild rose, held on for a dearer life. We could live under the wild rose wild as weasels, mute and uncomprehending. I could very calmly go wild. I could live two days in the den, curled, leaning on mouse fur, sniffing bird bones, blinking, licking, breathing musk, my hair tangled in the roots of grasses. Down is a good place to go, where the mind is single. Down is out, out of your ever-loving mind and back to your careless senses. I remember muteness as a prolonged and giddy fast, where every moment is a feast of utterance received. Time and events are merely poured, unremarked, and ingested directly, like blood pulsed into my gut through a jugular vein. Could two live that way? Could two live under the wild rose, and explore by the pond, so that the smooth mind of each is as everywhere present to the other, and as received and as unchallenged, as falling snow?

We could, you know. We can live any way we want. People take vows of poverty, chastity, and obedience—even of silence—by choice. The thing is to stalk your calling in a certain skilled and supple way, to locate the most tender and live spot and plug into that pulse. This is yielding, not fighting. A weasel doesn't "attack" anything; a weasel lives as he's meant to, yielding at every moment to the perfect freedom of single necessity.

I think it would be well, and proper, and obedient, and pure, to grasp your one necessity and not let it go, to dangle from it limp wherever it takes you. Then even death, where you're going no matter how you live, cannot you part. Seize it and let it seize you up aloft even, till your eyes burn out and drop; let your musky flesh fall off in shreds, and let your very bones unhinge and scatter, loosened over fields, over fields and woods, lightly, thoughtless, from any height at all, from as high as eagles.

| Thought

1. What attracts the author to Hollins Pond?

2. What does the author hope to learn from the weasel? Explain.

3. Distinguish between necessity and choice. Show how Dillard uses the weasel to exemplify necessity.

Style and Structure

4. Explain how Dillard uses the personal anecdote to entice the reader deeper into her own personal thoughts.

5. Show how Dillard develops the anecdote of the eagle to unify her essay.

6. In groups, choose sentences from the essay that are simultaneously outward-looking and inward-looking. How do these sentences serve to develop the theme?

7. Write a brief essay on Dillard's diction. Show how it reveals a very clear portrait of the author.

8. Explain how Dillard's phrase, "the perfect freedom of necessity," functions as a paradox.

Response and Extension

9. In your journal, speculate on Dillard's suggestion that we should be "living like weasels."
   a) What are the external forces that work against this kind of life, and the interior forces that work toward it?
   b) What is your own "calling," your "one necessity"—and where do you think it might lead you?

10. Compose an essay in which you recount a personal anecdote about an encounter with some element of nature. Develop this anecdote into a reflection on your own interior life. What did you discover about yourself through this experience?

11. If you could choose only one animal as a metaphor for human behaviour, which animal would you choose? Explain.

12. "I missed my chance." Read D. H. Lawrence's poem "Snake." Compare Dillard's response with Lawrence's when he says, "I missed my chance with one of the lords of life."

Unit Synthesis

1. Harry Bruce and Sydney J. Harris are both columnists. In what ways are their essays similar? Over a set period of time, search through newspapers and magazines and collect columns that interest you. How do each of these pieces demonstrate the author's particular powers of observation? How are their observations influenced by their viewpoints?

2. Make a list of the various expressions involving time, for example "time line" and "time consuming." What do each of these expressions reveal about how time is conceptualized?

3. Talk to some people older than yourself about time, including their experience of the dread of anticipation; of work time; of what it means to live "open to time and death painlessly." How does their conception of time differ from your own?

4. The essays in this unit all address questions of compulsion, choice, and responsiveness to the requirements of the moment. Explain how you can apply Annie Dillard's phrase, "the perfect freedom of necessity," to each of the other three essays.

5. Write a narrative account of the way you would spend a perfect day: a day free from necessity.

6. After considering two or more of the essays in this section, explain the importance—to both writer and reader—of observation via the senses.

Suggested Readings

Calvino, Italo *Time and the Hunter*
Costain, Thomas B. *Below the Salt*
Dillard, Annie *Pilgrim at Tinker Creek; Teaching a Stone to Talk; An American Childhood*
du Maurier, Daphne *The House on the Strand*
Finney, Jack *Time and Again*
Hawking, Stephen *A Brief History of Time*
Marquez, Gabriel Garcia *A Hundred Years of Solitude*
Woolf, Virginia *Orlando*

Writing to Describe

I did not know then that I would carry the land and town all my life within my skull, that they would form the mainspring and source of the writing I was to do; wherever and however far away I might live.

Margaret Laurence

Where the World Began

Margaret Laurence

A **strange** place it was, that place where the world began. A place of incredible happenings, splendours and revelations, despairs like multitudinous pits of isolated hells. A place of shadow-spookiness, inhabited by the unknowable dead. A place of jubilation and of mourning, horrible and beautiful.

It was, in fact, a small prairie town.

Because that settlement and that land were my first and for many years my only real knowledge of this planet, in some profound way they remain my world, my way of viewing. My eyes were formed there. Towns like ours, set in a sea of land, have been described thousands of times as dull, bleak, flat, uninteresting. I have had it said to me that the railway trip across Canada is spectacular, except for the prairies, when it would be desirable to go to sleep for several days, until the ordeal is over. I am always unable to argue this point effectively. All I can say is—well, you really have to live there to know that country. The town of my childhood could be called bizarre, agonizingly repressive or cruel at times, and the land in which it grew could be called harsh in the violence of its seasonal changes. But never merely flat or uninteresting. Never dull.

In winter, we used to hitch rides on the back of the milk sleigh, our moccasins squeaking and slithering on the hard rutted snow of the roads, our hands in ice-bubbled mitts hanging onto the box edge of the sleigh for dear life, while Bert grinned at us through his great frosted moustache and shouted the horse into speed, daring us to stay put. Those mornings, rising, there would be the perpetual fascination of the frost feathers on windows, the ferns and flowers and eerie faces traced there during the night by unseen artists of the wind. Evenings, coming back from skating, the sky would be black but not dark, for you could see a cold glitter of stars from one side of the earth's rim to the other. And then the sometime astonishment when you saw the Northern Lights flaring across the sky, like the scrawled signature of God. After a blizzard, when the snowploughs hadn't yet got through, school would be closed for the day, the assumption being that the town's young could not possibly flounder through five feet of snow in the pursuit of education. We would then gaily don snowshoes and flounder for miles out into the white dazzling deserts, in pursuit of a different kind of knowing. If you came back too close to night, through the woods at the foot of the town hill, the thin black branches of poplar and chokecherry now meringued with frost, sometimes you heard coyotes. Or maybe the banshee wolf-voices were really only inside your head.

Summers were scorching, and when no rain came and the wheat became bleached and dried before it headed, the faces of farmers and townsfolk would not smile much, and you took for granted, because it never seemed to have been any different, the frequent knocking at the back door and the young men standing there, mumbling or thrusting defiantly their requests for a drink of water and a sandwich if you could spare it. They were riding the freights, and you never knew where they had come from, or where they might end up, if anywhere. The Drought and Depression were like evil deities which had been there always. You understood and did not understand.

Yet the outside world had its continuing marvels. The poplar bluffs and the small river were filled and surrounded with a zillion different grasses, stones, and weed flowers. The meadowlarks sang undaunted from the twanging telephone wires along the gravel highway. Once we found an old flat-bottomed scow, and launched her, poling along the shallow brown waters, mending her with wodges of hastily chewed Spearmint, grounding her among the tangles of yellow marsh marigolds that grew succulently along the banks of the shrunken river, while the sun made our skins smell dusty-warm.

My best friend lived in an apartment above some stores on Main Street (its real name was Mountain Avenue, goodness knows why), an elegant apartment with royal-blue velvet curtains. The back roof, scarcely sloping at all, was corrugated tin, of a furnace-like warmth on a July afternoon, and we would sit there drinking lemonade and looking across the back lane at the Fire Hall. Sometimes our vigil would be rewarded. Oh joy! Somebody's house burning down! We had an almost-perfect callousness in some ways. Then the wooden tower's bronze bell would clonk and toll like a thousand speeded funerals in a time of plague, and in a few minutes the team of giant black horses would cannon forth, pulling the fire wagon like some scarlet chariot of the Goths, while the firemen clung with one hand, adjusting their helmets as they went.

The oddities of the place were endless. An elderly lady used to serve, as her afternoon tea offering to other ladies, soda biscuits spread with peanut butter and topped with a whole marshmallow. Some considered this slightly eccentric, when compared with chopped egg sandwiches, and admittedly talked about her behind her back, but no one ever refused these delicacies or indicated to her that they thought she had slipped a cog. Another lady dyed her hair a bright and cheery orange, by strangers often mistaken at twenty paces for a feather hat. My own beloved stepmother wore a silver fox neckpiece, a whole pelt, *with the embalmed (?) head still on*. My Ontario Irish grandfather said, "sparrow grass," a more interesting term than asparagus. The town dump was known as the "nuisance grounds," a phrase fraught with weird connotations, as though the effluvia of our lives was beneath contempt but at the same time was subtly threatening to the determined and sometimes hysterical propriety of our ways.

Some oddities were, as idiom had it, "funny ha ha"; others were "funny peculiar." Some were not so very funny at all. An old man lived, deranged, in a shack in the valley. Perhaps he wasn't even all that old, but to us he seemed a wild Methuselah figure, shambling among the underbrush and the tall couchgrass, muttering indecipherable curses or blessings, a prophet who had forgotten his prophesies. Everyone in town knew him, but no one knew him. He lived among us as though only occasionally and momentarily visible. The kids called him Andy Gump, and feared him. Some sought to prove their bravery by tormenting him. They were the medieval bear baiters, and he the lumbering bewildered bear, half blind, only rarely turning to snarl. Everything is to be found in a town like mine. Belsen, writ small but with the same ink.

All of us cast stones in one shape or another. In grade school, among the vulnerable and violet girls we were, the feared and despised were those few older girls from what was charmingly termed "the wrong side of the tracks." Tough in talk and tougher in muscle, they were said to be whores already. And may have been, that being about the only profession readily available to them.

The dead lived in that place, too. Not only the grandparents who had, in local parlance, "passed on" and who gloomed, bearded or bonneted, from the sepia photographs in old albums, but also the uncles, forever eighteen or nineteen, whose names were carved on the granite family stones in the cemetery, but whose bones lay in France. My own young mother lay in that graveyard, beside other dead of our kin, and when I was ten, my father, too, only forty, left the living town for the dead dwelling on the hill.

When I was eighteen, I couldn't wait to get out of that town, away from the prairies. I did not know then that I would carry the land and town all my life within my skull, that they would form the mainspring and source of the writing I was to do; wherever and however far away I might live.

This was my territory in the time of my youth, and in a sense my life since then has been an attempt to look at it, to come to terms with it. Stultifying to the mind it certainly could be, and sometimes was, but not to the imagination. It was many things, but it was never dull.

The same, I now see, could be said for Canada in general. Why on earth did generations of Canadians pretend to believe this country dull? We knew perfectly well it wasn't. Yet for so long we did not proclaim what we knew. If our upsurge of so-called nationalism seems odd or irrelevant to outsiders, and even to some of our own people (*what's all the fuss about?*), they might try to understand that for many years we valued ourselves insufficiently, living as we did under the huge shadows of those two dominating figures, Uncle Sam and Britannia. We have only just begun to value ourselves, our land, our abilities. We have only just begun to recognize our legends and to give shape to our myths.

There are, God knows, enough aspects to deplore about this country. When I see the killing of our lakes and rivers with industrial wastes, I feel rage and despair. When I see our industries and natural resources increasingly taken over by America, I feel an overwhelming discouragement, especially as I cannot simply say "damn Yankees." It should never be forgotten that it is we ourselves who have sold such a large amount of our birthright for a mess of plastic

Progress. When I saw the War Measures Act being invoked in 1970, I lost forever the vestigial remains of the naive wish-belief that repression could not happen here, or would not. And yet, of course, I had known all along in the deepest and often hidden caves of the heart that anything can happen anywhere, for the seeds of both man's freedom and his captivity are found everywhere, even in the microcosm of a prairie town. But in raging against our injustices, our stupidities, I do so as *family*, as I did, and still do in writing, about those aspects of my town which I hated and which are always in some ways aspects of myself.

The land still draws me more than other lands. I have lived in Africa and in England, but splendid as both can be, they do not have the power to move in the same way as, for example, that part of southern Ontario where I spent four months last summer in a cedar cabin beside a river. "Scratch a Canadian, and you find a phony pioneer," I used to say to myself in warning. But all the same it is true, I think, that we are not yet totally alienated from physical earth, and let us only pray we do not become so. I once thought that my lifelong fear and mistrust of cities made me a kind of old-fashioned freak; now I see it differently.

The cabin has a long window across its front western wall, and sitting at the oak table there in the mornings, I used to look out at the river and at the tall trees beyond, green-gold in the early light. The river was bronze; the sun caught it strangely, reflecting upon its surface the near-shore sand ripples underneath. Suddenly, the crescenting of a fish, gone before the eye could clearly give image to it. The old man next door said these leaping fish were carp. Himself, he preferred muskie, for he was a real fisherman and the muskie gave him a fight. The wind most often blew from the south, and the river flowed toward the south, so when the water was wind-riffled, and the current was strong, the river seemed to be flowing both ways. I liked this, and interpreted it as an omen, a natural symbol.

A few years ago, when I was back in Winnipeg, I gave a talk at my old college. It was open to the public, and afterward a very old man came up to me and asked me if my maiden name had been Wemyss. I said yes, thinking he might have known my father or my grandfather. But no. "When I was a young lad," he said, "I once worked for your great-grandfather, Robert Wemyss, when he had the sheep ranch at

Raeburn." I think that was a moment when I realized all over again something of great importance to me. My long-ago families came from Scotland and Ireland, but in a sense that no longer mattered so much. My true roots were here.

I am not very patriotic, in the usual meaning of that word. I cannot say "My country right or wrong" in any political, social or literary context. But one thing is inalterable, for better or worse, for life.

This is where my world began. A world which includes the ancestors—both my own and other people's ancestors who become mine. A world which formed me, and continues to do so, even while I fought it in some of its aspects, and continue to do so. A world which gave me my own lifework to do, because it was here that I learned the sight of my own particular eyes.

Thought

1. What does Laurence mean by the last words in her essay, "It was here that I learned the sight of my own particular eyes"?

2. **a)** How has Laurence caught a characteristic of childhood in her phrase, "You understood and did not understand"?
   b) To which anecdotes about her home town would this phrase best apply? Explain why.

3. Evaluate Laurence's attempt to show the following:
   a) "Everything is to be found in a town like mine."
   b) "Stultifying to the mind it certainly could be, and sometimes was, but not to the imagination."

Style and Structure

4. Analyze the rhetorical effect produced by the first two paragraphs.

5. Divide the essay into its various sections, according to each shift in focus. Why does the author arrange the sections in this manner?

6. Using several examples, demonstrate how Laurence's use of figurative language evokes a unique and colourful place.

Response and Extension

7. For discussion: "Why on earth did generations of Canadians pretend to believe this country dull? We knew perfectly well it wasn't."

8. Write a descriptive essay that evokes the place of your childhood. Focus on a time from your past when you felt your neighbourhood or town was the whole world. Describe that world, using precise details and vivid imagery. If you can, populate your essay with some colourful characters.

9. Create a photo essay which captures a sense of "place" that is significant to you.

10. Read one of Margaret Laurence's "Manawaka" novels. Write an essay comparing the author's descriptions of Manawaka with that of the town depicted in "Where the World Began."

11. Read "Reply to the U.S. Government" (p. 229) by Chief Seattle. Compare and contrast the attitudes of Chief Seattle and Margaret Laurence to the lands of their birth.

Shyly Slipping a Poem from the Purse

Bronwen Wallace

Okay out there, get ready. This is another piece about poetry. I can't help it. July is poetry month for me. I've been teaching at the Upper Canada Writers' Workshop in Kingston, Ontario for two weeks and now at the Summer School of the Arts for St. Lawrence College in Brockville. I think poetry and eat it and dream it and if I have a few minutes to weed my garden, I tell my plants about it too. I don't know if it's the poems or the mulch, but my cucumbers are doing fine.

Anyway, poetry. Most people I know think they hate it or that they don't understand it or that poetry is only written (and understood) by strange beings who sit around drinking black coffee and staring moodily at the moon.

At the same time—and this to me is stranger and more wonderful than the most obscure poem ever written—most people I know have written at least one poem in their lives. I mean, everybody. Supermarket checkout clerks and kindergarten kids and plumbers and taxi drivers and housewives and prison guards and police officers and nurses and babies. Everywhere I go, as soon as people ask me what I do for a living and I say "write poetry," I know what will happen next. A shy smile, first. Then a little giggle or a cough. Then, very softly, "Well I wrote a poem once too. Do you think you could read it?" And out of the pocket or the purse or the school scribbler or the memory will come a poem.

So what am I to make of all this? What do I make of the fact that every year, all over this country, all sorts of unlikely people, from stockbrokers to strippers, come out of the closet for a week or so at some workshop somewhere and reveal themselves as (blush, stammer) poets. The very same people—and you must understand this to understand how truly amazing this situation is—the very same people who might, in other situations say that they didn't understand poetry at all.

It would seem that we are a nation of poets too shy to admit it.

Let's get back to the bit about not understanding poetry, though. Why do we imagine that we don't? My own feeling is that some of this happens because of the way poetry is taught, when it is taught, in schools. There's a strong tendency to treat poetry as a problem that has to be solved, about something no ordinary mortal could understand, rather than as a communication from one human being to another, full of feelings and hopes and wishes and dreams that everyone shares, one way or another.

What I like about poetry is the economy of its communication, the way it uses the surprises of an image to say what it takes most of us paragraphs to say. In a poem called "When You Go Away," for example, W. S. Merwin says everything about the pain of being left and how hard it is to talk about it in two lines:

My words are the garment of what I shall never be
Like the tucked sleeve of a one-armed boy.

Besides being taught as a problem, the poetry we teach our children in school tends to ignore the fact that real poetry happens everywhere all the time, in every age. I meet hundreds of high-school students every year who say they hate poetry. When I ask them what they've read, they mention the usual classics—Keats, Shakespeare, Milton, etc. All great poets, true, but not the way to start enjoying poetry when you're fifteen. These same people listen to Talking Heads, David Bowie, Bruce Springsteen, and Kate Bush—all of whom are sophisticated, complex lyricists—with no trouble at all. In reading poetry, it seems to me we should follow the rule we have for writing poetry: Start with what you know, with what you love, and see where it takes you. Anyone who ignores rock and roll as a major 20th century poetic form is ignoring the energy, the surprise, the passion that is the basis of all good poetry in any age.

That's one problem. Another is the idea that poetry has to be about Great Themes without really thinking about what those Great Themes are. In the past, when most poems were written by white, upper-class men, both the content and the style, which were strong in classical references and biblical themes, reflected their world view as if it were the world view. The resistance that students have to this poetry is real and legitimate. To continue to teach this poetry as the only good poetry cuts us off from all sorts of other possibilities.

One example of other possibilities is the work of poet Tom Wayman. Wayman has constantly and quite rightly pointed out that one of the themes missing from the classical poetry of the past is that of work. One of the contributions that Wayman has made to Canadian poetry is to collect poems about work from other people. He has published several anthologies of work poetry. The best two are *A Government Job at Last* and *Going for Coffee*. Both contain wonderfully energetic examples of modern poetry written by ordinary people as well as established poets:

"Sometimes I pretend I'm stupid," writes cab-driver David Beaver in a poem called "Love Goes Out of Style," "and satisfied with the life / of a cabbie / After all, I tell myself / where else is there to go / that you haven't been to / at least twice today."

And British Columbia fisherman Kevin Roberts writes: "the fish come in dancing / iridescent / dark torpedoes / flurry of silver / spray / as they jump."

"Some day I'm gonna stand up on my desk / take all my clothes off / and hurl the typewriter at your head," begins a poem by secretary Diedre Gallagher. "Someday, I'm gonna claim compensation / for mind rot / and soul destruction."

In some countries—Nicaragua, for example—poets like Ernesto Cardinale and Chilean poet Pablo Neruda are national heroes. Everyone can recite some of their work. Their pictures appear on the streets and at large rallies. In other countries—Chile, El Salvador, Hungary, Guatemala—poets are imprisoned, sometimes tortured. Both these facts are testimonies to the power of poetry, to the fact that it manages to speak a truth and to demand a response in a way that no other art form can.

In our country we don't jail our poets, but we do silence them in other ways. We tend to say that poetry about work, poetry about women, by people of color, dub poetry (which is poetry that grows out of the language and music of West Indian people in Canada) is not "real" poetry. As a result, we deprive ourselves and our children of a whole world—and of their place in it.

A friend lends me an anthology of literature by women with disabilities, *With Wings*. I open it to a poem called "Diminishment" by Nancy Mairs, a woman whose disability is multiple sclerosis:

My body
is going away
It fades
to the transparency
of rubbed amber
held against the sun.
It shrinks
it grows quiet.
Small, quiet
it is a cold
and heavy
smoothed stone.
Who will have it
when it lies
pale and polished
as a clean bone?

What I want to know is why this poem does not appear in the anthologies we use in our high schools. Why can it only be found in an anthology by and about women with disabilities? What does that say about us as a society? What are we afraid of?

The poets themselves are not afraid. Every year I see them by the dozens. Some of them will end up being published poets some day. Many more will never do that, and what's more they don't care. They just want to write the poem for the joy of it, the sheer joy and power of making sense of their lives in words, on paper. Getting it down. Getting down to it.

The other evening I took some time off from poetry workshops to attend a party at a friend's house near Sydenham. Her four-year-old son Nicholas takes me for a walk. It's just about dark, a beautiful, still evening, the fire-flies are out and Nick has his sword with him just in case we run into dragons, which, as he and I know, are everywhere. Nick is telling me how he has a father and his father has a father, and his father has a father and how everyone has a mother too and some people have brothers and step-brothers and sisters and pets.

"It's all connected, you see," he says, taking my hand. "Dogs and frogs and cartoons and candy and fathers and sisters and dragons and everything. Everyone's different and it's all connected."

He pauses to let me take this in.

"And that," he says quietly just as the sun slips, finally, down, "that is why the world is such an exciting place."

See what I mean? Everyone's a poet.

Thought

1. According to the author, how is poetry being taught in school? How does her experience compare with your own? Explain.

2. Evaluate the author's recommendations for the way poetry should be taught in school. Justify your assessment.

3. What does Wallace imply about the way Canadians treat poets? Do you think she is correct? Why or why not?

Style and Structure

4. In this short essay the author quotes five poets. Explore what each quotation contributes to the development of the ideas contained within the essay.

5. Show that the anecdote about Nick is a fitting conclusion to this piece.

6. Explain how the author's diction and sentence structure establish the conversational tone of her essay.

7. Has Wallace succeeded in using an inviting tone to make the subject of her essay that much more involving? Explain.

Response and Extension

8. Are you one of those people whom Wallace describes, with a secret poem tucked away in a safe place? Bring in one of your poems and read it to your group.

9. Attend a poetry reading at your local library; invite a poet to your class to read his or her work; or hold a poetry reading of your own.

10. Read a collection of poems by Bronwen Wallace. Write an analysis of one or more of her poems, linking it to her views on poetry expressed in this essay.

11. Organize a poetry reading rotation in which every student will be responsible for reading a poem to the class over the course of the next thirty days.

12. Begin to compile a personal anthology of poems that are meaningful to you.

Seven Wonders

Lewis Thomas

A while ago I received a letter from a magazine editor inviting me to join six other people at dinner to make a list of the Seven Wonders of the Modern World, to replace the seven old, out-of-date Wonders. I replied that I couldn't manage it, not on short order anyway, but still the question keeps hanging around in the lobby of my mind. I had to look up the old biodegradable Wonders, the Hanging Gardens of Babylon and all the rest, and then I had to look up that word "wonder" to make sure I understood what it meant. It occurred to me that if the magazine could get any seven people to agree on a list of any such seven things you'd have the modern Seven Wonders right there at the dinner table.

Wonder is a word to wonder about. It contains a mixture of messages: something marvelous and miraculous, surprising, raising unanswerable questions about itself, making the observer wonder, even raising skeptical questions like, "I *wonder* about that." Miraculous and marvelous are clues; both words come from an ancient Indo-European root meaning simply to smile or to laugh. Anything wonderful is something to smile in the presence of, in admiration (which, by the way, comes from the same root, along with, of all telling words, "mirror").

I decided to try making a list, not for the magazine's dinner party but for this occasion: seven things I wonder about the most.

I shall hold the first for the last, and move along.

My Number Two Wonder is a bacterial species never seen on the face of the earth until 1982, creatures never dreamed of before, living violation of what we used to regard as the laws of nature, things literally straight out of Hell. Or anyway what we used to think of as Hell, the hot unlivable interior of the earth. Such regions have recently come into scientific view from the research submarines designed to descend twenty-five hundred meters or more to the edge of deep holes in the sea bottom, where open vents spew superheated seawater in plumes from chimneys in the earth's crust, known to oceanographic scientists as "black smokers." This is not just hot water, or steam, or even steam under pressure as exists in a laboratory autoclave (which we have relied upon for decades as the surest way to destroy all microbial life). This is extremely hot water under extremely high pressure, with temperatures in excess of 300 degrees centigrade. At such heat, the existence of life as we know it would be simply inconceivable. Proteins and DNA would fall apart, enzymes would melt away, anything alive would die instantaneously. We have long since ruled out the possibility of life on Venus because of that planet's comparable temperature; we have ruled out the possibility of life in the earliest years of this planet, four billion or so years ago, on the same ground.

B.J.A. Baross and J.W. Deming have recently discovered the presence of thriving colonies of bacteria in water fished directly from these deep-sea vents. Moreover, when brought to the surface, encased in titanium syringes and sealed in pressurized chambers heated to 250 degrees centigrade, the bacteria not only survive but reproduce themselves enthusiastically. They can be killed only by chilling them down in boiling water.

And yet they look just like ordinary bacteria. Under the electron microscope they have the same essential structure—cell walls, ribosomes, and all. If they were, as is now being suggested, the original archebacteria, ancestors of us all, how did they or their progeny ever learn to cool down? I cannot think of a more wonderful trick.

My Number Three Wonder is *oncideres*, a species of beetle encountered by a pathologist friend of mine who lives in Houston and has a lot of mimosa trees in his backyard. This beetle is not new, but it qualifies as a Modern Wonder because of the exceedingly modern questions raised for evolutionary biologists about the three consecutive things on the mind of the female of the species. Her first thought is for a mimosa tree, which she finds and climbs, ignoring all other kinds of trees in the vicinity. Her second thought is for the laying of eggs, which she does by crawling out on a limb, cutting a longitudinal slit with her mandible and depositing her eggs beneath the slit. Her third and last thought concerns the welfare of her offspring; beetle larvae cannot survive in live wood, so she backs up a foot or so and cuts a neat circular girdle all around the limb, through the bark and down into the cambium. It takes her eight hours to finish this cabinetwork. Then she leaves and where she goes I do not know. The limb dies from the girdling, falls to the ground in the next breeze, the larvae feed and grow into the next generation, and the questions lie there unanswered. How on earth did these three linked thoughts in her mind evolve together in evolution? How could any one of the three become fixed as beetle behavior by itself, without the other two? What are the odds favoring three totally separate bits of behavior—like a particular tree, cutting a slit for eggs, and then girdling the limb—happening together by random chance among a beetle's genes? Does this smart beetle know what she is doing? And how did the mimosa tree enter the picture in its evolution? Left to themselves, unpruned, mimosa trees have a life expectancy of twenty-five to thirty years. Pruned each year, which is what the beetle's girdling labor accomplishes, the tree can flourish for a century. The mimosa-beetle relationship is an elegant example of symbiotic partnership, a phenomenon now recognized as pervasive in nature. It is good for us to have around on our intellectual mantelpiece such creatures as this insect and its friend the tree, for they keep reminding us how little we know about nature.

The Fourth Wonder on my list is an infectious agent known as the scrapie virus, which causes a fatal disease of the brain in sheep, goats, and several laboratory animals. A close cousin of scrapie is the C-J virus, the cause of some cases of senile dementia in human beings. These are called "slow viruses," for the excellent reason that an animal exposed to infection today will not become ill until a year and a half or two years from today. The agent, whatever it is, can propagate itself in abundance from a few infectious units today to more than a billion next year. I use the phrase "whatever it is" advisedly. Nobody has yet been able to find any DNA or RNA in the scrapie or C-J viruses. It may be there, but if so it exists in amounts too small to detect. Meanwhile there is plenty of protein, leading to a serious proposal that the virus may indeed be all protein. But protein, so far as we know, does not replicate itself all by itself, not on this planet anyway. Looked at this way, the scrapie agent seems the strangest thing in all biology and, until someone in some laboratory figures out what it is, a candidate for Modern Wonder.

My Fifth Wonder is the olfactory receptor cell, located in the epithelial tissue high in the nose, sniffing the air for clues to the environment, the fragrance of friends, the smell of leaf smoke, breakfast, nighttime and bedtime, and a rose, even, it is said, the odor of sanctity. The cell that does all these things, firing off urgent messages into the deepest parts of the brain, switching on one strange unaccountable memory after another, is itself a proper brain cell, a certified neuron belonging to the brain but miles away out in the open air, nosing around the world. How it manages to make sense of what it senses, discriminating between jasmine and anything else non-jasmine with infallibility, is one of the deep secrets of neurobiology. This would be wonder enough, but there is more. This population of brain cells, unlike any other neurons of the vertebrate central nervous system, turns itself over every few weeks; cells wear out, die, and are replaced by brand-new cells rewired to the same deep centers miles back in the brain, sensing and remembering the same wonderful smells. If and when we reach an understanding of these cells and their functions, including the moods and whims under their governance, we will know a lot more about the mind than we do now, a world away.

Sixth on my list is, I hesitate to say, another insect, the termite. This time, though, it is not the single insect that is the Wonder, it is the collectivity. There is nothing at all wonderful about a single, solitary termite, indeed there is really no such creature, functionally speaking, as a lone termite, any more than we can imagine a genuinely solitary human being; no such thing. Two or three termites gathered together on a dish are not much better; they may move about and touch each other nervously, but nothing happens. But keep adding more termites until they reach a critical mass, and then the miracle begins. As though they had suddenly received a piece of extraordinary news, they organize in platoons and begin stacking up pellets to precisely the right height, then turning the arches to connect the columns, constructing the cathedral and its chambers in which the colony will live out its life for the decades ahead, air-conditioned and humidity-controlled, following the chemical blueprint coded in their genes, flawlessly, stone-blind. They are not the dense mass of individual insects they appear to be; they are an organism, a thoughtful, meditative brain on a million legs. All we really know about this new thing is that it does its architecture and engineering by a complex system of chemical signals.

The Seventh Wonder of the modern world is a human child, any child. I used to wonder about childhood and the evolution of our species. It seemed to me unparsimonious to keep expending all that energy on such a long period of vulnerability and defenselessness, with nothing to show for it, in biological terms, beyond the feckless, irresponsible pleasure of childhood. After all, I used to think, it is one sixth of a whole human life span! Why didn't our evolution take care of that, allowing us to jump catlike from our juvenile to our adult (and, as I thought) productive stage of life? I had forgotten about language, the single human trait that marks us out as specifically human, the property that enables our survival as the most compulsively, biologically, obsessively social of all creatures on earth, more interdependent and interconnected even than the famous social insects. I had forgotten that, and forgotten that children *do* that in childhood. Language is what childhood is for.

There is another related but different creature, nothing like so wonderful as a human child, nothing like so hopeful, something to worry about all day and all night. It is us, aggregated together in our collective, critical masses. So far, we have learned how to be useful to each other only when we collect in small groups—families, circles of friends, once in a while (although still rarely) committees. The drive to be useful is encoded in our genes. But when we gather in very large numbers, as in the modern nation-state, we seem capable of levels of folly and self-destruction to be found nowhere else in all Nature.

As a species, taking all in all, we are still too young, too juvenile, to be trusted. We have spread across the face of the earth in just a few thousand years, no time at all as evolution clocks time, covering all livable parts of the planet, endangering other forms of life, and now threatening ourselves. As a species, we have everything in the world to learn about living, but we may be running out of time. Provisionally, but only provisionally, we are a Wonder.

And now the first on my list, the one I put off at the beginning of making a list, the first of all Wonders of the modern world. To name this one, you have to redefine the world as it has indeed been redefined in this most scientific of all centuries. We named the place we live in the world long ago, from the Indo-European root *wiros*, which meant man. We now live in the whole universe, that stupefying piece of expanding geometry. Our suburbs are the local solar system, into which, sooner or later, we will spread life, and then, likely, beyond into the galaxy. Of all celestial bodies within reach or view, as far as we can see, out to the edge, the most wonderful and marvelous and mysterious is turning out to be our own planet earth. There is nothing to match it anywhere, not yet anyway.

It is a living system, an immense organism, still developing, regulating itself, making its own oxygen, maintaining its own temperature, keeping all its infinite living parts connected and interdependent, including us. It is the strangest of all places, and there is everything in the world to learn about it. It can keep us awake and jubilant with questions for millennia ahead, if we can learn not to meddle and not to destroy. Our great hope is in being such a young species, thinking in language only a short while, still learning, still growing up.

We are not like the social insects. They have only the one way of doing things and they will do it forever, coded for that way. We are coded differently, not just for binary choices, go or *no-go*. We can go four ways at once, depending on how the air feels: *go, no-go*, but also *maybe*, plus *what the hell let's give it a try*. We are in for one surprise after another if we keep at it and keep alive. We can build structures for human society never seen before, thoughts never thought before, music never heard before.

Provided we do not kill ourselves off, and provided we can connect ourselves by the affection and respect for which I believe our genes are also coded, there is no end to what we might do on or off this planet.

At this early stage in our evolution, now through our infancy and into our childhood and then, with luck, our growing up, what our species needs most of all, right now, is simply a future.

Thought

1. List Thomas's seven wonders.
   a) What criteria have determined his choices?
   b) What does this tell you about the author?

2. Do you agree with Thomas that "language is what childhood is for"? Explain your answer.

3. "The world will never starve for want of wonders, but only for want of wonder" (G. K. Chesterton). What do you think accounts for a shortage of wonder in a person? Consider both external and internal factors.

Style and Structure

4. How would your response to this essay be different if Thomas hadn't written his two introductory paragraphs? Explain the function of these paragraphs.

5. Which of Thomas's seven wonders do you find most interesting? How has Thomas made its description interesting to you?

6. Why does the author discuss his first "wonder" last?

7. Explain the relationship between the three concluding paragraphs and the rest of the essay.

Response and Extension

8. a) List your own seven wonders.
   b) Write a description of one of these wonders, making sure that you incorporate your reasons for choosing it.

9. Research the seven wonders of the ancient world.
   a) Do they strike you as "wonderful"? Why or why not?
   b) How do they compare to the sort of wonders that Thomas has described? How do they compare to your own?

10. Write a journal entry about some of the things that you wonder about. These could range from the small, everyday puzzlements to the larger questions about life. Try to be as clear and evocative as you can, both in your description of each wonder and in your reasons for wondering about it.

11. Many of Thomas's wonders are derived from nature. List wonders from other spheres, for example, inventions, music, technology, pre-eminent writers, composers, or scientists. Research one of these wonders and share your findings with the class.

The Monster

Deems Taylor

He was an undersized little man, with a head too big for his body—a sickly little man. His nerves were bad. He had skin trouble. It was agony for him to wear anything next to his skin coarser than silk. And he had delusions of grandeur.

He was a monster of conceit. Never for one minute did he look at the world or at people, except in relation to himself. He was not only the most important person in the world, to himself; in his own eyes he was the only person who existed. He believed himself to be one of the greatest dramatists in the world, one of the greatest thinkers, and one of the greatest composers. To hear him talk he was Shakespeare, and Beethoven, and Plato, rolled into one. And you would have had no difficulty in hearing him talk. He was one of the most exhausting conversationalists that ever lived. An evening with him was an evening spent in listening to a monologue. Sometimes he was brilliant; sometimes he was maddeningly tiresome. But whether he was being brilliant or dull, he had one sole topic of conversation: himself. What *he* thought and what *he* did.

He had a mania for being in the right. The slightest hint of disagreement, from anyone, on the most trivial point, was enough to set him off on a harangue that might last for hours, in which he proved himself right in so many ways, and with such exhausting volubility, that in the end his hearer, stunned and deafened, would agree with him for the sake of peace.

It never occurred to him that he and his doing were not of the most intense and fascinating interest to anyone with whom he came in contact. He had theories about almost any subject under the sun, including vegetarianism, the drama, politics, and music; and in

43

support of these theories he wrote pamphlets, letters, books . . . thousands upon thousands of words, hundreds and hundreds of pages. He not only wrote these things, and published them—usually at somebody else's expense—but he would sit and read them aloud, for hours, to his friends and his family.

He wrote operas; and no sooner did he have the synopsis of a story, but he would invite—or rather summon—a crowd of his friends to his house and read it aloud to them. Not for criticism. For applause. When the complete poem was written, the friends had to come again, and hear that read aloud. Then he would publish the poem, sometimes years before the music that went with it was written. He played the piano like a composer, in the worst sense of what that implies, and he would sit down at the piano before parties that included some of the finest pianists of his time, and play for them, by the hour, his own music, needless to say. He had a composer's voice. And he would invite eminent vocalists to his house, and sing them his operas, taking all the parts.

He had the emotional stability of a six-year-old child. When he felt out of sorts, he would rave and stamp, or sink into suicidal gloom and talk darkly of going to the East to end his days as a Buddhist monk. Ten minutes later, when something pleased him, he would rush out of doors and run around the garden, or jump up and down on the sofa, or stand on his head. He could be grief-stricken over the death of a pet dog, and he could be callous and heartless to a degree that would have made a Roman emperor shudder.

He was almost innocent of any sense of responsibility. Not only did he seem incapable of supporting himself, but it never occurred to him that he was under any obligation to do so. He was convinced that the world owed him a living. In support of this belief, he borrowed money from everybody who was good for a loan—men, women, friends, or strangers. He wrote begging letters by the score, sometimes groveling without shame, at others loftily offering his intended benefactor the privilege of contributing to his support, and being mortally offended if the recipient declined the honour. I have found no record of his ever paying or repaying money to anyone who did not have a legal claim upon it.

What money he could lay his hands on he spent like an Indian rajah. The mere prospect of a performance of one of his operas was enough to set him running up bills amounting to ten times the amount of his prospective royalties. On an income that would reduce a more scrupulous man to doing his own laundry, he would keep two servants. Without enough money in his pocket to pay his rent, he would have the walls and ceiling of his study lined with pink silk. No one will ever know—certainly he never knew—how much money he owed. We do know that his greatest benefactor gave him 6,000 dollars to pay the most pressing of his debts in one city, and a year later had to give him 16,000 dollars to enable him to live in another city without being thrown into jail for debt.

He was equally unscrupulous in other ways. An endless procession of women marches through his life. His first wife spent twenty years enduring and forgiving his infidelities. His second wife had been the wife of his most devoted friend and admirer, from whom he stole her. And even while he was trying to persuade her to leave her first husband he was writing to a friend to inquire whether he could suggest some wealthy woman—*any* wealthy woman—whom he could marry for her money.

He was completely selfish in his other personal relationships. His liking for his friends was measured solely by the completeness of their devotion to him, or by their usefulness to him, whether financial or artistic. The minute they failed him—even by so much as refusing a dinner invitation—or began to lessen in usefulness, he cast them off without a second thought. At the end of his life he had exactly one friend left whom he had known even in middle age.

He had a genius for making enemies. He would insult a man who disagreed with him about the weather. He would pull endless wires in order to meet some man who admired his work, and was able and anxious to be of use to him—and would proceed to make a mortal enemy of him with some idiotic and wholly uncalled-for exhibition of arrogance and bad manners. A character in one of his operas was a caricature of one of the most powerful music critics of his day. Not content with burlesquing him, he invited the critic to his house and read him the libretto aloud in front of his friends.

The name of this monster was Richard Wagner. Everything that I have said about him you can find on record—in newspapers, in police reports, in the testimony of people who knew him, in his own letters, between the lines of his autobiography. And the curious thing about this record is that it doesn't matter in the least.

Because this undersized, sickly, disagreeable, fascinating little man was right all the time. The joke was on us. He was one of the world's great dramatists; he was a great thinker; he was one of the most stupendous musical geniuses that, up to now, the world has ever seen. The world did owe him a living. People couldn't know those things at the time, I suppose; and yet to us, who know his music, it does seem as though they should have known. What if he did talk about himself all the time? If he talked about himself for twenty-four hours every day for the span of his life he would not have uttered half the number of words that other men have spoken and written about him since his death.

When you consider what he wrote—thirteen operas and music dramas, eleven of them still holding the stage, eight of them unquestionably worth ranking among the world's great musico-dramatic masterpieces—when you listen to what he wrote, the debts and heartaches that people had to endure from him don't seem much of a price. Eduard Hanslick, the critic whom he caricatured in *Die Meistersinger* and who hated him ever after, now lives only because he was caricatured in *Die Meistersinger*. The women whose hearts he broke are long since dead; and the man who could never love anyone but himself has made them deathless atonement, I think, with *Tristan und Isolde*. Think of the luxury with which for a time, at least, fate rewarded Napoleon, the man who ruined France and looted Europe; and then perhaps you will agree that a few thousand dollars' worth of debts were not too heavy a price to pay for the Ring trilogy.

What if he was faithless to his friends and to his wives? He had one mistress to whom he was faithful to the day of his death: music. Not for a single moment did he ever compromise with what he believed, with what he dreamed. There is not a line of his music that could have been conceived by a little mind. Even when he is dull, or downright bad, he is dull in the grand manner. There is a greatness about his worst mistakes. Listening to his music, one does not forgive him for what he may or may not have been. It is not a matter of forgiveness. It is a matter of being dumb with wonder that his poor brain and body didn't burst under the torment of the demon of creative energy that lived inside him, struggling, clawing, scratching to be released; tearing, shrieking at him to write the music that was in him. The miracle is that what he did in the little space of seventy years could have been done at all, even by a great genius. Is it any wonder that he had no time to be a man?

Thought

1. Is this essay an indictment or a defence of Richard Wagner? Explain.

2. Look up the etymology of the word "monster." In what sense does Taylor use this word?

3. If Wagner were a contemporary composer, would society's reaction to his behaviour be any different? Why or why not?

Style and Structure

4. What does Taylor achieve by not identifying his subject until near the end of the essay?

5. Show that Taylor makes effective use of comparison in illuminating the life and significance of his subject.

6. What answer is Taylor inviting with his final question?

Response and Extension

7. Do you think Taylor has justified his assertion that Wagner's personal qualities and life do not "matter in the least" when balanced against his importance and contributions as a composer? Explain.

8. Invite a music teacher into your class to provide more information about the life and work of Richard Wagner.

9. Present to your class a biographical analysis of a famous person from the past, for example Napoleon Bonaparte, Cesare Borgia, The Duke of Wellington, Evita Peron, Eleanor of Aquitaine, Georgia O'Keefe, Anais Nin. Provide an interpretation of the personal qualities and the historical context that contributed to this person's eminence.

10. Richard Wagner composed operas on such a scale that an opera house had to be designed in order to house them. Research and compose a description of Wagner's opera house in the town of Bayreuth, Germany.

Unit Synthesis

1. Consider one of the novels or poems in your English course in terms of its description of a particular place or person. How does the depiction of the specific evoke the universal?

2. What are the "wonders" of your own home town? Be sure to explain the criteria for your choices.

3. Write an essay that recalls a journey you took in your childhood. Use vivid imagery to describe the place, or places, of most intense significance to you.

4. Each of the essayists in this unit insist, explicitly or implicitly, on the significance of the particular—whether it be obscure, grandiose, wondrous, or everyday. Write a description of a very specific aspect of your life; for example, a certain person, or a moment of perception or realization. Make your account as original as you can by investing it with a meaning that might otherwise be overlooked.

Suggested Readings

Ackerman, Diane *A Natural History of the Senses*
Beston, Henry *The Outermost House*
Craven, Margaret *I Heard the Owl Call My Name*
Houston, James *The White Dawn*
Kroetsch, Robert *Badlands*
Mayle, Peter *A Year in Provence*
McGuane, Thomas *Keep the Change*
Mitchell, W.O. *Jake and the Kid; Who Has Seen the Wind*
Paton, Alan *But Your Country Is Beautiful*
Pinsent, Gordon *John and the Missus*
Thomas, Lewis *Lives of a Cell; The Medusa and the Snail; Late Night Thoughts on Listening to Mahler's Ninth Symphony*
Tisdale, Sallie *Stepping Westward*

Writing to Define

The highest form of moral courage requires us to look at ourselves
from another perspective ... and to reown our own shadows. True
self-knowledge introduces self-doubt into our minds.

Sam Keen

Faces of the Enemy

Sam Keen

The world, as always, is debating the issues of war and peace. Conservatives believe safety lies in more arms and increased firepower. Liberals place their trust in disarmament and a nuclear freeze. I suggest we will be saved by neither fire nor ice, that the solutions being offered by the political right and left miss the mark. Our problem lies not in our technology, but in our minds, in our ancient tendency to create our enemies in our own imagination.

Our best hope for avoiding war is to understand the psychology of this enmity, the ways in which our mind works to produce our habits of paranoia, projection, and the making of propaganda. How do we create our enemies and turn the world into a killing ground?

We first need to answer some inevitable objections, raised by the advocates of power politics, who say: "You can't psychologize political conflict. You can't solve the problem of war by studying perception. We don't *create* enemies. There are real aggressors—Hitler, Stalin, Qaddafi."

True: There are always political, economic, and territorial causes of war. Wars come and go; the images we use to dehumanize our enemies remain strangely the same. The unchanging projections of the hostile imagination are continually imposed onto changing historical circumstances. Not that the enemy is innocent of these projections—as popular wisdom has it, paranoids sometimes have *real* enemies. Nevertheless, to understand the hostile imagination we need to temporarily ignore the question of guilt and innocence. Our quest is for an understanding of the unchanging images we place on the enemy.

The Enemy as Created by Paranoia

Paranoia is not an occasional individual pathology, but rather it is the human condition. History shows us that, with few exceptions, social cohesion within tribes is maintained by paranoia: when we do not have enemies, we invent them. The group identity of a people depends on division between insiders and outsiders, us and them, the tribe and the enemy.

The first meaning of *the enemy* is simply the stranger, the alien. The bond of tribal membership is maintained by projecting hostile and divisive emotions upon the outsider. Paranoia forms the mold from which we create enemies.

In the paranoid imagination, *alien* means the same as *evil*, while the tribe itself is defined as good: a single network of malevolent intent stretches over the rest of the world. "They" are out to get "us." All occurrences prove the basic assumption that an outside power is conspiring against the community.

The Enemy as Enemy of God

In the language of rhetoric, every war is a crusade, a "just" war, a battle between good and evil. Warfare is a ritual in which the sacred blood of our heroes is sacrificed to destroy the enemies of God.

We like to think that theocracies and holy wars ended with the coming of the Industrial Revolution and the emergence of secular cultures in the West. Yet in World War I the kaiser was pictured as the devil; in World War II both Germany and the U.S. proclaimed *Gott mit uns*, "In God We Trust"; each accused the other of being Christ-killers. Sophisticated politicians may insist that the conflict between the U.S. and the USSR is a matter of pragmatic power politics, but theological dimensions have not disappeared. President Reagan warns us against "the aggressive impulses of an evil empire" and asks us to "pray for the salvation of all those who live in totalitarian darkness, pray they will discover the joy of knowing God."

By picturing the enemy as the enemy of God we convert the guilt associated with murder into pride. A warrior who kills such an enemy strikes a blow for truth and goodness. Remorse isn't necessary. The warrior engaged in righteous battle against the enemies of God may even see himself as a priest, saving his enemy from the grip of evil by killing him.

The Enemy as Barbarian

The enemy not only is a demon but is also a destroyer of culture. If he is human at all, he is brutish, dumb, and cruel, lower on the scale of evolution than The People. To the Greeks he was a barbarian. To the Americans he was, most recently, a "gook" or "slant." To the South African he is a black or "colored."

The barbarian theme was used widely in World War II propaganda by all participants. Nazi anti-semitic tracts contrasted the sunny, healthy Aryan with the inferior, dark, and contaminated races—Jews, Gypsies, Eastern Europeans. American soldiers were pictured as Chicago-style gangsters. Blacks were portrayed as quasi-gorillas despoiling the artistic achievements of European civilization. One poster used in Holland warned the Dutch that their supposed "liberators" were a mélange of KKK, jazz-crazed blacks, convicts, hangmen, and mad bombers. In turn, the U.S. frequently pictured the Germans as a Nazi horde of dark monsters on a mindless rampage.

The image of the barbarian represents a force to be feared: power without intelligence, matter without mind, an enemy that must be conquered by culture. The warrior who defeats the barbarian is a culture hero, keeping the dark powers in abeyance.

The Enemy as Rapist

Associated with the enemy as barbarian is the image of the enemy as rapist, the destroyer of motherhood.

As rapist, the enemy is lust defiling innocence. He is according to Nazi propaganda the Jew who lurks in the shadows waiting to seduce Aryan girls. Or in the propaganda of the Ku Klux Klan he is the black man with an insatiable lust for white women. In American war posters he is the Jap carrying away the naked Occidental woman.

The portrait of the enemy as rapist, destroyer of the madonna, warns us of danger and awakens our pornographic imagination by reminding us of the enticement of rape. The appeal to sexual adventure is a sine qua non in motivating men to go to war: To the warrior belong the spoils, and chief among the spoils are the enemy's women.

The Enemy as Beast, Insect, Reptile

The power of bestial images to degrade is rooted in the neurotic structure of the hostile imagination. Karen Horney has shown that neurosis always involves a movement between glorified and degraded images of the self. In warfare we act out a mass neurosis whereby we glorify ourselves as agents of God and project our feelings of degradation and impotence upon the enemy. We are suprahuman; therefore they must be subhuman. By destroying the bestial and contaminated enemy we can gain immortality, escape evil, transcend decay and death.

The Enemy as Death

In the iconography of propaganda, the enemy is the bringer of death. He is Death riding on a bomb, the Grim Reaper cutting down youth in its prime. His face is stripped of flesh, his body a dangling skeleton.

War is an irrational ritual. Generation after generation we sacrifice our substance in a vain effort to kill some essential enemy. Now he wears an American or Soviet face. A moment ago he was a Nazi, a Jew, a Moslem, a Christian, a pagan. But the true face of the enemy, as Saint Paul said, is Death itself. The unconscious power that motivates us to fight for Peace, kill for Life, is the magical assumption that if we can destroy this particular enemy we can defeat Death.

Lying within each of us is the desire for immortality. And because this near-instinctive desire for immortality is balanced by the precariously repressed fear that death might really eradicate all traces of our existence, we will go to any extreme to reassure ourselves. By submitting to the divine ordeal of war, in which we are willing to die or kill the enemy who is Death, we affirm our own deathlessness.

The Reluctant Killers

It is easy to despair when we look at the human genius for creating enemies in the image of our own disowned vices. When we add our mass paranoia and projection to our constantly progressing weapons technology, it seems we are doomed to destroy ourselves.

But the persistent archetypal images of the enemy may point in a more hopeful direction. We demean our enemies not because we are instinctively sadistic, but because it is difficult for us to kill others whom we recognize as fully human beings. Our natural empathy, our instinct for compassion, is strong: society does what it must to attempt to overcome the moral imperative that forbids us from killing.

Even so, the effort is successful only for a minority. In spite of our best propaganda, few men and women will actually try to kill an enemy. In his book *Men Against Fire*, Brigadier General S.L.A. Marshall presents the results of his study of American soldiers under fire during World War II. He discovered that *in combat* the percentage of men who would fire their rifle at the enemy *even once* did not rise above 25 percent, and the more usual figure was 15 percent. He further discovered that the fear of killing was every bit as strong as the fear of dying.

If it is difficult to mold men into killers, we may still hope to transform our efforts from fighting an outward enemy to doing battle with our own paranoia. Our true war is our struggle against the antagonistic mind. Our true enemy is our propensity to make enemies. The highest form of moral courage requires us to look at ourselves from another perspective, to repent, and to reown our own shadows. True self-knowledge introduces self-doubt into our minds. And self-doubt is a healthy counterbalance to the dogmatic, self-righteous certainty that governs political rhetoric and behavior; it is, therefore, the beginning of compassion.

Thought

1. Paraphrase Keen's thesis. Do you agree with it? Why or why not?

2. a) According to Keen, why and how are enemies created?
   b) Do any of your own experiences with "group identity" have bearing on Keen's analysis of "paranoia"? Explain.

3. This essay was first published in the mid-eighties. What political situations alluded to in the essay have changed since then?

4. "War is an irrational ritual." To what extent do you think this statement is true?

Style and Structure

5. Consider the tone in which Keen writes, and the effect of the language he employs. Citing quotes from the essay, analyze how Keen's writing style conveys his message in so powerful and provocative a manner.

6. How does Keen address obvious objections to his thesis in the first four paragraphs of the essay?

7. How do the headings serve the purposes of Keen's definition?

8. Each section of Keen's essay depends upon a set of contrasts and paradoxes. Identify these, and describe the effect they produce.

9. How has Keen used repetition to strengthen his conclusion?

Response and Extension

10. To whom are you the enemy? Why? Examine, for example, the school culture for your answers, and explain the reasons and context in your journal.

11. In groups, choose a contemporary figure featured in the media and compile a list of the reasons why he or she is considered by some to be an "enemy." Do you think the enmity is justified? Analyze the media portrayal of this figure, and make your own assessment.

12. Analyze the image of an "enemy" portrayed in a contemporary film or television series, using the categories that Keen suggests.

13. "True self-knowledge introduces self-doubt into our minds." Recount in your journal an experience you've had with a person who in your mind was an "enemy"—but whom you later came to like. With reference to the above quote, define the process of overcoming your enmity.

Arks Can't Save Aardvarks

Stan Rowe

Humans discovered their environment as all-encompassing with the first outer-space photos that revealed the Ecosphere: a blue cloud-swathed globe in whose watery skin a marvelous variety of protoplasmic bits and pieces are enclosed and sustained. Suddenly we were given a breathtaking new perspective on ourselves: self-conscious deep-air animals, a dependent and integral part of it all.

Suppose that this vision, this reality, had preceded the development of today's science. Suppose that we had been given the outside perspective to see the Earth entire, ourselves immersed in it, and had taken the vision to heart before we decided what was important, what was real.

Had such transcendent insight been granted, would we not have recognized the Ecosphere, the Home-sphere, as the unitary thing to be valued above all else? Only afterwards would we have studied and analyzed it, dissecting it into its component water bodies, atmosphere, continental platforms, plants and animals in their communities and as individuals—in order to better understand its miraculous integrity.

Unfortunately, submerged in it we were unaware of the whole. Like the blind men in the fable who mistook the legs or tusks, the trunk or tail for the elephant itself, we have assumed that the parts of the Earth are autonomous things-in-themselves, starting with humans and working out from there, identifying as most important the objects with properties similar to our own: animals and plants.

Various other things around us—apparently peripheral odds and ends—in turn forced their importance on our attention: the aerial climate, soils, sediments, salt water, surface and subsurface geological rocks and ores. These we called "raw materials" and "resources" when we perceived human uses for them, while to those dimly perceived to be indispensable we gave the name "environment," meaning that which surrounds objects of greater importance: namely, organic things like us. An inadequate conception, this view from inside.

The view from outside came too late. The un-sensed Ecosphere had already been dissected from the inside out. Philosophers and theologians had pronounced their final Truths about its parts. Disciplines had been defined and disciplinary knowledge had hardened. Universities and governments were departmentalized to deal with the fragments, their adherents assured of certain certainties. In millions of books and learned treatises, the components of the Ecosphere were confirmed by the savants to be self-standing entities. "The proper study of mankind is man," we have been taught. "Soils are natural bodies at the surface of the earth." "Rare and endangered plants and animals can be saved." All part truths and all misleading.

Ideas are changing. The new perspective from outside casts yesterday's assumptions in a critical light. More aware of our evolutionary history and our dependencies, we know intellectually that the segments of the world we study in the disciplines are indeed segments. Geoscience tells us that what we call atmosphere, lithosphere, hydrosphere and biosphere developed together; they have no separate reality, except in thought. Ecology tells us that what we call organisms and environment are inseparable, except as words. But these facts have not been assimilated. We do not know them in the way that counts: in our affections as well as in our heads.

How difficult it is to accept in our hearts and imaginations that the authentic thing, the important thing, the primary reality, is the Ecosphere, one of whose attributes is the phenomenon called life. Life is not a property of organisms, nor of cells, nor of strands of protoplasm, nor of complex molecules like DNA. Life is a property of the skin of the planet and of the ecological systems that the marvelous skin comprises.

One-eyed biology, lacking depth perception, has misled us into conceiving a world divided into the biotic and the abiotic, the organic and the inorganic, the animate and the inanimate, the living and the dead. The divisions are false and mischievous. For what would qualify as animate, living, organic and biotic without sunlight, water, soil, air? These latter components are as vital and as important as the organisms whose life-giving environment they are. The Ecosphere, the most perfect ecological system, comprises all-of-them-together. It is an evolving, adjusting, self-repairing *Supra-organismic Unit*, transcending the organic, and not just a super organism.

One of the tools of human understanding is reduction, anatomizing objects of interest into their parts. Into what parts should the Ecosphere be dissected to aid comprehension? The answer, the wrong one, has already been provided: primarily important are organisms, and secondarily their nebulous environments or habitats. But that is the myopic view from inside the system, not the comprehensive view from outside.

If we take to heart the truths that the three-dimensional skin of the planet, the Ecosphere, is the unit of importance and that life is not a phenomenon that exists apart from it, then clearly the most significant parts are volumetric landscapes and waterscapes. Anatomizing the Ecosphere into sectoral three-dimensional ecosystems whose components include plants and animals along with their matrix of atmosphere, soil and water, provides simplified but almost complete homologues of the Real Thing. Such ecosystems, chunks of the Ecosphere, can very nearly exist on their own, like large terraria and aquaria. Plants, animals and people, individually or in their populations and communities, cannot do that!

Endangered organisms *per se* cannot be preserved. Ecosystems of which organisms are interesting ingredients can, however be preserved—as long as the Ecosphere of which they are parts continues to function in the old natural and healthy way.

This realization should turn attention more and more to the absolute necessity of preserving wildernesses and natural areas, ecological reserves and sanctuaries, endangered *spaces* before endangered *species*. Unless natural ecological systems are preserved, the native flora and fauna will not be preserved. Organisms will still exist in the truncated environments fashioned by well-meaning people but only as cultivars, zoo freaks, the living dead.

In practical terms this means that we never deal just with organisms but always and necessarily with ecological systems of which organisms are notable parts. Preserving a rare plant population in any but a temporary sense must mean preserving the rare ecosystem of which it is one component among others of equal importance. Taking a threatened species on board an ark to save it from the industrial deluge is to immerse it in a tame ecosystem from which—if kept there for more than a generation—it will emerge as something else, on its way to becoming a tame species, a cultivar.

Unless our various arks—zoos, arboreta, seed banks and propagation gardens—are looked on as temporary life-boats whose occupants are to be landed as speedily as possible on whatever Mount Ararats and other sanctuaries protrude above the human flood, all the current discourse about preservation will be only fine talk. The survival of some threads of biological history that we knew to be valuable may be secured, but their texture will no longer be that which drew us to them in the first place. Somewhere along the way, full of good intentions, we will have killed the things we love.

In this there lies a lesson for ourselves. We too have built and boarded an ark, a cultural vehicle that is carrying us into the future. We have cast off from our native shore, left it behind and plan never to land there again. Unlike Noah we have made room for few other passengers, preferring to exterminate rather than to save. Our brave new world will be a people-only world, an ark expanded—electronically and chemically bigger and better, like the metal-and-glass space-ships of science fiction—in time entirely replacing the old world. True, we have not thought out whether the idea is good or bad, but meanwhile build and sail onward, to a richer and more abundant future!

Humanity is already suffering from having been on board its particular monospecific ark too long, from solitary confinement in the plastic and asphalt environment, shut off by choice from its roots in the ancestral world, not enough bird song, too little spongy turf underfoot. More and more the human species is out of touch with Nature, too citified, at risk from its own seed-bank environment—rows and rows of boxes in which we have voluntarily imprisoned ourselves and where with less and less success we attempt to bring up good and natural progeny.

We will not save the riverine forests without protecting the flood plains, nor will the orchids be preserved without preserving the marshes. Our own fate is linked to the limits we set on the domestication of the world around us and to the offsetting effort we devote to maintaining the life-blood of the Home Place, the natural beauty and health of the creative, sustaining, enveloping Ecosphere.

Thought

1. Do Rowe's assertions in paragraph 3 follow logically from his premise in paragraph 2? Explain.

2. List five ways in which the "inside view" differs from the "outside view."

3. Do you agree with the author's assertion that the view from "inside" is "myopic"? Why or why not?

4. Discuss the relationship between the title and the content of the essay.

5. What is Stan Rowe defining in this essay? How does he define it?

Style and Structure

6. Assess the degree to which the author uses comparison and contrast to develop his argument.

7. Identify and explain the effectiveness of two of Rowe's metaphors.

8. Show how Rowe uses concrete examples to illustrate abstract concepts.

9. Divide into groups to create a point-form outline of Rowe's ideas. On the basis of this outline summarize the "shape" of this essay; that is, in what manner the author has chosen to build his argument. Compare your outline and your conclusions with those of the other groups.

Response and Extension

10. Investigate the current conditions of the East and West Coast fisheries, and how these conditions developed. Carefully consider as much relevant data as possible. How would a "comprehensive view from outside" have prevented current problems?

11. Research an endangered species in your region. Comment on the ways in which endangering the "spaces" in which the species lives contributes to its demise.

12. Research the "nature" of zoos, aquaria, etc. which are deemed "natural environments" or as "fair" to the species they include. What qualities make them "fair"? What aspects are unfair or unnatural?

13. Write a spirited defence of an "endangered space" that is of particular importance to you. Send it to the "Op Ed" editor of your local newspaper.

Marginal Men

Barbara Ehrenreich

Crime seems to change character when it crosses a bridge or a tunnel. In the city, crime is taken as emblematic of the vast injustices of class and race. In the suburbs, though, it's intimate and psychological—resistant to generalization, a mystery of the individual soul. Recall the roar of commentary that followed the murderous assault on a twenty-eight-year-old woman jogging in Central Park. Every detail of the assailants' lives was sifted for sociological significance: Were they poor? How poor? Students or dropouts? From families with two parents or one? And so on, until the awful singularity of the event was lost behind the impersonal grid of Class, Race, and Sex.

Now take the Midtown Tunnel east to the Long Island Expressway, out past the clutter of Queens to deepest suburbia, where almost every neighborhood is "good" and "social pathology" is something you learn about in school. Weeks before the East Harlem youths attacked a jogger, Long Islanders were shaken by two murders which were, if anything, even more inexplicably vicious than the assault in Central Park. In early March, the body of thirteen-year-old Kelly Tinyes was found in the basement of a house just down the block from her own. She had been stabbed, strangled, and hit with a blunt instrument before being mutilated with a bayonet. A few weeks later, fourteen-year-old Jessica Manners was discovered along the side of a road in East Setauket, strangled to death, apparently with her own bra, and raped.

Suspects have been apprehended. Their high-school friends, parents, and relatives have been interviewed. Their homes and cars have been searched; their photos published. We know who they hung out with and what they did in their spare time. But on the scale of large social meanings, these crimes don't rate. No one is demanding that we understand—or condemn—the white communities that nourished the killers. No one is debating the roots of violence in the land of malls and tract homes. Only in the city, apparently, is crime construed as something "socioeconomic." Out here it's merely "sick."

But East Setauket is not really all that far from East Harlem. If something is festering in the ghetto, something very similar is gnawing away at Levittown and East Meadow. A "way of life," as the cliché goes, is coming to an end, and in its place a mean streak is opening up and swallowing everything in its path. Economists talk about "deindustrialization" and "class polarization." I think of it as the problem of *marginal men*: they are black and white, Catholic and Pentecostal, rap fans and admirers of technopop. What they have in common is that they are going nowhere—nowhere legal, that is.

Consider the suspects in the Long Island murders. Twenty-one-year-old Robert Golub, in whose basement Kelly Tinyes was killed, is described in *Newsday* as an "unemployed bodybuilder." When his high-school friends went off to college, he stayed behind in his parents' home in Valley Stream. For a while, he drove a truck for a cosmetics firm, but he lost that job, in part because of his driving record: his license has been suspended twelve times since 1985. At the time of the murder, he had been out of work for several months, constructing a life around his weight-lifting routine and his dream of becoming an entrepreneur.

Christopher Loliscio, the suspect in the Manners case, is nineteen, and, like Golub, lives with his parents. He has been in trouble before, and is charged with third-degree assault and "menacing" in an altercation that took place on the campus of the State University at Stony Brook last December. Loliscio does not attend college himself. He is employed as a landscaper.

The suburbs are full of young white men like Golub and Loliscio. If they had been born twenty years earlier, they might have found steady work in decent-paying union jobs, married early, joined the volunteer fire department, and devoted their leisure to lawn maintenance. But the good blue-collar jobs are getting sparser, thanks to "deindustrialization"—which takes the form, in Long Island, of cutbacks in the defense and aerospace industries. Much of what's left is likely to be marginal, low-paid work. Nationwide, the earnings of young white men dropped 18 percent between 1973 and 1986, according to the Census Bureau, and the earnings of male high-school dropouts plunged 42 percent.

Landscaping, for example—a glamorous term for raking and mowing—pays four to five dollars an hour; truck driving for a small firm is in the same range: not enough to pay for a house, a college education, or even a mid-size wedding reception at the VFW hall.

And even those modest perquisites of life in the subyuppie class have become, in some sense, "not enough." On Long Island, the culture that once sustained men in blue-collar occupations is crumbling as more affluent settlers move in, filling the vacant lots with their new, schooner-shaped, $750,000 homes. In my town, for example, the last five years saw the bowling alley close and the blue-collar bar turn into a pricey dining spot. Even the volunteer fire department is having trouble recruiting. The prestigious thing to join is a $500-a-year racquetball club; there's just not much respect anymore for putting out fires.

So the marginal man lives between two worlds—one that he aspires to and one that is dying, and neither of which he can afford. Take "Rick," the twenty-two-year-old son of family friends. His father is a machinist in an aerospace plant which hasn't been hiring anyone above the floor-sweeping level for years now. Not that Rick has ever shown any interest in his father's trade. For one thing, he takes too much pride in his appearance to put on the dark green company-supplied work clothes his father has worn for the past twenty years. Rick has his kind of uniform: pleated slacks, high-tops, Italian knit cardigans, and a $300 leather jacket, accessorized with a gold chain and earring stud.

To his parents, Rick is a hard-working boy for whom things just don't seem to work out. For almost a year after high school, he worked behind a counter at Crazy Eddie's, where the pay is low but at least you can listen to rock and roll all day. Now he has a gig doing valet parking at a country club. The tips are good and he loves racing around the lot in the Porsches and Lamborghinis of the stockbroker class. But the linchpin of his economic strategy is living at home, with his parents and sisters, in the same room he's occupied since third grade. Rick is a long way from being able to afford even a cramped, three-bedroom house like his family home; and, given the choice, he'd rather have a new Camaro anyway.

If this were the seventies, Rick might have taken up marijuana, the Grateful Dead, and vague visions of a better world. But like so many of his contemporaries in the eighties, Rick has no problem with "the system," which, in his mind, embraces every conceivable hustle, legal or illegal. Two years ago, he made a tidy bundle dealing coke in a local dance club, bought a $20,000 car, and smashed it up. Now he spends his evenings as a bouncer in an illegal gambling joint—his parents still think he's out "dancing"—and is proud of the handgun he's got stowed in his glove compartment.

Someday Rick will use that gun, and I'll probably be the first to say—like Robert Golub's friends—"but he isn't the kind of person who would hurt *anyone*." Except that even now I can sense the danger in him. He's smart enough to know he's only a cut-rate copy of the upscale young men in *GQ* ads and MTV commercials. Viewed from Wall Street or Southampton, he's a peon, a member of the invisible underclass that parks cars, waits on tables, and is satisfied with a five-dollar tip and a remark about the weather.

He's also proud. And there's nowhere for him to put that pride except into the politics of gesture: the macho stance, the seventy-five-mile-per-hour takeoff down the expressway, and eventually maybe, the drawn gun. Jobs are the liberal solution; conservatives would throw in "traditional values." But what the marginal men—from Valley Stream to Bedford-Stuyvesant—need most of all is *respect*. If they can't find that in work, or in a working-class lifestyle that is no longer honored, they'll extract it from someone weaker—a girlfriend, a random jogger, a neighbor, perhaps just any girl. They'll find a victim.

Thought

1. With specific reference to the essay, define Ehrenreich's term "marginal men."

2. a) What, in the author's view, is the connection between crime and "marginal men"?

   b) Discuss in groups the extent to which you agree or disagree with Ehrenreich's conclusions.

3. Does Ehrenreich suggest any answers to the problem of marginal men? Why or why not?

4. Do you feel the author's viewpoint is biased in any way? Explain.

Style and Structure

5. How does Ehrenreich create her dominant mood of doom and gloom?

6. Do you think Ehrenreich has relied too heavily on sensational anecdotes to construct a compelling argument? Explain.

7. Ehrenreich uses the examples from Rick's life to intensify her argument. In your view, is Rick a real person or a psychological construct? Explain.

Response and Extension

8. This piece was written in the 1980s. Is it still valid today? Explain.

9. As a group devise some solutions to the problem of "marginal men." Present your proposals to the class.

10. Research another place and time for evidence of the activities of "marginal men" in the context of warfare, colonization, or imperialism. Consider, for example, knights in the Crusades; the Samurai; or early Australian settlers. Present your findings to the class.

11. Write an essay that defines and describes the circumstances and behaviour of "marginal women."

12. In groups, discuss the ways in which society treats adolescents differently from adults. What are some of the results of this treatment?

In Bed

Joan Didion

Three, four, sometimes five times a month, I spend the day in bed with a migraine headache, insensible to the world around me. Almost every day of every month, between these attacks, I feel the sudden irrational irritation and the flush of blood into the cerebral arteries which tell me that migraine is on its way, and I take certain drugs to avert its arrival. If I did not take the drugs, I would be able to function perhaps one day in four. The physiological error called migraine is, in brief, central to the given of my life. When I was 15, 16, even 25, I used to think that I could rid myself of this error by simply denying it, character over chemistry. "Do you have headaches *sometimes? frequently? never?*" the application forms would demand. "Check one." Wary of the trap, wanting whatever it was that the successful circumnavigation of that particular form could bring (a job, a scholarship, the respect of mankind and the grace of God), I would check one. "*Sometimes,*" I would lie. That in fact I spent one or two days a week almost unconscious with pain seemed a shameful secret, evidence not merely of some chemical inferiority but of all my bad attitudes, unpleasant tempers, wrongthink.

For I had no brain tumor, no eyestrain, no high blood pressure, nothing wrong with me at all: I simply had migraine headaches, and migraine headaches were, as everyone who did not have them knew, imaginary. I fought migraine then, ignored the warnings it sent, went to school and later to work in spite of it, sat through lectures in Middle English and presentations to advertisers with involuntary tears running down the right side of my face, threw up in washrooms, stumbled home by instinct, emptied ice trays onto my bed and tried to freeze the pain in my right temple, wished only for a neurosurgeon who would do a lobotomy on house call, and cursed my imagination.

68

It was a long time before I began thinking mechanistically enough to accept migraine for what it was: something with which I would be living, the way some people lived with diabetes. Migraine is something more than the fancy of a neurotic imagination. It is an essentially hereditary complex of symptoms, the most frequently noted but by no means the most unpleasant of which is a vascular headache of blinding severity, suffered by a surprising number of women, a fair number of men (Thomas Jefferson had migraine, and so did Ulysses S. Grant, the day he accepted Lee's surrender), and by some unfortunate children as young as two years old. (I had my first when I was eight. It came on during a fire drill at the Columbia School in Colorado Springs, Colorado. I was taken first home and then to the infirmary at Peterson Field, where my father was stationed. The Air Corps doctor prescribed an enema.) Almost anything can trigger a specific attack of migraine: stress, allergy, fatigue, an abrupt change in barometric pressure, a contretemps over a parking ticket. A flashing light. A fire drill. One inherits, of course, only the predisposition. In other words I spent yesterday in bed with a headache not merely because of my bad attitudes, unpleasant tempers and wrongthink but because both my grandmothers had migraine, my father has migraine and my mother has migraine.

No one knows precisely what it is that is inherited. The chemistry of migraine, however, seems to have some connection with the nerve hormone named serotonin, which is naturally present in the brain. The amount of serotonin in the blood falls sharply at the onset of migraine, and one migraine drug, methysergide, or Sansert, seems to have some effect on serotonin. Methysergide is a derivative of lysergic acid (in fact Sandoz Pharmaceuticals first synthesized LSD-25 while looking for a migraine cure), and its use is hemmed about with so many contraindications and side effects that most doctors prescribe it only in the most incapacitating cases. Methysergide, when it is prescribed, is taken daily, as a preventive; another preventive which works for some people is old-fashioned ergotamine tartrate, which helps to constrict the swelling blood vessels during the "aura," the period which in most cases precedes the actual headache.

Once an attack is under way, however, no drug touches it. Migraine gives some people mild hallucinations, temporarily blinds others, shows up not only as a headache but as a gastrointestinal disturbance, a painful sensitivity to all sensory stimuli, an abrupt overpowering fatigue, a strokelike aphasia, and a crippling inability to make even the most routine connections. When I am in a migraine aura (for some people the aura lasts fifteen minutes, for others several hours), I will drive through red lights, lose the house keys, spill whatever I am holding, lose the ability to focus my eyes or frame coherent sentences, and generally give the appearance of being on drugs, or drunk. The actual headache, when it comes, brings with it chills, sweating, nausea, a debility that seems to stretch the very limits of endurance. That no one dies of migraine seems, to someone deep into an attack, an ambiguous blessing.

My husband also has migraine, which is unfortunate for him but fortunate for me: perhaps nothing so tends to prolong an attack as the accusing eye of someone who has never had a headache. "Why not take a couple of aspirin," the unafflicted will say from the doorway, or "I'd have a headache, too, spending a beautiful day like this inside with all the shades drawn." All of us who have migraine suffer not only from the attacks themselves but from this common conviction that we are perversely refusing to cure ourselves by taking a couple of aspirins, that we are making ourselves sick, that we "bring it on ourselves." And in the most immediate sense, the sense of why we have a headache this Tuesday and not last Thursday, of course we often do. There certainly is what doctors call a "migraine personality," and that personality tends to be ambitious, inward, intolerant of error, rather rigidly organized, perfectionist. "You don't look like a migraine personality," a doctor once said to me. "Your hair's messy. But I suppose you're a compulsive housekeeper." Actually my house is kept even more negligently than my hair, but the doctor was right nonetheless: perfectionism can also take the form of spending most of a week writing and rewriting and not writing a single paragraph.

But not all perfectionists have migraine, and not all migrainous people have migraine personalities. We do not escape heredity. I have tried in most of the available ways to escape my own migrainous heredity (at one point I learned to give myself two daily injections of histamine with a hypodermic needle, even though the needle so frightened me that I had to close my eyes when I did it), but I still have migraine. And I have learned how to live with it, learned when to expect it, and how to outwit it, even how to regard it, when it does come, as more friend than lodger. We have reached a certain understanding, my migraine and I. It never comes when I am in real trouble. Tell me that my house is burned down, my husband has left me, that there is gunfighting in the streets and panic in the banks, and I will not respond by getting a headache. It comes instead when I am fighting not an open but a guerrilla war with my own life, during weeks of small household confusions, lost laundry, unhappy help, cancelled appointments, on days when the telephone rings too much and I get no work done and the wind is coming up. On days like that my friend comes uninvited.

And once it comes, now that I am wise in its ways, I no longer fight it. I lie down and let it happen. At first every small apprehension is magnified, every anxiety a pounding terror. Then the pain comes, and I concentrate only on that. Right there is the usefulness of migraine, there in that imposed yoga, the concentration on the pain. For when the pain recedes, ten or twelve hours later, everything goes with it, all the hidden resentments, all the vain anxieties. The migraine has acted as a circuit breaker, and the fuses have emerged intact. There is a pleasant convalescent euphoria. I open the windows and feel the air, eat gratefully, sleep well. I notice the particular nature of a flower in a glass on the stair landing. I count my blessings.

Thought

1. Why does Didion refer to migraine as "the physiological error . . . central to the given of my life"?

2. List the features of the "migraine personality." Explain the connection, as described in this essay, between perfectionism and migraine.

3. How has her acceptance of migraine influenced Didion's personality and behaviour?

Style and Structure

4. a) List the symptoms of migraine.
   b) List four or five of Didion's non-clinical descriptions of her own migraine. Which mode of expression conveys more information about the experience of migraine? Explain.

5. Construct an outline for this essay that Didion might have used before writing "In Bed."

6. What is Didion implying about herself by referring to migraine as "more friend than lodger"?

Response and Extension

7. a) Describe to the members of your group the worst headache or the most painful experience you have ever endured.

   b) Consider the words you have used to describe your headaches. What conclusions can you draw about the effectiveness of words used to describe pain?

8. Write an essay in which you define and describe a condition "central to the given" of your life; for example, being a twin or an only child. Try to develop a central metaphor which conveys the essence of this condition.

9. For discussion: Why do some people define themselves in terms of a specific illness or condition, e.g. "I'm an asthmatic," as opposed to saying, "I suffer from asthma"?

10. Examine an overview of the latest therapies used to treat migraines.

11. Interview someone who is or has been ill to determine the degree and kind of societal reponse to the illness. Write an essay defining this response, and whatever conclusions you think you can draw from it.

Unit Synthesis

1. Using Keen's definitions of the enemy, analyze the enmity between the protagonist and antagonists in a novel such as *The Wars* by Timothy Findley; *A Separate Peace* by John Knowles; *Lord of the Flies* by William Golding; *A Farewell to Arms* by Ernest Hemingway; *In Country* by Bobbie Ann Mason; *The Gate to Women's Country* by Sherri S. Tepper; *The Left Hand of Darkness* by Ursula K. Le Guin; *A Thousand Acres* by Jane Smiley.

2. Applying what you have learned in Keen's essay, analyze Shakespeare's "propaganda techniques" in plays such as *Richard III, Hamlet, King Lear,* and *Romeo and Juliet.*

3. Each of the essays in this unit establish contexts which give rise to alienation in one form or another. The separation that alienation involves lends itself well to the task of "writing to define," since here the writer's purpose is to distinguish outlines, to mark out boundaries.

   Consider an alienating situation that you have experienced in your own life. Define the context that led to this alienation, and the feelings of separation that resulted.

4. "An inadequate conception, this view from inside," writes Stan Rowe in his essay. How does this limited view that Rowe describes relate to Keen's and to Ehrenreich's theses? Define the links between these ideas, quoting key phrases or sentences from each essay to support your argument.

5. Read, view, or listen to a number of reports in the media dealing with specific illnesses, paying close attention to their descriptions. Following a structure similar to Keen's "Faces of the Enemy," develop an essay defining the "faces of illness" as portrayed in the media. Do you think we view the "enemy within" much differently from the "enemy without"? Why or why not?

Suggested Readings

Ackerman, Diane *The Moon by Whale Light; A Natural History of the Senses*

Bly, Robert *Iron John*

Bly, Robert et al., *The Rag and Bone Shop of the Heart*

Coté, James and Anton Allahar, *Generation on Hold*

Johnson, Robert A., *The Fisher King and the Handless Maiden*

McKibben, Bill *The End of Nature*

Pollan, Michael *Second Nature*

Sontag, Susan, *Illness as Metaphor*

Styron, William *Darkness Visible*

Weiner, Jonathan *The Next Hundred Years*

Works by Rachel Carson, Jane Goodall, Diane Fossey

Writing to Explain

We want, need, the stories of others. We need, too, to place our own stories beside theirs, to compare, weigh, judge, forgive, and to find, by becoming something other than ourselves, an angle of vision that renews our image of the world.

Carol Shields

The Leering That Has to Stop

Ann Fuller

My body stiffens with surprise as I feel the supervisor's arm pressed against mine.

"I must be in his way," I say to myself.

I take a step away, embarrassed for thinking anything dirty. The supervisor stands beside me as I do my work. He takes a step closer and again presses his arm to mine. I feel the warmth of his arm through my shirt. And I'm sure he can feel my body tremble. It's too intimate. Too personal. I don't want to feel his body heat.

Afraid to move, I feel my face grow red. If I jump away I could just fuel the problem. Maybe he didn't even notice he was touching me. But if I stay still I might lead him on.

The pen falls from my hand. I bend down to pick it up. Then I walk away.

This episode took place within a month of my starting a job. I didn't tell anyone. But that's not because I didn't want to. It just seemed that on this topic my tongue was paralyzed.

I wasn't sure if it was sexual harassment. I could have been misinterpreting his actions. My greatest fear was blowing things out of proportion. So I kept quiet.

I stayed quiet for weeks, even when his attentions continued and grew more pointed.

When I was the object in his eye, his look was never casual or innocent. His eyes fixed me with a strong, pointed gaze. They would travel the length of my body and return to my face with a sliver-trace of a smile.

I grew to hate that smile. And his comments. He would stand with the other male workers and look at me. He would make a comment and they'd all laugh. Were they talking about me? About my body? My movements? Or was I just growing paranoid?

He left his business card and phone number lying on my books. He cracked jokes about giving me a map to his house. The other guys would laugh. My face would redden and they would laugh more.

Then one day I was talking to a male co-worker when I felt the back of my skirt being slowly lifted. Quickly I turned to find the supervisor behind me. Without stopping or thinking, I punched him in the stomach. He laughed. So did the male co-worker.

"There was something on your skirt. I was just taking it off," he said.

Embarrassed by my actions and the laughter of my co-worker, I apologized.

Later that day I told a female co-worker everything. She said she noticed, but she didn't think he'd ever cheat on his wife.

I don't know why, but after that he left me alone. Maybe she spoke to him. Or maybe my efforts to avoid and ignore him were finally enough.

It was my first experience with sexual harassment, but not my last. The paralyzing effect I'll always remember—too scared to say anything, too embarrassed to move.

But the laughter of my co-workers also hurt. They saw me, I am sure, as a sexual object.

Experts say the increase in sexual harassment in the workplace directly corresponds with the increase in working women.

The solution is the change of attitudes of working men.

I'm not insinuating that most men would sexually harass someone. Or that they share the same values or the same views of women. But the majority of men perpetuate the attitudes that lead the few to their twisted attitudes about women.

At a hockey game last year, I stopped for a second in the aisle to look for my friends. The view was momentarily, and I stress momentarily, obstructed for the man sitting in the section above.

"Get moving or get naked, —" he yelled.

And his friends just laughed.

These kinds of attitudes find their way into working relationships. Talking on the phone last year, I was again reminded.

"Is there a naked picture of you we can put up?" asked a client.

"I don't think so," I said sarcastically, surprised and angry.

"Would you like me to take one?" he offered.

I was shocked. I'd never even met this man—how dare he address me in such a manner. I am a professional. Why does he think he can humiliate me, as if I'm just some object for his amusement?

Women can yell and holler, write and protest as much as they want, but it won't fundamentally change until men's attitudes change. That has to start with the men themselves.

To tell a sexist joke is to perpetuate the twisted attitudes of some men. To laugh at a sexist joke is just as bad.

I don't really like sexist jokes. And when I hear guys in a bar making crude, sexual comments when I walk by, I don't merely feel insulted. I feel embarrassed, dirty, and hurt.

When they leer, I feel belittled.

When I punch a total stranger in a bar for grabbing my breast, and he just laughs, I feel helpless.

I'm only twenty-two. But already I've reached that borderline where I just can't take it any more.

It is up to men to destroy these persisting sexist attitudes. It's similar to a two-year old child doing something naughty—if you laugh, he'll keep doing it.

If men keep laughing at these jokes and comments, they are only encouraging them. They are justifying such behaviour.

I respect a man who is strong and secure enough in himself to need no part of these childish antics. Until there are more such men, I will not feel safe.

Last year I walked down a street in Ottawa with a friend. It was late at night, and dark. We were coming from a dance bar on the Market. Three or four guys were standing on the corner talking. We walked by.

"Hey baby, come over here for a minute."

We just kept walking.

One of them stepped forward.

"Arrogant, eh? That's okay, if you had come over I would have — you and beat your head in with a rock."

We didn't turn around and we didn't stop. Fortunately, he didn't follow us. But I'll always remember the sound of his friends when we walked away.

Laughter.

He'll remember the laughter, too. And do it again.

Thought

1. For what reasons did Fuller "keep quiet" about sexual harassment in the workplace? Would you have done the same in her situation? Explain.

2. Explain why Fuller apologizes for punching her supervisor.

3. Account for the "paralyzing effect" as experienced by the author.

4. "The majority of men perpetuate the attitudes that lead the few to their twisted attitudes about women." Is Fuller justified in this assertion? Explain.

5. a) What are the types of power relationships that underly the author's various experiences of sexual harassment?
   b) Which do you think is more entrenched, more fundamental to the problem of sexual harassment: "power" or "attitude"?

Style and Structure

6. What effects does the author achieve by her frequent quotations?

7. a) Why does Fuller use the first-person point of view in presenting her argument?
   b) What is Fuller's purpose in shifting from present to past tense in the essay?

8. Comment on the effectiveness of Fuller's terse sentences and short paragraphs.

Response and Extension

9. For discussion: "It is up to men to destroy persisting sexist attitudes."

10. In groups, compose a definition of sexual harassment and devise practical ways of dealing with it, both in school and in the workplace.

Unreasonable Facsimile

Frederick Allen

In 1950, in the optimistic early morning of the computer age, the British mathematician Alan Turing predicted that computers would become intelligent enough to pass for human beings in conversation. "I believe that in about fifty years' time it will be plausible . . . to make them play the imitation game so well that an average interrogator will not have more than a 70 percent chance of making the right identification after five minutes of questioning," he wrote. A field soon grew up to make his prediction come true, led by Marvin Minsky, who co-founded the Artificial Intelligence Laboratory at the Massachusetts Institute of Technology. For a while the possibilities seemed limitless. One MIT professor asserted that "a modern computer system . . . can be made to develop a sense of itself . . . a kind of self-consciousness." Another writer went so far as to warn, in a book titled *Machines Who Think*, that "there will be very little communication between machines and humans because unless the machines condescend to talk to us about something that interests us, we'll have no communication."

Today traditional artificial intelligence, or AI, is a backwater at best, and the confidence with which it was once pursued seems unimaginable. Nobody has ever designed a program that can converse at all convincingly on a single subject, and the field has splintered into disparate parts. People work to simulate bits of the neural networks that are the raw material of mind; they design robots to perform simple tasks involving vision and coordinated movement; they struggle to come up with useful language translators; they devise programs to digest medical diagnostic data and calculate suggested courses of treatment. The grand vision has nearly vanished. As one critic of the field wrote in 1984, "The world of artificial intelligence programs is populated by idiot savants and well-behaved children."

Still, there are diehards. A small group of them run the Loebner Prize Competition in Artificial Intelligence, which sponsors an actual Turing test, in which judges converse with computer terminals and then try to identify which have computers behind them and which have human confederates. I was one of the eight judges in the third Loebner contest, last December. I got to meet some of the best conversational AI programs existing, and I came away with the conviction that real humanlike artificial intelligence is not just far off but impossible—and that the goal is misguided and pointless anyway.

The eight judges gathered in a defense contractor's headquarters in San Diego (I had to sign a paper avowing my U.S. citizenship to be let in) and huddled in a room with eight computer terminals. Next to each terminal was a sign indicating a single topic for conversation, such as "Abortion" or "Baseball." We spent three hours taking turns at the terminals and then privately casting ballots on which were human and which were humanoid.

I began at "Pets." The conversation, with me going first, commenced as follows:

"Hello. What kind of pets do you have yourself?"

"I have two cats."

"What are their names?"

"My cats are called Spats and Bowtie."

"How do you feel about declawing?"

"What kind of pets did you have as a child?"

"Won't you answer my question? How do you feel about declawing?"

"Guinea pigs are about as smart as cucumbers."

It was clearly a program and already at sea. It never again attained the apparent coherence of its first two answers.

Next I went to "Baseball." That conversation started with my asking, "What team are you a fan of?"

"The Baltimore Orioles!" came the reply.

"Have you always been an Orioles fan?"

"I would like to say yes, but at one time when I was small I was a Tiger fan."

"Didn't what's-his-name Robinson play third base for the Orioles?"

"You have that right! The best ever to play 3rd base!!"

"What was his first name?"

"Brooks, of course!"

Now I was just as obviously talking to a human being—who, I soon learned, had played some minor-league ball himself. I could always tell instantly if a terminal had a program or a person behind it. There was no comparison. The programs were elaborate, digitized versions of the old magic Eight Ball. They could look for a few key words and try to recognize very basic kinds of questions, but then all they could do was choose from a long list of prepared questions and answers.

As soon as we'd all had a turn at each terminal, we voted. Not one of the judges was fooled into thinking that any of the three computer programs was a human being, but five of my seven colleagues were fooled in the other direction, which wasn't supposed to happen at all. Each of them guessed that at least one of the five human confederates was in fact a computer program, even though the human beings had been instructed to act as honestly human as possible. The confederates had happened to be very humanly inarticulate and illogical. The judges had been too humanly eager to equate humanity with eloquence to recognize this.

The winner—the computer program we judged most nearly human, a more or less arbitrary choice—turned out to have been designed by the same person who had won the prize both years before. All three of the programs were hopeless at conversation. The winner, "Liberal or Conservative?", gave itself away by churning out non sequiturs and rote wisecracks about *Star Trek*. The runner-up, "Bad Marriage," had obviously been designed only to ask questions, not to answer them.

Because the contest has been so disappointing, the chairman of the prize committee, the Tufts University philosopher Daniel Dennett, who is the author of the popular *Consciousness Explained* (1991), sought to persuade the prize's benefactor, a New York businessman named Hugh Loebner, to cut it back at least to every two years. (Shortly after I judged the prize, Loebner said he could not, and three members of the prize committee quit.)

If the computer programs gave themselves away with their crudeness, the human beings gave themselves away too, I found—but not with sophistication so much as with simple humanness. People inevitably had distinct personalities that shone through fast and clear, even though we were conversing over computer terminals, about narrowly defined topics.

I quickly became aware that all the confederates' knowledge and how they expressed it must be tied up with their backgrounds, their moods, their reactions to being part of this test. The "Cooking" confederate told me, "My favorite cuisine is oriental food, but I am an excellent Mexican food cook." I asked how mole sauce is made, and she answered, "I've heard you use chocolate, and that sounds awful!" Then she remembered that she had made it once. I asked if she had ever made pad Thai, and she said, "No, what is that?" I mentioned that I am married to a professional gourmet cook; she was fascinated and a bit abashed: "Well, I am not a professional cook—I am self-taught. I had to teach myself because I was married at an early age and it was sink or swim."

Every conversation I had with a human confederate had a similar quality, and so I found myself wondering how anyone could hope ever to teach a computer to converse in a way that would seem at all human. No machine could possibly pass for human without manifesting such a rich, vital context. As the contest made plain, being human isn't about knowledge and syntax—or if it is, it is about mysteriously accumulated, emotion-distorted, often forgotten, confused knowledge, and how you got your knowledge and how you communicate it, which depends on whom you're communicating it to, and what kind of day you're having, and much more. Even the most mundane conversation has this kind of texture—and so, for that matter, does time spent in idleness without saying a word. This may be recognized more often by novelists and poets than by scientists. After all, Marcel Proust built literary immortality on knowing it, and more recently Nicholson Baker knew it well enough to set an entire novel, *The Mezzanine*, in a single silent escalator ride.

And so I came to suspect that the only truly believable computer program would be one able to ape life itself, since thinking as we know it exists only as a purposive tool of living organisms. And even if the thing were created, what purpose would it serve? We already have at our disposal the all-too-easy means for creating human beings with fully human brains and bodies. What's more, creating a human being (or its facsimile) means creating something passionate, demanding, selfish, neurotic, fallible, and often fog-bound. If it isn't, it will never pass.

Computers, it seems to me, are valuable exactly insofar as they are inhuman—they can do enormously complex calculations at lightning speed with no chance for error; they can contain volumes of information without forgetting or confusing it, and with immediate access to all of it; they can be emptied out and refilled to tackle totally new problems with no preconceptions except those explicitly fed to them; and so on. Their great strength is their very lack of humanness. What good would a computer be at any of that if it had the power to change its mind, or get bored, or forget, or wonder?

One area of human intelligence that AI researchers have particularly wanted to simulate is our ability to associate—to retrieve appropriate but disparate memories and to think metaphorically. But isn't our genius for making farfetched associations also the source of many of our neuroses and prejudices and stupidities? The ingenious mind that foresaw an enormous market for automobiles and figured out how to meet that demand by reversing the concept behind the disassembly lines at meat-packing houses—the mind of Henry Ford— was also the anti-Semitic mind that blamed the Jews for the First World War and for a personal difficulty in dealing with investors.

So perhaps creating a program to pass a Turing test is both impossible in the conceivable future and futile. Perhaps there's no reason why anyone should want to create one. I asked Hugh Loebner about this. He is a dreamer who also envisions long-distance gravity railroads, but he is especially devoted to AI, which he concedes is an extremely long way from fulfilling its promise. When I asked him what one would do with a humanlike computer that had what I saw as crippling human weaknesses, he talked of "unstrapping" it from those human frailties when they got in the way. But that sounds an awful lot like backtracking toward a traditional computer.

Mightn't there be a more fundamental urge behind all this activity? The classicist J. David Bolter, who also has a degree in computer science, has pointed out in his book *Turing's Man* that "there was perhaps never a moment in the ancient or modern history of Europe when no one was pursuing the idea of making a human being by other than the ordinary reproductive means." That is to say, he adds, "the cultural equivalent of artificial intelligence can be found throughout the history of Western cultures." Is that what it's all about? Is the quest for AI really at heart an expression of that essential, timeless Promethean urge?

"Of course it is," Loebner said. "Of course."

Thought

1. Provide three examples from the essay which prove Allen's assertion that "nobody has ever designed a program that can converse at all convincingly on a single subject."

2. Why is it so difficult for a computer program to simulate "simple humanness"?

3. Why does Allen conclude that AI programs are "misguided and pointless"?

4. According to Allen, what are the strengths of computers and computer programs?

Style and Structure

5. How does Allen reveal himself to be a qualified judge of AI programs?

6. Show that Allen has used a blend of subjective and objective points of view to support his argument.

7. Why does Allen conclude his essay by quoting a classicist?

Response and Extension

8. What current or anticipated advance in computer technology do you think will have the greatest effect on human interaction? Explain.

9. Read Mary Shelly's Gothic novel *Frankenstein* for another account of the "essential, timeless Promethean urge."

10. Compose a short story or poem involving the interaction between a human intelligence and an artificial one.

The Same Ticking Clock

Carol Shields

My friend Sarah was worried about her five-year-old son, Simon. "I hear voices in my head," he told her, "and they're talking all the time."

It took her a few days to figure out that the buzzings in his brain were nothing more than his own thoughts, the beginning of that life-long monologue that occupies and imprisons the self.

It's here in the private, talky cave of our minds that we spend the greater part of our lives—whether we like it or not. And mostly, it seems, we do like it—"The soul selects her own society"—but there are times when the interior tissues thin and when the endless conversation grows unbearably monotonous, when it seems to be going back and forth across the same grooves of experience, the same channels of persuasion, and we long for release. Long, in fact, to become someone else. Even the most fortunate of us lead lives that are sadly limited; we can inhabit only so many places, follow so many lines of work, and can love a finite number of people. We're enclosed not just by the margins of time and by the accident of geography, but by gender and perspective, and by the stubborn resistance of language to certain modes of meditation.

Our own stories, moreover, are not quite enough; why else are our newspapers filled with Dear Abby and Ann Landers, with problem columns for golden-agers, for adolescents, mid-lifers, parents, consumers, patients and professionals? It's not for the solutions that we devour this often execrable journalese, but for a glimpse of human dilemma, the inaccessible stories of others. Even the smallest narrative fragments have the power to seduce. School children read in their arithmetic books about Mary Brown who buys three pounds of turnips at twenty cents a pound and a kilo and a half of cheese at five dollars a kilo. How much change will she get back from a twenty-dollar bill? The answer arrives easily, or not so easily, but leaves us hungering after the narrative thread—who is this Mary Brown, what will she do with all that cheese, and what of her wider life, her passions and disappointments? A phrase overheard on a bus or perhaps a single name scratched on a wall have the power to call up the world. We want, need, the stories of others. We need, too, to place our own stories beside theirs, to compare, weigh, judge, forgive, and to find, by becoming something other than ourselves, an angle of vision that renews our image of the world.

Of course we draw on our own experiences, though only a few writers draw directly. We want to imbue our fictions with emotional truth, but does this require that we stay imprisoned in the tight little outline of our official résumés, that we must write about the prairies because that's where we live, that we cannot make forays into the swamps of Florida or Mars or Baloneyland, that we must concentrate our steady eyes on the socio-economic class we come from and know best, that we must play it safe—because this is what it amounts to—and write about people of our own generation? A lot of energy has been lost in the name of authenticity; we fear far too much that critical charge—"it doesn't ring true"—and worry too little that it may not ring at all.

"When I write I am free," Cynthia Ozick argues in one of her essays, collected in her book *Art and Ardor*—and she means utterly free, free to be "a stone, or a raindrop, or a block of wood, or a Tibetan, or the spine of a cactus." Our circumscription is largely of our own making, and at least a portion of it flows from a peculiar reluctance—whether caused by a stance of political purity or a fear of trespassing or "getting it wrong"—to experiment with different points of view, and, in particular, with shifts of gender.

We all know that a fully-furnished universe is made up of men and women, and that women writers are often called upon to write about men, and male writers about women. Writers go even further at times, not just writing about the other sex, but speaking through its consciousness, using its voice. The question can be asked, and often is, how successful is this gender-hopping? Does any truth at all seep through? Maybe more than we think. Oscar Wilde had the notion that we can hear more of the author's true voice in her or his fictional impersonations than we can hear in any autobiography. (Not that he bothered with the niceties of gender pronouns.) "Man is least himself," he said, "when he talks in his own person. Give him a mask, and he will tell you the truth." A mask, he said, but he might also have said, a skirt. Or a small pointy beard.

This is not to say that crossing gender lines consists of trickery or sleight of hand, nor is it a masquerade as Anne Robinson in her book, *Male Novelists and their Female Voices*, would like us to think; and certainly not an impersonation as Oscar Wilde suggests. To believe this is to deny the writer the powers of observation and imagination and also to resist the true composition of the universe, real or created, in which men and women exist in more or less equal numbers.

Nevertheless it is still considered a rare achievement for a man to have created a believable and significant woman, and a woman a believable and significant man. We point to these gender trips as exceptions, as marvels. Isn't it amazing, we say, that Brian Moore could get inside the head of Judith Hearne and make us believe in her? And Flaubert—how remarkable that he was able to comprehend the temperament of a French housewife, her yearnings and passion! And there must be a couple of others out there—aren't there? Jane Austen gave us a few men who were worth waiting four hundred pages for, although there's a chilliness about even the best of them. Charlotte Brontë uses the male voice in her novel *The Professor*, but the tone is painfully awkward. In writing the male character, Brontë says, she was working under a disadvantage; when writing about women she was surer of her ground. Joyce Carol Oates once remarked that she did badly with male narrators because for her the angle of vision was restricted, and too much feeling and self-awareness had to be sacrificed.

A few years ago women could point to their own lack of experience in the world of men, but this situation has been extraordinarily altered by legislation and by a revolution in thinking. What has also been altered is the kind of experience that can legitimately be brought to art—birth, motherhood, the rhythms of the female body, a yearning for love, and the domestic component of our lives—which serious literature had previously suppressed. But the news is out: we all, male and female alike, possess a domestic life. The texture of the quotidian is rich with meaning, and the old problem-solution trick is beginning to look like a set-up, a photo opportunity for artificial crisis and faked confrontation. Acknowledgement of that fact leads us to the hypothesis that we are all born with a full range of sympathy toward both men and women—yet something, somewhere, gets in our way and makes us strangers. This is puzzling since, despite the inequities of the power structure, men have always had mothers, sisters, wives, daughters, just as women have had access, albeit limited, to the lives of fathers and brothers, husbands and sons. We have been living under the same roofs all these years and listening to the same ticking clock.

It seems baffling, then, that in this day there should be so few men and women writing well about the other sex and even sadder that they are not writing *for* the other sex. The world we are being offered as readers is only half-realized, a world divided down its middle. As readers we are being misled; as writers we are cheated. I wonder sometimes if the loneliness writers complain about isn't a result of scraping a single personality, our own, down to its last nuance.

What is needed is permission to leave our own skins, worrying less about verisimilitude and trusting the human core we all share. Of course our experiences are necessarily limited—this is part of the human conundrum—but observation and imagination may lead us to what we intuitively know, and have known all along.

Thought

1. a) Identify and explain the implied and explicit metaphors in the opening three paragraphs.

    b) Do you agree with Shields's inferences about personal experience and the nature of our lives? Explain.

2. According to the author, what is the value of other people's narratives in evaluating our own lives? Do you agree? Explain.

3. Summarize Shields's thinking about successfully crossing gender lines in literature.

4. Evaluate Shields's conclusions in the last paragraph. Do you agree that we intuitively understand the perspective of the opposite gender?

Style and Structure

5. Analyze how Shields makes the transition from the general to the particular in this essay. Has she used an effective structure for her ideas? Explain why or why not.

6. Is the personal anecdote in the opening paragraph a fitting introduction to the theme? Explain.

7. Show that Shields makes effective use of quotations in the body of her essay.

8. How does the image of the ticking clock illuminate the theme of this essay?

Response and Extension

9. "The soul selects her own society" is a line taken from an Emily Dickinson poem. Search through a volume of Dickinson's collected works to find other poems that express this, or related, ideas. Write an essay that explains the meaning and significance of these poems. Incorporate your own response to the above statement into your analysis.

10. Consider your own English course of study for writers who cross gender lines, and evaluate their success.

11. Write a personal essay describing how, for you, "the texture of the quotidian is rich with meaning."

12. Compose a short story in which the protagonist is a member of the opposite sex. Before you write, consider the "observation and imagination" required to make this leap in perspective.

"On a Field, Sable, the Letter A, Gules": Signs, Symbols, and Possession of Thought

Neil McDonald

Last fall, across from the southbound platform of the "Museum" subway stop in Toronto, there was a billboard advertisement promoting AIDS awareness. If I recall it accurately, the background was mostly white or cream-coloured, and perhaps there was an outline of the lapel of a coat. This background was blurred and slightly indistinct, but imposed upon it, equally rough-edged, was an image of the red ribbon—a single loop and two tails—that is the accepted symbol of support for the fight against AIDS. Beside the ribbon, in tall, black letters, were the only words on the sign: "Or you could close your eyes and wish it would go away."

The message is clear, direct, and unavoidable. The poster is an effective piece of advertising. What I found interesting at first glance was that the ad chose to use the AIDS ribbon as its provocative symbol. After a while, this choice seemed understandable, and, in fact, it seemed to be the key to the ad's effectiveness. The red ribbon is now ubiquitous. It is a necessary accessory to the dinner jacket or formal gown at any gala event, especially in the arts community. Television and other media often highlight the cause of AIDS, and their coverage always makes use of the movement's symbol. It is also a common adornment on the street and in casual wear; its closest rivals appear in December when white ribbons and white buttons signal the struggle to end violence against women, but the former do not seem to stand out, and the latter, for this year at least, seem to have lost their impact because of an unfortunate similarity with the briefly popular "Trudeau Is Back" buttons issued by McClelland and Stewart.

The timing is right for the red ribbon to be popular. AIDS is no longer a disease confined to homosexuals, IV drug-users, and prostitutes; it has the potential to touch the life of anyone at any time and is regarded by many as the plague of the 1990s. Its own form also makes the ribbon a successful symbol. It is visually striking, especially against black, and its elegant simplicity raises it above the commonness of a standard button. It also bears a stylized resemblance to the letter A, and is therefore easily associated with both the disease and the cause of aiding the fight against it. The red ribbon is a fitting symbol for this fight: its understatement captures the defiance and nobility of the battle against a deadly and cruelly indiscriminate disease. Its colour is that of blood, the colour of our life and the colour of the means of exchanging the HIV virus, the colour of death. The red ribbon is a red letter. It is a scarlet letter.

In 1850, Nathaniel Hawthorne published his now-famous novel, *The Scarlet Letter*. Set in seventeenth-century Puritan New England, the story follows the consequences that a young woman named Hester Prynne faces in her community after giving birth to an illegitimate child. Within the strict morality of the time, it falls to the magistrates of the town to decide upon the punishment: for the duration of her life, Hester Prynne must wear without lapse a red "A" as an outward and visible sign of her corruption. Initially, there is nothing more similar between Hester Prynne's scarlet letter and the red ribbon of AIDS than their coincidental resemblance. And even then, the two symbols seem to oppose one another: the modern one is simple while the fictional one is richly adorned; one stands for a struggle against what is seen as an injustice, while the other represents justice in requital of contravention of divine law. One shows support for a victim while the other marks the victim.

The two letters, though, bear a similarity stronger than what is immediately obvious. When Hester first emerges from prison, the entire community is there to view not only her, but also her baby and the letter. Collectively, the three are the object of everyone's scorn, and the letter is a symbol of sin used by the ministers for its didactic purpose. The reaction of the Puritan community is perhaps often closer to the reality of AIDS than we allow. Some see the disease as fit punishment for irresponsible, if not immoral, lifestyles. As much as we know of how the virus travels and how it can strike randomly, there is still, even among more liberal communities, a fascination with how one contracts it and a stigma attached by some to its carriers. "How did he get it?" is an initial response, whether voiced or not. There is a reluctance to view oneself in the same position. The searing gaze of the Puritans is not as distant as we might hope.

Hester's daily struggle likewise parallels that of AIDS sufferers. She holds up emotionally during her public disgrace with instinctive combativeness, but after the initial rush of the shock, she finds herself alone, as each one who knows she has been condemned to death must feel: "Tomorrow would bring its own trial with it; so would the next day, and so would the next; each its own trial, and yet the very same that was now so unutterably grievous to be borne." Both Hester and the modern victim face these trials for the rest of their lives, but the length of one's life after contracting the virus is indefinite. One can remain HIV positive for years, and AIDS itself does not kill—it takes another sickness to do that. The course of the full-blown disease is often a horribly indecisive series of sicknesses encompassing everything from shingles to pneumonia. Here too, then, the yoke under which these people labour is similar: each inmate faces an oppressively dismal future that nevertheless must be lived out.

The fight in defiance of the sentence, however, allows the nobility of the battle for life to emerge. Just as Hester's selfless devotion to her community causes some to reverse the signification of her 'A' from Adulteress to Able, so do the frequent examples of those who continue to work and teach—to function and function for the benefit of others—earn our respect. *Maclean's* magazine chose a couple as one of its outstanding Canadians of 1993. The man has AIDS and the woman is HIV positive. They earned the distinction for their victory in their fight for compensation from their provincial government for tainted blood the hemophiliac husband was given years ago.

Though Hester's letter takes on its former ignominy near the end of her story, its final revelation is liberating. So, too, is the death of an AIDS sufferer. Drawn out, painful, and often disgusting, the final step, I presume, is one gladly taken by those completing their journey. The symbol of the scarlet letter shares more with the red ribbon of AIDS than we might expect. Both can be seen to stand for endurance, strength of will, and ultimately victory over forces that seem unjust and oppressive.

Despite my admiration for what it may stand for, I will not wear an AIDS ribbon. For a long time, I didn't know why there was something that made me uncomfortable about it, let alone exactly what that something was. I have reason to wear one, if the question comes down to personal experience with the disease, but I don't think that personal history is necessarily relevant. It was that billboard in the subway station that made me realize where my own instinctive reluctance comes from.

The message of the ad is clear: you could wear a red ribbon, "or you could close your eyes and wish it [the disease] would go away." It is direct. It addresses you and prevents you from hiding. It demands that you confront your own attitudes on the disease and the fight against it. That done, it places you in a paradox: if you're not part of the solution, you're part of the problem. Specifically, it tells us that to wear a red ribbon is to support the cause, while not to wear one is to hinder the cure. The paradox is compelling because it galvanizes support by focusing it on the red ribbon; this symbol is portrayed as the only acceptable token of empathy.

The paradox of the ad is more than compelling; it's inescapable. If you're not part of the solution, you're part of the problem. Insofar as the first step to defeating AIDS is understanding it—how the virus travels, how it affects us, and how to protect against it—then ignorance of these questions may well be contributing to its spread. But the ad involves more than this in its technique. It demands not only that supporting the cause of AIDS entails wearing a red ribbon, but also that wearing a red ribbon indicates support. Neither of these assumptions is necessarily true.

There are many ways to support a cause such as the fight against AIDS. Apart from actual research, financial contributions, and volunteer work, basic understanding and empathy are steps that are crucial to preventing its spread and making life bearable for the victims. These, though, are personal actions; they involve our own attitudes and characters, our own confrontation with the disease. There is no necessary connection between supporting the fight against AIDS, between thinking about one's own behaviour and attitudes, and a specific symbol of that support; yet the ad makes this connection. The AIDS ribbon is a wonderful and effective sign that focuses attention, and for many it is a symbol that carries emotional baggage no less burdensome than Hester Prynne's. However, to identify this symbol exclusively with support that one is compelled to give (or remain part of the problem) is a dangerous reduction. Wearing a red ribbon is a choice that each one of us has the right to make free of the pressure of conformity, but the ad exerts its own pressure, and this is the source of its effectiveness: it requires a certain kind of action by defining any other action as unacceptable. "Or you could close your eyes and wish it would go away."

Admittedly, the billboard may be more ambiguous than I am allowing. Its intent may be to use the ribbon as a symbol for AIDS awareness and encourage awareness of the problem without actually demanding that one actually wear a ribbon. The ad, though, uses the ribbon as its sole image, and this reduces ambiguity. The image condenses the complex personal relationship with the issue to a neat symbol; the symbol in turn stands for this relationship and dispenses with variances and exceptions. There are two parts to the equation, and neither admits doubt. The reality beyond the piece, however, is obviously more complicated. Wearing a ribbon does not necessarily indicate that I am aware of AIDS problems any more than wearing a white ribbon guarantees that I do not condone or engage in violence against women. The ad (and the society that encourages it) seeks to invest our visible symbols with power over our behaviour. This kind of connection between outward signs and inner status is a fiction best left to the realm of fiction: Hester Prynne's lover, as a result of his hidden guilt, appears to be scarred by a greater force with his own scarlet letter on his flesh.

Contrary to what the ad in the subway station suggests, the red ribbon cannot stand as the exclusive symbol of the fight against AIDS. Nor should we allow that symbol, for all that it is simple and provocative, to stand for more than it can. The poster is an ad and therefore wants to achieve a desired effect. I do not find it disturbing because it wants us to confront our own attitudes and actions towards AIDS and question whether we are addressing or ignoring its realities. I find the ad disturbing for the precise reason that it is good: it uses a simple image and a simple message to put us in an uncomfortable situation.

I have often wondered at my own reluctance to wear this ribbon and those of other worthy causes. Are my reasons legitimate? Or am I simply refusing to stand for something? Am I afraid to proclaim that I believe in something on the grounds that I may be judged (how or by whom I don't know and don't suppose it matters)? I've come to realize, I think, that the admonishing voice of my anti-self is actually my anticipation of the voices of others, of the same ones, in fact, whose initial judgement I fear. In my thought, I'm caught on both sides: either I'm afraid of being judged by my actions, or I'm afraid of being judged by my non-actions. In this sense, I suppose the ad is not entirely effective with me: while I appreciate its paradox, I cannot accede readily or quickly to its demands. Nevertheless, it is powerful enough to make me feel guilty for my reluctance and consequently question why I question it.

The ad fosters my guilt because it makes me feel as though I am questioning the cause. This is not true, of course; I am questioning techniques of promotion generally and what the red ribbon stands for specifically. It would be easy to make excuses, to allow the ad its leeway and be part of the solution by contributing to the visibility of the struggle. But the more general problem nags too persistently. The ad equates the ribbon with the cause and thereby limits my or anyone's ability to question the symbol in good conscience. This moral and emotional blackmail is its strength and its most distressing feature, for it aligns this cause with some of today's most distressing attitudes: it sends the message that you can't question this issue, for to do so is to be part of the problem. There are many issues today that are "too serious" to be questioned, mocked, disagreed with, or even joked about, and it is unfortunate that the defenses of the politically correct have been erected around this particular one, for it doesn't need them. No worthwhile argument does, and the presence of these defenses is ultimately, and ironically, belittling.

Some commentators have likened the speech codes and behavioural demands of political correctness to a new puritanism, and this brings us back to the Puritan world of Hester Prynne. We are not really so much different. Positions have been reversed, the causes of outrage and acts of sin have changed, and all of the influences on our behaviour are perhaps a little more subtle (if only because we are bombarded with so many); but the dominant, or at least the most loudly proclaimed, attitudes with which we are expected to conform are not as distanced from the severe Puritan morality of *The Scarlet Letter* as we may hope.

We are all faced with a challenge similar to that of Hester and her lover. They struggle under the burden of their sin until they find the means to escape it, and their solution is its own path that is separate from the conventional options which surround them. It is individual and unique. Today we have the difficulty of taking possession of our own ideas, even of claiming our language as our own. We are incessantly barraged with messages telling us how to act, how to speak, and, ultimately, how to think. These messages do not themselves all conform to one view. To break away from some is only to conform to others; the backlash against political correctness can be as harsh and as limiting as the most extreme and ridiculous examples of the original movement. Conflicting signals abound, and the lure of simple answers to the problems these messages address is based on an illusion of comfort: formulations like "do this or be ignorant" oversimplify and reduce without allowing or respecting thoughtful engagement with the issue.

The path out of the confusion is as narrow and rugged as Hester's path out of the forest. Every step must be considered and questioned, and self-examination is critical. As Hester's lover knows, conforming is not the answer; and as the couple discover, running away, choosing the easiest solution, is equally futile. To engage with any of today's controversial issues requires time and thought to allow us to come to our own understanding. But the forces around us work against allowing this process to take place by focusing on the symbols of responses. Ultimately, though, responses cannot be judged on their own, for the process one goes through to possess them is more important—this is how we come to own our actions. An end result may conform, it may conform to non-conformity, or it may be original. Whatever the outward sign, it should not be taken to stand for something simple. A response may be as complicated as not wearing a scarlet letter.

Thought

1. **a)** List and explain three similarities between the red ribbon and the scarlet letter, as outlined by McDonald.
   b) Are these similarities valid, in your view? Explain.

2. **a)** Explain the logic behind McDonald's refusal to wear an AIDS ribbon.
   b) Do you agree with his conclusion? Discuss.

3. "To engage with any of today's controversial issues requires time and thought to allow us to come to our own understanding. But the forces around us work against allowing this process to take place by focusing on the symbols of responses." How does McDonald use the AIDS ribbon and his own perceptions of neo-Puritanism and political correctness to arrive at this conclusion?

4. What is the meaning of the title of this essay?
   a) Explain the use of heraldry in the title.
   b) Why are the words sequenced in this way?

Style and Structure

5. How successfully does McDonald link the AIDS ribbon and the scarlet letter in developing his argument? Explain.

6. The word "essay" comes from the French word *essai*, meaning "attempt."
   a) How is the word particularly appropriate for this piece?
   b) Write an analysis of how McDonald involves the reader in his own musings.

7. Explain how the author interprets the AIDS ribbon as sign, symbol, and paradox.

8. How does McDonald arrive at the conclusion that identifying "this symbol exclusively with support . . . is a dangerous reduction"?

Response and Extension

9. For debate: "Today we have the difficulty of taking possession of our own ideas, even of claiming our language as our own."

10. Do you think McDonald is over-intellectualizing his response to the AIDS ribbon? Discuss.

11. **a)** Why do we use metaphors to describe illness?

    b) In what ways do these metaphors reflect the society in which we live?

12. Compose an essay that comments upon society's attitudes towards the way people contract AIDS. What are the beliefs underlying these attitudes?

13. The author perceives that the ad is "disturbing for the precise reason that it is good: it uses a simple image and a simple message to put us in an uncomfortable situation." In groups, collect ads from newspapers and magazines that you find particularly disturbing and thought-provoking. Together, analyze how they achieve their effect.

14. Design a symbol to represent something you believe people should support or reject. Create the ad that promotes your symbol and your purpose for bringing the issue to awareness.

Unit Synthesis

1. Frederick Allen writes that "people inevitably had distinct personalities that shone through fast and clear, even though we were conversing over computer terminals . . . ." If you established a connection with someone through the Internet, to what extent do you think a satisfying relationship is possible without ever actually meeting them? How might Carol Shields's observation, "The texture of the quotidian is rich with meaning," be considered in this context?

2. What if AI were considerably more advanced than what Frederick Allen describes in his essay? Write a short story about an "artificial intelligence" which forms a romantic attachment with a human being. Try narrating it from the point of view of the opposite gender.

3. Shields observes that "we are all born with a full range of sympathy toward both men and women—yet something, somewhere, gets in our way and makes us strangers."
   a) To what extent do you agree, or disagree, with this remark?
   b) What do you think is the "something" (or things) to which Shields refers?
   c) To what extent are these responsible for the problems Ann Fuller describes in her essay?

4. Neil McDonald laments that "conflicting signals abound, and the lure of simple answers to the problems these messages address is based on an illusion of comfort . . . ." Choose a contemporary issue that interests you, for example AIDS; gender relations; the appropriation of voice. Consider how the questions that this issue raises have been simplified in the popular media. Explore and develop your own ideas by writing an essay that expresses your "thoughtful engagement" with the subject.

Suggested Readings and Viewing

2001: A Space Odyssey (film)

Adams, Douglas *The Hitchhiker's Guide to the Galaxy*

Faludi, Susan *Backlash*

Flagg, Fanny *Fried Green Tomatoes at the Whistle Stop Cafe*

Hawthorne, Nathaniel *The Scarlet Letter*

Hoffman, William *As Is*

Hofstadter, Daniel *Godel, Escher, Bach; Metamagical Themas*

Kingsolver, Barbara *Animal Dreams; The Bean Trees; Pigs in Heaven*

Lem, Stanislaw *The Cyberiad*

Le Guin, Ursula K. *Dancing at the Edge of the World*

Lorenzo's Oil (film)

Philadelphia (film)

Second Best (film)

Shields, Carol *The Stone Diaries*

Smiley, Jane *A Thousand Acres*

Sontag, Susan *Illness as Metaphor*

Walker, Alice *The Color Purple*

Wolf, Naomi *The Beauty Myth; Fire with Fire*

Writing to Analyze a Process

Among the most amazing and hopeful things about us is that we show up, from our day of birth, programmed to receive and transmit even in the most difficult circumstances.

Michael Bérubé

Why Leaves Turn Color in the Fall

Diane Ackerman

The stealth of autumn catches one unaware. Was that a goldfinch perching in the early September woods, or just the first turning leaf? A red-winged blackbird or a sugar maple closing up shop for the winter? Keen-eyed as leopards, we stand still and squint hard, looking for signs of movement. Early-morning frost sits heavily on the grass, and turns barbed wire into a string of stars. On a distant hill, a small square of yellow appears to be a lighted stage. At last the truth dawns on us: Fall is staggering in, right on schedule, with its baggage of chilly nights, macabre holidays, and spectacular, heart-stoppingly beautiful leaves. Soon the leaves will start cringing on the trees, and roll up in clenched fists before they actually fall off. Dry seedpods will rattle like tiny gourds. But first there will be weeks of gushing color so bright, so pastel, so confettilike, that people will travel up and down the East Coast just to stare at it—a whole season of leaves.

Where do the colors come from? Sunlight rules most living things with its golden edicts. When the days begin to shorten, soon after the summer solstice on June 21, a tree reconsiders its leaves. All summer it feeds them so they can process sunlight, but in the dog days of summer the tree begins pulling nutrients back into its trunk and roots, pares down, and gradually chokes off its leaves. A corky layer of cells forms at the leaves' slender petioles, then scars over. Undernourished, the leaves stop producing the pigment chlorophyll, and photosynthesis ceases. Animals can migrate, hibernate, or store food to prepare for winter. But where can a tree go? It survives by dropping its leaves, and by the end of autumn only a few fragile threads of fluid-carrying xylem hold leaves to their stems.

A turning leaf stays partly green at first, then reveals splotches of yellow and red as the chlorophyll gradually breaks down. Dark green seems to stay longest in the veins, outlining and defining them. During the summer, chlorophyll dissolves in the heat and light, but it is also being steadily replaced. In the fall, on the other hand, no new pigment is produced, and so we notice the other colors that were always there, right in the leaf, although chlorophyll's shocking green hid them from view. With their camouflage gone, we see these colors for the first time all year, and marvel, but they were always there, hidden like a vivid secret beneath the hot glowing greens of summer.

The most spectacular range of fall foliage occurs in the northeastern United States and in eastern China, where the leaves are robustly colored, thanks in part to a rich climate. European maples don't achieve the same flaming reds as their American relatives, which thrive on cold nights and sunny days. In Europe, the warm, humid weather turns the leaves brown or mildly yellow. Anthocyanin, the pigment that gives apples their red and turns leaves red or red-violet, is produced by sugars that remain in the leaf after the supply of nutrients dwindles. Unlike the carotenoids, which color carrots, squash, and corn, and turn leaves orange and yellow, anthocyanin varies from year to year, depending on the temperature and amount of sunlight. The fiercest colors occur in years when the fall sunlight is strongest and the nights are cool and dry (a state of grace scientists find vexing to forecast). This is also why leaves appear dizzyingly bright and clear on a sunny fall day: The anthocyanin flashes like a marquee.

Not all leaves turn the same colors. Elms, weeping willows, and the ancient ginkgo all grow radiant yellow, along with hickories, aspens, bottlebrush buckeyes, cottonweeds, and tall, keening poplars. Basswood turns bronze, birches bright gold. Water-loving maples put on a symphonic display of scarlets. Sumacs turn red, too, as do flowering dogwoods, black gums, and sweet gums. Though some oaks yellow, most turn a pinkish brown. The farmlands also change color, as tepees of cornstalks and bales of shredded-wheat-textured hay stand drying in the fields. In some spots, one slope of a hill may be green and the other already in bright color, because the hillside facing south gets more sun and heat than the northern one.

An odd feature of the colors is that they don't seem to have any special purpose. We are predisposed to respond to their beauty, of course.

They shimmer with the colors of sunset, spring flowers, the tawny buff of a colt's pretty rump, the shuddering pink of a blush. Animals and flowers color for a reason—adaptation to their environment—but there is no adaptive reason for leaves to color so beautifully in the fall any more than there is for the sky or ocean to be blue. It's just one of the haphazard marvels the planet bestows every year. We find the sizzling colors thrilling, and in a sense they dupe us. Colored like living things, they signal death and disintegration. In time, they will become fragile and, like the body, return to dust. They are as we hope our own fate will be when we die: Not to vanish, just to sublime from one beautiful state into another. Though leaves lose their green life, they bloom with urgent colors, as the woods grow mummified day by day, and Nature becomes more carnal, mute, and radiant.

We call the season "fall," from the Old English *feallan*, to fall, which leads back through time to the Indo-European *phol*, which also means to fall. So the word and the idea are both extremely ancient, and haven't really changed since the first of our kind needed a name for fall's leafy abundance. As we say the word, we're reminded of that other Fall, in the garden of Eden, when fig leaves never withered and scales fell from our eyes. Fall is the time when leaves fall from the trees, just as spring is when flowers spring up, summer is when we simmer, and winter is when we whine from the cold.

Children love to play in piles of leaves, hurling them into the air like confetti, leaping into soft unruly mattresses of them. For children, leaf fall is just one of the odder figments of Nature, like hailstones or snowflakes. Walk down a lane overhung with trees in the never-never land of autumn, and you will forget about time and death, lost in the sheer delicious spill of color. Adam and Eve concealed their nakedness with leaves, remember? Leaves have always hidden our awkward secrets.

But how do the colored leaves fall? As a leaf ages, the growth hormone, auxin, fades, and cells at the base of the petiole divide. Two or three rows of small cells, lying at right angles to the axis of the petiole, react with water, then come apart, leaving the petioles hanging on by only a few threads of xylem. A light breeze, and the leaves are airborne. They glide and swoop, rocking in invisible cradles. They are all wing and may flutter from yard to yard on small whirlwinds or updrafts, swiveling as they go. Firmly tethered to earth, we love to see things rise up and fly—soap bubbles, balloons, birds, fall leaves. They remind us that the end of a season is capricious, as is the end of life. We especially like the way leaves rock, careen, and swoop as they fall. Everyone knows the motion. Pilots sometimes do a maneuver called a "falling leaf," in which the plane loses altitude quickly and on purpose, by slipping first to the right, then to the left. The machine weighs a ton or more, but in one pilot's mind it is a weightless thing, a falling leaf. She has seen the motion before, in the Vermont woods where she played as a child. Below her the trees radiate gold, copper, and red. Leaves are falling, although she can't see them fall, as she falls, swooping down for a closer view.

At last the leaves leave. But first they turn color and thrill us for weeks on end. Then they crunch and crackle underfoot. They *shush*, as children drag their small feet through leaves heaped along the curb. Dark, slimy mats of leaves cling to one's heels after a rain. A damp, stuccolike mortar of semidecayed leaves protects the tender shoots with a roof until spring, and makes a rich humus. An occasional bulge or ripple in the leafy mounds signals a shrew or a field mouse tunneling out of sight. Sometimes one finds in fossil stones the imprint of a leaf, long since disintegrated, whose outlines remind us how detailed, vibrant, and alive are the things of this earth that perish.

| Thought

1. Why *do* leaves turn colour in the fall?

2. **a)** Summarize Ackerman's thoughts about the effects of fall on human nature.

   b) Do you think Ackerman may be overstating a common and straightforward biological process? Explain.

3. What do you think Ackerman means when she writes that the changing colour of the leaves is "just one of the haphazard marvels the planet bestows every year"? Explain.

Style and Structure

4. Compare Ackerman's figurative and scientific language. Why do you think she has chosen this particular combination of styles?

5. What does Ackerman's diction reveal about the purpose of her essay?

6. **a)** Consider Ackerman's depiction of how leaves fall.
   b) Describe in your own words how this movement illustrates the theme of this essay.

7. Eliminate everything from the essay that does not deal strictly with the changing colours or falling of leaves. What does the essay then become?

Response and Extension

8. Compare Ackerman's evocation of fall with Harry Bruce's evocation of Labour Day ("Labour Day is a Dreaded Bell in the Schoolyard of the Mind" p. 3). Describe what you think are the most interesting links between these essays.

9. Investigate and write an essay about another biological process, such as metamorphosis; the fertilization of an egg; the attack of white blood cells; the pollination of a blossom. In the style of Ackerman, be sure to evoke the human response to this natural process.

10. Write an essay analyzing a non-biological process—crystallization, how a car engine runs, getting over a broken heart. Try to make your analysis as compelling as possible by using vivid description, a sense of awe, humour, personal anecdote, or flights of imaginative speculation.

Life as We Know It

Michael Bérubé

In my line of work I don't think very often about carbon or potassium, much less about polypeptides or transfer RNA. I teach American and African-American literature; Janet Lyon, my legal spouse and general partner, teaches modern British literature and women's studies. Nothing about our jobs requires us to be aware of the biochemical processes that made us—and, more recently, our children—into conscious beings. But in 1985-86, when Janet was pregnant with our first child, Nicholas, I would lie awake for hours, wondering how the baseball-size clump of cells in her uterus was really going to form something living, let alone something capable of thought. The fact that self-replicating molecules had eventually come up with a life-form that could actually pick apart the workings of self-replicating molecules . . . well, let's just say I found this line of thought something of a distraction. At the time, I thought that I would never again devote so much attention to such ideas. I figured the miracle of human birth, like that of humans landing on the moon, would be more routine than miracle the second time around. It wasn't.

Five years later, in September 1991, Janet was pregnant again, another fall semester was beginning, and I was up late writing. At 2:00 A.M., Janet asked when I was coming to bed. At 4:00 A.M., she asked again. "Soon," I said. "Well, you should probably stop working now," she replied, "because I think I'm going into labor." At which point she presented me with an early birthday present, a watch with a second hand.

That was the first unexpected thing: James wasn't due for another two weeks. Then came more unexpected things in rapid succession.

Eight hours later, in the middle of labor, Janet spotted a dangerous arrhythmia on her heart monitor. The only other person in the room was an obstetrics staff nurse; Janet turned to her and barked, "That's

V-tach. We need a cardiologist in here. Get a bolus of lidocaine ready, and get the crash cart." (Being an ex-cardiac-intensive-care nurse comes in handy sometimes.) Pounding on her chest and forcing herself to cough, she broke out of what was possibly a lethal heart rhythm. Labor stalled; Janet and I stared at each other for an hour. Suddenly, at a strange moment when she and I were the only people in the room, James's head presented. I hollered down the hall for help. James appeared within minutes, an unmoving baby of a deep, rich, purple hue, tangled in his umbilical cord. "He looks Downsy around the eyes," I heard. Downsy? He looks stillborn, I thought. They unwrapped the cord, cut it, gave him oxygen. Quickly, incredibly, he revived. No cry, but who cared? They gave him an Apgar score of 7, on a scale of 1 to 10. I remember feeling an immense relief. My wife was alive, my second child was alive. At the end of a teeth-grating hour during which I'd wondered if either of them would see the end of the day, Down syndrome somehow seemed like a reprieve.

Over the next half hour, as the nurses worked on James, and Janet and I tried to collect our thoughts, I realized I didn't know very much about Down's, other than that it meant James had an extra chromosome and would be mentally retarded. I knew I'd have some homework to do.

But what kind of homework were we talking about? Would we ever have normal lives again? We'd struggled for eight years on salaries that left us able to peer at the poverty line only if one of us stood on the other's shoulders. A mere three weeks earlier, the university had hired Janet, thus making us one of the extremely rare dual-career academic couples working in the same department; we knew how lucky we were, and we thought we were finally going to be "comfortable." But now were we going to spend the rest of our days caring for a severely disabled child? Would we have even an hour to ourselves? Christ, we'd only just finished paying off the bills for *Nick's* birth two months earlier, and now were we facing the kind of catastrophic medical debt that fills the op-ed pages? These were selfish thoughts, and the understanding that such thoughts are "natural" didn't make them any less bitter or insistent.

Back in the present, over on his table in the birthing room, James wasn't doing very well. He still wasn't moving, he had no sucking reflex, and he was getting bluer. It turned out that the fetal opening in his heart hadn't closed fully. You and I had the same arrangement until around the time of birth, when our heart's ventricles sealed themselves off in order to get us ready to start conducting oxygen from our lungs into our bloodstream. But James still had a hole where no hole should be, and wasn't oxygenating properly.

There was more. Along with his patent ductus arteriosus and his trisomy 21, there was laryngomalacia (floppy larynx), jaundice, polycythemia (an abnormal increase in red blood cells), torticollis, vertebral anomaly, scoliosis, hypotomia (low muscle tone), and (not least of these) feeding problems. That's a lot of text to wade through to get to your kid.

Within days things got better, and one anxiety after another peeled away: Jamie's duct closed, and as I entered the intensive-care unit one morning I found that the staff had erased from his chart the phone number of the emergency helicopter service that would have flown him to Peoria for heart surgery. He still wasn't feeding, but he was opening an eye now and then and looking out at his brother and his parents.

I got hold of everything I could on genetics, reproduction, and "abnormal" human development, dusting off college textbooks I hadn't touched since before Nick was born. At one point a staff nurse was sent in to check on our mental health; she found us babbling about meiosis and monoploids, wondering anew that Jamie had "gotten" Down syndrome the second he became a zygote. When the nurse inadvertently left behind her notes, Janet sneaked a peek. "Parents seem to be intellectualizing," we read. "Well," Janet shrugged, "that seems accurate enough."

What's odd about Down's is how extraordinarily subtle it can be. Mental retardation is one well-known effect, and it can sometimes be severe, but anyone who's watched Chris Burke in TV's *Life Goes On* or "Mike" in McDonald's commercials knows that the extent of such retardation can be next to negligible. The *real* story of Down's lies not in intelligence tests but in developmental delays across the board, and for the first two years of James's life the most important of these were physical rather than mental (though thanks to James I've come to see how interdependent the mental and physical really are). His muscles are weaker than those of most children his age, his nasal passages imperceptibly narrower. His tongue is slightly thicker, one ear is crinkly. His fingers would be shorter and stubbier but for the fact that his mother's are long, thin, and elegant. His face is a few degrees flatter through the middle, his nose delicate.

Down's doesn't cut all children to one mold. It's sort of like what happens in Ray Bradbury's short story "A Sound of Thunder," in which a time traveller accidentally steps on a butterfly while hunting dinosaurs 65 million years ago and returns home to find that he's changed the conventions of English spelling and the outcome of the previous day's election. As he hit the age of two, James was very pleased to find himself capable of walking; by three, he had learned to say the names of colors, to count to ten, and to claim that he would *really* be turning four. Of all our genetic nondisjunctions (with the possible exception of hermaphroditism), only Down syndrome produces so nuanced, so finely articulated a variation on "normal" reproduction. James is less mobile and more susceptible to colds than his peers, but—as his grandparents have often attested—you could play with him for hours and never see anything "wrong."

There has never been a better time than now to be born with Down syndrome—and that's really saying something, since it has recently been reported in chimpanzees and gorillas. Because our branch of the evolutionary tree split off from the apes' around 15 to 20 million years ago, these reports would seem to suggest that we've produced offspring with Down syndrome with great regularity at every point in our history as hominids—even though it's a genetic anomaly that's not transmitted hereditarily (except in extremely rare instances) and has no obvious survival value. The statistical incidence of Down's in the current human population is no less staggering: there may be 10 million people with Down's worldwide, or just about one on every other street corner.

But although *Homo sapiens* (as well as our immediate ancestors) has always experienced some difficulty dividing its chromosomes, it wasn't until 1866 that British physician J. Langdon Down diagnosed it as "mongolism" (because it produced children with almond-shaped eyes reminiscent, to at least one nineteenth-century British mind, of central Asian faces). At the time, the average life expectancy of children with Down's was under ten. And for a hundred years thereafter—during which the discovery of antibiotics lengthened the life span of Down's kids to around twenty—Down syndrome was formally known as "mongoloid idiocy."

The 1980 edition of my college genetics textbook, *The Science of Genetics: An Introduction to Heredity*, opens its segment on Down's with the words, "An important and tragic instance of trisomy in humans involves Down's syndrome, or mongoloid idiocy." It includes a picture of a "mongoloid idiot" along with a karyotype of his chromosomes and the information that most people with Down's have IQs in the low 40s. The presentation is objective, dispassionate, and strictly "factual," as it should be. But reading it again in 1991, I began to wonder: is there a connection between the official textual representation of Down syndrome and the social policies by which people with Down's are understood and misunderstood?

You bet your life there is. Anyone who has paid attention to the "political correctness" wars on American campuses knows how stupid the academic left can be: we're always talking about language instead of reality, whining about "lookism" and "differently abled persons" instead of changing the world the way the real he-man left *used* to do. But you know, there really is a difference between calling someone "a mongoloid idiot" and calling him or her "a person with Down syndrome." There's even a difference between calling people "retarded" and calling them "delayed." Though these words may appear to mean the same damn thing when you look them up in Webster's, I remember full well from my days as an American male adolescent that I never taunted my peers by calling them "delayed." Even from those of us who were shocked at the frequency with which "homo" and "nigger" were thrown around in our fancy Catholic high school, "retard" aroused no comment, no protest. In other words, a retarded person is just a retard. But *delayed* persons will get where they're going eventually, if you'll only have some patience.

It's impossible to say how deeply we're indebted to those parents, children, teachers, and medical personnel who insisted on treating people with Down's as if they *could* learn, as if they *could* lead "meaningful" lives. In bygone eras, parents who didn't take their children home didn't really have the "option" of doing so; you can't talk about "options" (in any substantial sense of the word) in an ideological current so strong. But in the early 1970s, some parents did bring their children home, worked with them, held them, provided them physical therapy and "special learning" environments. These parents are saints and sages. They have, in the broadest sense of the phrase, uplifted the race. In the 15-million-year history of Down syndrome, they've allowed us to believe that we're finally getting somewhere.

Of course, the phrase "mongoloid idiocy" did not cause Down syndrome any more than the word "homo" magically induces same-sex desire. But words and phrases are the devices by which we beings signify what homosexuality, or Down syndrome, or anything else, will mean. There surely were, and are, the most intimate possible relations between the language in which we spoke of Down's and the social practices by which we understood it—or refused to understand it. You don't have to be a poststructuralist or a postmodernist or a post-*anything* to get this; all you have to do is meet a parent of a child with Down syndrome. Not long ago, we lived next door to people whose youngest child had Down's. After James was born, they told us of going to the library to find out more about their baby's prospects and wading through page after page of outdated information, ignorant generalizations, and pictures of people in mental institutions, face down in their feeding trays. These parents demanded the library get some better material and throw out the garbage they had on their shelves. Was this a "politically correct" thing for them to do? Damn straight it was. That garbage has had its effects *for generations*. It may only look like words, but perhaps the fragile little neonates whose lives were thwarted and impeded by the policies and conditions of institutionalization can testify in some celestial court to the power of mere language, to the intimate links between words and social policies.

Some of my friends tell me this sounds too much like "strict social constructionism"—that is, too much like the proposition that culture is everything and biology is only what we decide to make (of) it. But although James is pretty solid proof that human biology "exists" independently of our understanding of it, every morning when he gets up, smiling and babbling to his family, I can see for myself how much of his life depends on our social practices. On one of those mornings I turned to my mother-in-law and said, "He's always so full of mischief, he's always so glad to see us—the only thought I can't face is the idea of this little guy waking up each day in a state mental hospital." To which my mother-in-law replied, "Well, Michael, if he were waking up every day in a state mental hospital, he wouldn't *be* this little guy."

As it happens, my mother-in-law doesn't subscribe to any strict social constructionist newsletters; she was just passing along what she took to be good common sense. But every so often I wonder how common that sense really is. Every ten minutes we hear that the genetic basis of something has been "discovered," and we rush madly to the newsweeklies: Disease is genetic! Homosexuality is genetic! Infidelity, addiction, obsession with mystery novels—all genetic! Such discourses, it would seem, bring out the hidden determinist in more of us than will admit it. Sure, there's a baseline sense in which our genes "determine" who we are: we can't play the tune unless the score is written down somewhere in the genome. But one does not need or require a biochemical explanation for literary taste, or voguing, or faithless lovers. In these as in all things human, including Down's, the genome is but a template for a vaster and more significant range of social and historical variation. Figuring out even the most rudimentary of relations between the genome and the immune system (something of great relevance to us wheezing asthmatics) involves so many trillions of variables that a decent answer will win you an all-expenses-paid trip to Stockholm.

And yet there's something very seductive about the notion that Down syndrome wouldn't have been so prevalent in humans for so long without good reason. Indeed, there are days when, despite everything I know and profess, I catch myself believing that people with Down syndrome are here for a specific purpose—perhaps to teach us patience, or humility, or compassion, or mere joy. A great deal can go wrong with us in utero, but under the heading of what goes wrong, Down syndrome is among the most basic, the most fundamental, the most common, and the most innocuous, leavening the species with children who are somewhat slower, and usually somewhat gentler, than the rest of the human brood. It speaks to us strongly of design, if design may govern in a thing so small.

After seventeen days in the ICU, James was scheduled for release. We would be equipped with the materials necessary for his care, including oxygen tanks and an apnea monitor that would beep if his heart slowed, became extremely irregular, or stopped. To compensate for his inability to take food orally, James would have a gastrostomy tube surgically introduced through his abdominal wall into his stomach. Janet and I balked. James had recently made progress in his bottle feeding; why do preemptive surgery? We nixed the gastrostomy tube, saying we'd prefer to augment his bottle feedings with a nasal tube and we'd do it ourselves. James stayed three more days in the ICU, and came home to a house full of flowers and homemade dinners from our colleagues.

For the most part, I've repressed the details of that autumn. But every once in a while, rummaging through the medicine closet for Ace bandages or heating pads, I come across the Hypafix adhesive tape with which we attached James's feeding tube to the bridge of his nose, or the strap we wrapped around his tiny chest for his apnea monitor. It's like discovering evidence of another life, dim but indelible, and you realize that once upon a time you could cope with practically anything. Running a small tube through your baby's nose to his stomach is the worst kind of counterintuitive practice. You have to do it carefully, measuring your length of tubing accurately and listening with a stethoscope to make sure you haven't entered the lung. Whenever James pulled out his tubes, we had to do the whole thing over again, in the other nostril this time, lubricating and marking and holding the tube while fumbling with the world's stickiest tape. It's a four-handed job, and I don't blame the staff doctors for assuming we wouldn't undertake such an enterprise alone.

But slowly we got James to bottle feed. After all, for our purposes, Jamie's nasal tube, like unto a thermonuclear weapon, was there precisely so that we wouldn't use it. Each week a visiting nurse would set a minimum daily amount for Jamie's milk intake, and whatever he didn't get by bottle would have to go in by tube. So you can see the incentive at work here. Within a month we began to see glimpses of what James would look like sans tube. Then we stopped giving him oxygen during the night, and gradually his tiny nostrils found themselves a lot less encumbered. He still didn't have a voice, but he was clearly interested in his new home and very trusting of his parents and brother.

In the midst of that winter James began physical therapy and massages. We stretched his neck every night, and whenever we could afford it we took him to a local masseuse who played ambient music, relaxed us all, and worked on James for an hour. His physical therapist showed us how everything about James was connected to everything else: His neck, if left uncorrected, would reshape the bones of his face. The straighter his neck, the sooner he'd sit up, the sooner he'd walk. If he could handle simple solid foods with equal facility in both sides of his mouth, he could center himself more easily; and the sooner he could move around by himself, the more he'd be able to explore and learn. In other words, his eating would affect his ability to walk, and his thighs and torso would impinge upon his ability to talk. I suppose that's what it means to be an organism.

Not only did we realize the profound interdependence of human hearts and minds; we also discovered (and had to reconfigure) our relations to a vast array of social practices and institutions. "Developmental" turns out to be a buzzword for a sprawling nexus of agencies, state organizations, and human disabilities. Likewise, "special needs" isn't a euphemism; it's a very specific marker. We're learning about the differences between "mainstreaming" and "inclusion," and we'll be figuring out the Americans with Disabilities Act for the rest of our lives. Above all else, we know that James is extremely lucky to be so well provided for; when every employer is as flexible as ours, when parental leave is the law of the land, when private insurers can't drop families from the rolls because of "high risk" children, when every child can be fed, clothed, and cared for—*then* we can start talking about what kind of a choice "life" might be.

Because, after all he's been through, James is thriving. He's thrilled to be here and takes a visible, palpable delight in seeing his reflection in the oven door as he toddles across the kitchen, or hearing his parents address him in the voices of the *Sesame Street* regulars, or winging a Nerf ball to his brother on the couch. He knows perfectly well when he's doing something we've never seen before, like riding his toddler bicycle down the hall into the laundry room or calling out "Georgia" and "Hawaii" as he flips through Nick's book of the fifty states. He's been a bibliophile from the moment he learned to turn pages. His current favorite is Maurice Sendak's classic *Where the Wild Things Are*, surely a Great Book by any standard; he began by identifying with Max and then, in one of those "oscillations" described by reader-response criticism and feminist film theory, switched over to identifying with the wild things themselves—roaring his terrible roar and showing his terrible claws.

He has his maternal aunts' large deep eyes, and a beautiful smile that somehow involves his whole body. He's not only an independent cuss, but he also has an attention span of about twenty minutes—eighteen minutes longer than the average American political pundit. He's blessed with a preternaturally patient, sensitive brother in Nick, who, upon hearing one of his classmates' parents gasp "Oh my God" at the news that Jamie had Down's, turned to her and said with a fine mixture of reassurance and annoyance, "He's perfectly all *right*." Like Nick, James has a keen sense of humor; the two of them can be set agiggle by pratfalls, radical incongruities, and mere sidelong looks. He's just now old enough to be curious about what he was like as a baby: as he puts it, all he could do was go "waaah" (holding his fists to his eyes). Barring all the contingencies that can never be barred, James can expect a life span of anywhere from thirty-five to fifty-five years. For tomorrow, he can expect to see his friends at day care, to put all his shapes in his shapes box, and to sing along with Raffi as he shakes his sillies out and wiggles his waggles away.

Before James was born I frankly didn't think very highly of appeals to our "common humanity." I thought such appeals were well intentioned but basically inconsequential. Clearly, Muslim and Christian do not bond over their common ancestor in *Australopithecus*. Rwandan Hutu and Rwandan Tutsi do not toast to the distinctive size of their cerebral cortices. The rape of Bosnia, and Bosnian women, does not stop once Serbian soldiers realize that they too will pass from the earth.

And yet we possess one crucial characteristic: the desire to communicate, to understand, to put ourselves in some mutual, reciprocal form of contact with one another. This desire hasn't proven any better at disarming warheads than any of the weaker commonalities enumerated above, but it stands a better chance nonetheless. For among the most amazing and hopeful things about us is that we show up, from our day of birth, programmed to receive and transmit even in the most difficult circumstances; the ability to imagine mutual communicative relations is embedded in our material bodies, woven through our double-stranded fibers. Granted, it's only one variable among trillions, and it's not even "fundamentally" human—for all we know, dolphins are much better at communication than we are. And the sociohistorical variables of human communication will always be more significant and numerous than any genetic determinism can admit. All the same, it's in our software somewhere, and, better still, it's a program that teaches itself how to operate each time we use it.

Whether you want to consider reciprocal communication a constant or a variable, though, the point remains that it's a human attribute requiring other people if it's going to work. Among the talents we have, it's one we could stand to develop more fully. It's only natural: among our deepest, strongest impulses is the impulse to mutual cuing. Nothing will delight James so much as the realization that you have understood him—except the realization that he has understood you, and recursively understood his own understanding and yours. Perhaps I could have realized our human stake in mutual realization without James's aid; any number of other humans would have been willing to help me out. But now that I get it, I get it for good. Communication is itself self-replicating. Sign unto others as you'd have them sign unto you. Pass it on.

Thought

1. **a)** What are the characteristics of Down syndrome?
   b) What are the causes?

2. What relationship does Bérubé perceive between language and social practices? Provide three examples.

3. **a)** Why did these two parents reject received opinion about Down syndrome?
   b) What have been the results for them and for their sons?

4. What implications for child-rearing lie in the statement made by James's grandmother?

5. Summarize Bérubé's thoughts about language and communication. Do you agree with his conclusions? Explain.

6. According to the author, how might humanity be served by people with Down syndrome? Do you agree with this way of thinking?

Style and Structure

7. What is the purpose of the opening paragraph?

8. Show with examples how the author uses narrative style to convey technical information.

9. Trace the three recurring threads of the essay: personal narrative, scientific exposition, and exploration of moral issues. Using a graphic flow chart, show how the author weaves these strands in order to build his argument.

10. Has Bérubé effectively connected the final three paragraphs to the body of the essay? Explain.

11. Using specific references from the text, characterize Bérubé's voice.

Response and Extension

12. View the film *Lorenzo's Oil*, and compare the characters and behaviours of Lorenzo's parents with James's.

13. Research the development of a contemporary social practice that has introduced new expressions into our lexicon, for example, "wheelchair access" or "closed captioned."

14. In groups, discuss your own hopes and fears about parenthood.

15. Write a journal entry from the point of view of Nick.

16. Compose a letter from the mother or father of James which they might have written to him on the occasion of his twenty-first birthday.

Deficits

Michael Ignatieff

It begins the minute Dad leaves the house.

"Where is George?"

"He is out now, but he'll be back soon."

"That's wonderful," she says.

About three minutes later she'll look puzzled: "But George . . ."

"He's away at work, but he'll be back later."

"I see."

"And what are you doing here? I mean it's nice, but . . ."

"We'll do things together."

"I see."

Sometimes I try to count the number of times she asks me these questions but I lose track.

I remember how it began, five or six years ago. She was 66 then. She would leave a pot to boil on the stove. I would discover it and find her tearing through the house, muttering, "My glasses, my glasses, where the hell are my glasses?"

I took her to buy a chain so that she could wear her glasses around her neck. She hated it because her mother used to wear *her* glasses on a chain. As we drove home, she shook her fist at the windscreen.

"I swore I'd never wear one of these damned things."

I date the beginning to the purchase of the chain, to the silence that descended over her as I drove her home from the store.

The deficits, as the neurologists call them, are localized. She can tell you what it felt like when the Model T Ford ran over her at the school gates when she was a girl of seven. She can tell you what a good-looking man her grandfather was. She can tell you what her grandmother used to say, "A genteel sufficiency will suffice," when turning down another helping at dinner. She remembers the Canadian summer nights when her father used to wrap her in a blanket and take her out to the lake's edge to see the stars.

But she can't dice an onion. She can't set the table. She can't play cards. Her grandson is five, and when they play pairs with his animal cards, he knows where the second penguin will be. She just turns up cards at random.

He hits her because she can't remember anything, because she keeps telling him not to run around quite so much.

Then I punish him. I tell him he has to understand.

He goes down on the floor, kisses her feet, and promises not to hit her again.

She smiles at him, as if for the first time, and says, "Oh, your kiss is so full of sugar."

After a week with him, she looks puzzled and says, "He's a nice little boy. Where does he sleep? I mean, who does he belong to?"

"He's your grandson."

"I see." She looks away and puts her hand to her face.

My brother usually stays with her when Dad is out of town. Once or twice a year, it's my turn. I put her to bed at night. I hand her the pills—small green ones that are supposed to control her moods— and she swallows them. I help her out of her bra and slip, roll down her tights, and lift the nightie over her head. I get into the bed next to hers. Before she sleeps she picks up a Len Deighton and reads a few paragraphs, always the same paragraphs, at the place where she has folded down the page. When she falls asleep, I pick the book off her chest and I pull her down in the bed so that her head isn't leaning against the wall. Otherwise she wakes up with a crick in her neck.

Often when I wake in the night, I see her lying next to me, staring into the dark. She stares and then she wanders. I used to try to stop her, but now I let her go. She is trying to hold on to what is left. There is a method in this. She goes to the bathroom every time she wakes, no matter if it is five times a night. Up and down the stairs silently, in her bare feet, trying not to wake me. She turns the lights on and off. Smooths a child's sock and puts it on the bed. Sometimes she gets dressed, after a fashion, and sits on the downstairs couch in the dark, clutching her handbag.

When we have guests to dinner, she sits beside me at the table, holding my hand, bent forward slightly to catch everything that is said. Her face lights up when people smile, when there is laughter. She doesn't say much any more; she is worried she will forget a name and we won't be able to help her in time. She doesn't want anything to show. The guests always say how well she does. Sometimes they say, "You'd never know, really." When I put her to bed afterward I can see the effort has left her so tired she barely knows her own name.

She could make it easier on herself. She could give up asking questions.

"Where we are now, is this our house?"

"Yes."

"Where is our house?"

"In France."

I tell her: "Hold my hand, I'm here. I'm your son."

"I know."

But she keeps asking where she is. The questions are her way of trying to orient herself, of refusing and resisting the future that is being prepared for her.

She always loved to swim. When she dived into the water, she never made a splash. I remember her lifting herself out of the pool, as sleek as a seal in a black swimsuit, the water pearling off her back. Now she says the water is too cold and taking off her clothes too much of a bother. She paces up and down the poolside, watching her grandson swim, stroking his towel with her hand, endlessly smoothing out the wrinkles.

I bathe her when she wakes. Her body is white, soft, and withered. I remember how, in the changing-huts, she would bend over as she slipped out of her bathing suit. Her body was young. Now I see her skeleton through her skin. When I wash her hair, I feel her skull. I help her from the bath, dry her legs, swathe her in towels, sit her on the edge of the bath and cut her nails: they are horny and yellow. Her feet are gnarled. She has walked a long way.

When I was as old as my son is now I used to sit beside her at the bedroom mirror watching her apply hot depilatory wax to her legs and upper lip. She would pull her skirt up to her knees, stretch her legs out on the dresser, and sip beer from the bottle, while waiting for the wax to dry. "Have a sip," she would say. It tasted bitter. She used to laugh at the faces I made. When the wax had set, she would begin to peel it off, and curse and wince, and let me collect the strips, with fine black hairs embedded in them. When it was over, her legs were smooth, silky to touch.

Now I shave her. I soap her face and legs with my shaving brush. She sits perfectly still; as my razor comes around her chin we are as close as when I was a boy.

She never complains. When we walk up the hill behind the house, I feel her going slower and slower, but she does not stop until I do. If you ask her whether she is sad, she shakes her head. But she did say once, "It's strange. It was supposed to be more fun than this."

I try to image what the world is like for her. Memory is what reconciles us to the future. Because she has no past, her future rushes toward her, a bat's wing brushing against her face in the dark.

"I told you. George returns on Monday."

"Could you write that down?"

So I do. I write it down in large letters, and she folds it in her white cardigan pocket and pats it and says she feels much less worried.

In half an hour, she has the paper in her hand and is showing it to me.

"What do I do about this?"

"Nothing. It just tells you what is going to happen."

"But I didn't know anything of this."

"Now you do," I say and I take the paper away and tear it up.

It makes no sense to get angry at her, but I do.

She is afraid Dad will not come back. She is afraid she has been abandoned. She is afraid she will get lost and never be able to find her way home. Beneath the fears that have come with the forgetting, there lie anxieties for which she no longer has any names.

She paces the floor, waiting for lunch. When it is set before her, she downs it before anyone else, and then gets up to clear the plates.

"What's the hurry?" I ask her.

She is puzzled. "I don't know," she says. She is in a hurry, and she does not know why. She drinks whatever I put before her. The wine goes quickly.

"You'll enjoy it more if you sip it gently."

"What a good idea," she says and then empties the glass with a gulp.

I wish I knew the history of this anxiety. But I don't. All she will tell me is about being sprawled in the middle of Regent Street amid the blood and shop glass during an air raid, watching a mother sheltering a child, and thinking: I am alone.

In the middle of all of us, she remained alone. We didn't see it. She was the youngest girl in her family, the straggler in the pack, born cross-eyed till they straightened her eyes out with an operation. Her father was a teacher and she was dyslexic, the one left behind.

In her wedding photo, she is wearing her white dress and holding her bouquet. They are side by side. Dad looks excited. Her eyes are wide open with alarm. Fear gleams from its hiding place. It was her secret and she kept it well hidden. When I was a child, I thought she was faultless, amusing, regal. My mother.

She thinks of it as a happy family, and it was. I remember them sitting on the couch together, singing along to Fats Waller records. She still remembers the crazy lyrics they used to sing:

There's no disputin'
That's Rasputin
The high-falutin loving man.

I don't know how she became so dependent on him, how she lost so many of the wishes she once had for herself, and how all her wishes came to be wishes for him.

She is afraid of his moods, his silences, his departures, and his returns. He has become the weather of her life. But he never lets her down. He is the one who sits with her in the upstairs room, watching television, night after night, holding her hand.

People say: it's worse for you, she doesn't know what is happening. She used to say the same thing herself. Five years ago, when she began to forget little things, she knew what was in store, and she said to me once, "Don't worry. I'll make a cheerful old nut. It's you who'll have the hard time." But that is not true. She feels everything. She has had time to count up every loss. Every night, when she lies awake, she stares at desolation.

What is a person? That is what she makes you wonder. What kind of a person are you if you only have your habits left? She can't remember her grandson's name, but she does remember to shake out her tights at night and she never lets a dish pass her by without trying to clean it, wipe it, clear it up, or put it away. The house is littered with dishes she is putting away in every conceivable cupboard. What kind of a person is this?

It runs in the family. Her mother had it. I remember going to see her in the house with old carpets and dark furniture on Prince Arthur Avenue. The windows were covered with the tendrils of plants growing in enormous Atlas battery jars, and the parquet floors shone with wax. She took down the giraffe, the water buffalo, and the leopard—carved in wood—that her father had brought back from Africa in the 1880s. She sat in a chair by the fire and silently watched me play with them. Then—and it seems only a week later—I came to have Sunday lunch with her and she was old and diminished and vacant, and when she looked at me she had no idea who I was.

I am afraid of getting it myself. I do ridiculous things: I stand on my head every morning so that the blood will irrigate my brain; I compose suicide notes, always some variant of Captain Oates's: "I may be gone for some time." I never stop thinking about what it would be like for this thing to steal over me.

She has taught me something. There are moments when her pacing ceases, when her hunted look is conjured away by the stillness of dusk, when she sits in the garden, watching the sunlight stream through all the trees they planted together over 25 years in this place, and I see something pass over her face which might be serenity.

And then she gets up and comes toward me looking for a glass to wash, a napkin to pick up, a child's toy to rearrange.

I know how the story has to end. One day I return home to see her and she puts out her hand and says: "How nice to meet you." She's always charming to strangers.

People say I'm already beginning to say my farewells. No, she is still here. I am not ready yet. Nor is she. She paces the floor, she still searches for what has been lost and can never be found again.

She wakes in the night and lies in the dark by my side. Her face, in profile, against the pillow has become like her mother's, the eye sockets deep in shadow, the cheeks furrowed and drawn, the gaze ancient and disabused. Everything she once knew is still inside her, trapped in the ruined circuits—how I was when I was little, how she was when I was a baby. But it is too late to ask her now. She turns and notices I am awake too. We lie side by side. The darkness is still. I want to say her name. She turns away from me and stares into the night. Her nightie is buttoned at the neck like a little girl's.

Thought

1. Why do you think Ignatieff chose "Deficits" as the title of his essay? What levels of meaning does it convey?

2. In your groups decide upon which of Ignatieff's mother's deficits you find most poignant. Explain the reasons for your decision.

3. "Memory is what reconciles us to the future." What do you think the author means by this?

4. Ignatieff writes, "I wish I knew the history of that anxiety." Considering his account of his mother's past, list and analyze all those factors that you think could have contributed to her present fears.

5. The author's mother remembers thinking to herself, "I am alone." What levels of meaning does this evoke?

6. What do you think the author has in mind when he writes that "she still searches for what has been lost and can never be found again"? Make a list of everything you think Ignatieff's mother has lost. What do you think she might have gained?

7. Ignatieff writes, "What is a person? That is what she makes you wonder. What kind of a person are you if you only have your habits left?" Do you agree that his mother has only her habits remaining? Explain your answer.

Style and Structure

8. How effective is the dialogue at the beginning of the essay? Explain.

9. How does Ignatieff use incidents from his mother's present to evoke aspects of her past?

10. Show that Ignatieff never loses sight of his mother as a person, rather than regarding her as a patient.

11. Choose several sentences or phrases that you feel best characterize the tone of the essay, and explain why.

12. Why do you think the author chose to end his essay with the analogy of the little girl?

Response and Extension

13. In groups, discuss what makes a person "alone."

14. Write a monologue in which you assume the character of someone who has no memory.

15. Compose a letter to a real or imaginary person whom you love, but who has no memory of you.

16. Construct an autobiography of yourself, making liberal use of photographs.

Thunderstrokes and Firebolts

Janice McEwen

Imagine the chagrin of a Renfrew, Ontario farmer who pulled on the handle of a recently repaired barn door one morning following a thunderstorm only to have the door crumble into a heap of individual boards at his feet.

The man was left sheepishly wondering about his carpentry skills until a local lightning protection contractor examined the door and explained that, unknown to the farmer, a bolt of lightning had hit the barn during the storm. Leapfrogging from nail-to-nail along the Z-shaped bracing boards that supported the door, the lightning made its way to the ground. In the process the heat produced by the bolt reduced the nails to dust.

For the 118 passengers aboard an Air Canada DC-8 jetliner, lightning had much more serious consequences: the ill-fated plane crashed in a swampy field shortly after take-off from Montreal in November, 1963. When investigators finished sifting through the rubble of what is still Canada's worst airplane disaster, lightning was high on the list of probable causes.

Lightning is the most awesome of nature's weather phenomena—a single stroke of lightning produces more electricity than the combined output of all electrical power plants in the United States. The average cloud-to-ground lightning bolt averages only six inches in diameter, but attains a core temperature of about 50 000 degrees Fahrenheit—five times the temperature at the surface of the sun.

Each day some 44 000 thunderstorms break out around the globe, the greatest concentration of them within the belt extending 30 degrees north and south of the equator. As you read this there are 1800 electrical storms raging throughout the world, and by the time you finish this sentence, lightning will have struck earth 100 times.

Too frequently, lightning strikes spell disaster. Each year several hundred North Americans are killed by lightning, and others die in the fires that follow in the wake of electrical storms. Ten thousand forest fires and more than 30 000 building blazes are caused by lightning. Damages to property and loss of timber are estimated at more than 50 million dollars annually.

Yet the scientific study of lightning is still in pioneering stages, leaving unexplained many aspects of the complicated series of events that take place in the five thousandths of a second required for the average lightning bolt to strike.

Scientists are, for example, at a loss to explain "ball" lightning, a rare occurrence in which an orb about eight inches in diameter forms at the lightning impact point. This blinding ball of energy is able to move around at a speed of several metres per second and is said to be accompanied by a hissing sound. Ball lightning is able to pass through closed windowpanes and often disappears with an explosion.

Little wonder that this astounding natural force has always aroused man's curiosity and fear.

For our ancient forefathers, there was no doubt about what caused lightning: various gods were flamboyantly expressing their disapproval of somebody's actions.

Zeus, as legend would have it, was particularly keen to use a handy supply of lightning bolts to express his frequent outbursts of rage. Unfortunate were the troops that attacked friends of this surly deity— Zeus would often step in when his side was losing and tip the tides of battle with a few well-placed bolts among the enemy ranks.

But recent findings by Nobel Prize winner Dr. Harold Urey suggest that the ancients may not have underestimated the nearly divine role lightning plays in terrestrial life.

Through laboratory reconstruction of the atmosphere of the young, lifeless earth—an atmosphere composed of ammonia, methane, hydrogen and water—students of Urey found that when electrical sparks, much like lightning, were passed through this medium, amino acids were created—the first building blocks in the evolution of life.

Recent findings also suggest that we can thank lightning (at least partially) for giving the world plants. Although nitrogen makes up 80 per cent of the earth's atmosphere, in its pure state it is useless to plants.

It has been found that lightning causes atmospheric nitrogen to combine with oxygen, forming nitric-oxide gas. This gas dissolves in rain and falls to the earth as usable nitrates. Some scientists estimate that hundreds of millions of tons of these nitrates are produced by lightning each year. It's enough to make a purveyor of bagged 20-20-20 weep.

Benjamin Franklin, that portly Renaissance man of the eighteenth century, made the first real breakthrough in man's understanding of lightning by determining that it was, indeed, a huge electrical spark. But it is ironic (in light of his factual discoveries) that one of the most prevalent schoolboy myths still surrounding lightning features Mr. Franklin as its main character.

Everyone has heard about Franklin's kite flying antics. What few people realize is that his kite was never struck by lightning. Had it been, either the string would have burned and Mr. Franklin would have lost his kite, or the experimenter himself would have been struck, and the world would have lost an able scholar and statesman.

What happened during this famous flight was that there was enough difference in the electrical charge between the earth and the air at the level of the kite to create a small finger-tingling flow of electrical current through Mr. Franklin's string.

Today we know that conditions leading to electrical storms begin when a strong negative charge builds in rain (cumulo-nimbus) clouds. How this charge develops is still a matter of scientific debate, but an accepted theory is that air turbulence in the clouds creates a build-up of negatively-charged electrons.

Free electrons on the earth directly below the cloud are repelled by the huge numbers of electrons above, and therefore the charge of the earth becomes more positive.

Because opposing charges are attracted to each other, the electrons in the cloud yearn to get to the positive earth.

Air, however, is a poor conductor of electricity. As the cloud matures, the charge continues to build until pressure becomes great enough to permit the electrons to leap through the insulative layer of air.

The first tentative electrons probe toward the earth in a series of steps that gives a lightning bolt its irregular shape. These first electrons clear a path for those in the cloud, and as soon as the first electrons connect with the ground, an avalanche of electricity surges from the sky.

Lightning has struck.

Lightning bolts range from 1000 to 9000 feet long, and can attain speeds over 60 000 miles per second.

A lightning bolt seeks the route offering the least electrical resistance in its journey from cloud to ground. Almost any solid object offers an easier path for electricity than air: it could be a tree, a utility pole, a high patch of ground; it could also be your barn, one of your outbuildings—or your house.

Lightning is a hazard deserving special attention from rural dwellers. Grim statistics show that nine out of ten lightning-caused deaths occur outside city limits. Fire authorities estimate that lightning causes up to 37 per cent of all rural building fires.

G.A. Pelletier, chief of technical services in the Ontario Fire Marshall's Office and one of Canada's foremost authorities on lightning, attributes part of this phenomenal loss of life and property in rural areas to people being misinformed about this frightening natural force.

"Most people are totally unaware of what lightning is, how it behaves and what it can do," he said. "Take the old wives' tale about lightning never hitting the same place twice—a common enough belief. It's totally false. As a matter of fact, if a place has been hit once, it shows that it is a prime site for future strikes."

Pelletier also says that many people believe their homes to be safe from lightning because of the proximity of tall trees or a high television aerial. Neither is necessarily true.

We can thank Ben Franklin's inquisitive (and financially long-sighted) mind for the protection we now have against destruction of property caused by lightning.

"It has pleased God in His goodness to mankind, at length to discover to them the means of securing their habitations and other buildings from mischief by thunder and lightning," wrote Franklin in the 1753 edition of *Poor Richard's Almanack*. He went on to outline a system that not only worked, but which remains, almost unchanged, as the most efficient form of lightning protection.

The heart of a lightning protection system is a series of rods extending at least 12 inches above a structure at lightning vulnerable places: peaks, gable ends, chimneys, etc.

These lightning rods (or "air terminals" in the jargon of lightning experts) are connected to each other by a woven copper cable roughly one-half inch thick. The cable, in turn, is grounded on at least two sides of the building to rods driven 10 feet into the earth, although the depth will vary somewhat in accordance with soil conditions. It is often said that a lightning rod gives protection within a circle whose radius is the height of the tip of the rod from the ground. Unfortunately, lightning does not always adhere to this rule, but the Canadian Standards Association says that "a properly installed lightning rod system, if not 100 per cent effective, will ensure that in nearly all cases of lightning strikes to buildings, little or no damage will result."

Fire statistics support these claims: in 1975, the most recent year for which figures are available, only 91 of the 2559 structural fires started by lightning in Ontario occurred in buildings protected by lightning rod systems.

Pelletier explains that a properly working lightning rod system creates an easy route for the electrical charges to follow, diverting them away from the building and allowing them to dissipate harmlessly in the ground.

This, of course, is preferable to the unprotected alternative—where the bolt strikes the roof of the building and passes through the structure itself, leaping through walls, appliances, plumbing fixtures, radiators (and in some cases human beings) en route to the earth . . . .

Your chances of being killed by lightning this summer are roughly one in a million—certainly no reason to cancel plans for boating, picnics and hiking during the warm season, but reason enough to implement precautions.

An electrical storm that swept the New York City area took a typical toll of human victims. A golfer whose foursome had sought refuge from the rain beneath a tree (a common mistake that accounts for one-third of thunderstorm fatalities) died when lightning slammed into the tree. His companions were unharmed. The storm's next victim was a fisherman holding a metal casting rod. Lightning leapt from the rod to his jacket zipper. His single companion was injured but recovered. The final victim, a young man, died while standing near a beachhouse.

All of these deaths could have been prevented had the victims followed commonsense safety measures.

A car is perhaps the safest place to be during an electrical storm.

There have been few, if any, substantiated cases of lightning striking an automobile, but laboratory experiments show that the charge would pass harmlessly over the metal shell of the car and then leap from the undercarriage to the pavement.

Second only to a car (and virtually 100 per cent safe) is a dry building protected by lightning rods. When the first signs of thunder make themselves manifest, the sensible thing to do is go straight to the shelter of a protected building. Two-thirds of lightning-caused deaths occur outdoors.

When you are caught by a storm in an open area, do not, under any circumstances, take shelter under an isolated tree. If you cannot reach a protected building, seek a low-lying area of open land.

Trees are favourite targets for lightning, and electrical charges that surge from the base of a struck tree can kill for a considerable distance.

In one instance, a single bolt of lightning struck a tree in a Utah pasture and killed 500 sheep. There are recorded cases of cattle being killed while standing 100 yards from a struck tree.

Few people are killed by direct lightning strikes. If someone were directly hit, he would be severely burned. In most cases, the lightning victim is not burned but dies because currents cast off from a nearby lightning strike pass through his body, stopping his breathing and heartbeat.

Lightning frequently strikes water and electrical charges travel freely through this medium. Boats are high on the list of undesirable places to be when there is an approaching electrical storm. If you are in a boat, get to shore immediately and move some distance inland; shoreline trees are prime candidates for lightning strikes.

Swimmers, too, are in danger of being injured or killed by electrical charges that surge through water as a result of lightning.

If you find yourself in a protected house at the outbreak of a thunderstorm, take heart; you are safe.

Still, it is wise to stay away from sinks and bathtubs—your plumbing system is connected to a metal vent pipe protruding through the roof and is a potential lightning target.

Avoid touching refrigerators, stoves and other large metal objects. Do not use telephones or other electrical appliances, and stay away from stovepipes, chimneys and fireplaces. Windows and doors should be closed.

If your home or one of your outbuildings is struck by lightning, an immediate check-over is due to insure that no hidden fires have started. (Old-timers often referred to hot and cold lightning—the former causing fires and the latter merely hitting with one explosive bolt.) When lightning fells a human, it is often possible to revive him with prolonged artificial respiration. Many victims have recovered fully, while others were left with sight or hearing impairments.

But even when nestled in the security of a snug, lightning-protected house, there are still some people who find themselves quivering under the bed with the dog at the faintest rumble of thunder. This unfortunate segment of the population might consider moving to the Arctic or Antarctic—areas which see only one thunderstorm per decade.

If relocation does not fit your plans, we can only offer the slim comfort of words spoken by one lightning protection expert: "If you heard the thunder, the lightning did not strike you. If you saw the lightning, it missed you; and if it did strike you, you would not have known it."

Thought

1. **a)** Why do you think thunder and lightning exert such a hold on our psyches?

   b) How, and to what extent, does this essay address this question? Explain your answer.

2. **a)** In your own words, describe first the process that culminates in an electrical storm, and then the physics involved in a lightning discharge.

   b) Does McEwan's explanation of these two processes raise any further questions for you, scientific or otherwise?

3. Make a list from the essay of common misconceptions about lightning. How do you account for the prevalence of each of these misconceptions?

Style and Structure

4. Explain why you think McEwan chose to open her essay with the incidents recounted in the first three paragraphs.

5. How would you describe the "shape" of this essay, the structure of its ideas? Support your answer with specific references to the essay.

6. This essay presents an abundance of facts about lightning.
   a) Show how the author uses a convincing blend of statistical and anecdotal evidence.
   b) Which approach do you find most effective? Explain.

Response and Extension

7. Devise a method to harness the energy of lightning. Your method may or may not be based on scientific data. Write an analytical essay outlining the process.

8. Write a short story that centres on an experience with lightning. Try to make the particular circumstances as dramatic and original as you can.

9. Thunder, lightning, and storms in general have enriched our lexicon with a number of metaphors and similes. In small groups, "brainstorm" a list of these images and expressions, and then compile a list of your own. Compare your list with the other groups in your class.

10. McEwan writes that "the ancients may not have underestimated the nearly divine role lightning plays in terrestrial life." The phenomena she goes on to describe could rival those found in Lewis Thomas's essay, "Seven Wonders" (p. 36). Write an imaginary, mythological account which elaborates on one of the two processes McEwan outlines here.

11. Compare the style and intent of McEwan's essay to Diane Ackerman's "Why Leaves Turn Color in the Fall" (p. 105) What are the similarities and differences? What do you find most interesting about these two approaches to natural phenomena?

Imelda

Richard Selzer

I heard the other day that Hugh Franciscus had died. I knew him once. He was the Chief of Plastic Surgery when I was a medical student at Albany Medical College. Dr. Franciscus was the archetype of the professor of surgery—tall, vigorous, muscular, as precise in his technique as he was impeccable in his dress. Each day a clean lab coat monkishly starched, that sort of thing. I doubt that he ever read books. One book only, that of the human body, took the place of all others. He never raised his eyes from it. He read it like a printed page as though he knew that in the calligraphy there just beneath the skin were all the secrets of the world. Long before it became visible to anyone else, he could detect the first sign of granulation at the base of a wound, the first blue line of new epithelium at the periphery that would tell him that a wound would heal, or the barest hint of necrosis that presaged failure. This gave him the appearance of a prophet. "This skin graft will take," he would say, and you must believe beyond all cyanosis, exudation and inflammation that it would.

He had enemies, of course, who said he was arrogant, that he exalted activity for its own sake. Perhaps. But perhaps it was no more than the honesty of one who knows his own worth. Just look at a scalpel, after all. What a feeling of sovereignty, megalomania even, when you know that it is you and you alone who will make certain use of it. It was said, too, that he was a ladies' man. I don't know about that. It was all rumor. Besides, I think he had other things in mind than mere living. Hugh Franciscus was a zealous hunter. Every fall during the season he drove upstate to hunt deer. There was a glass-front case in his office where he showed his guns. How could he shoot a deer? we asked. But he knew better. To us medical students he was someone heroic, someone made up of several gods, beheld at a distance, and always from a lesser height. If he had grown accustomed to his miracles, we had not. He had no close friends on the staff. There was something a little sad in that. As though once long ago he had been flayed by friendship and now the slightest breeze would hurt. Confidences resulted in dishonor. Perhaps the person in whom one confided would scorn him, betray. Even though he spent his days among those less fortunate, weaker than he—the sick, after all— Franciscus seemed aware of an air of personal harshness in his environment to which he reacted by keeping his own counsel, by a certain remoteness. It was what gave him the appearance of being haughty. With the patients he was forthright. All the facts laid out, every question anticipated and answered with specific information. He delivered good news and bad with the same dispassion.

I was a third-year student, just turned onto the wards for the first time, and clerking on Surgery. Everything—the operating room, the morgue, the emergency room, the patients, professors, even the nurses— was terrifying. One picked one's way among the mines and booby traps of the hospital, hoping only to avoid the hemorrhage and perforation of disgrace. The opportunity for humiliation was everywhere.

It all began on Ward Rounds. Dr. Franciscus was demonstrating a cross-leg flap graft he had constructed to cover a large fleshy defect in the leg of a merchant seaman who had injured himself in a fall. The man was from Spain and spoke no English. There had been a comminuted fracture of the femur, much soft tissue damage, necrosis. After weeks of débridement and dressings, the wound had been made ready for grafting. Now the patient was in his fifth postoperative day. What we saw was a thick web of pale blue flesh arising from the man's left thigh, and which had been sutured to the open wound on the right thigh. When the surgeon pressed the pedicle with his finger, it blanched; when he let up, there was a slow return of the violaceous color.

"The circulation is good," Franciscus announced. "It will get better." In several weeks, we were told, he would divide the tube of flesh at its site of origin, and tailor it to fit the defect to which, by then, it would have grown more solidly. All at once, the webbed man in the bed reached out, and gripping Franciscus by the arm, began to speak rapidly, pointing to his groin and hip. Franciscus stepped back at once to disengage his arm from the patient's grasp.

"Anyone here know Spanish? I didn't get a word of that."

"The cast is digging into him up above," I said. "The edges of the plaster are rough. When he moves, they hurt."

Without acknowledging my assistance, Dr. Franciscus took a plaster shears from the dressing cart and with several large snips cut away the rough edges of the cast.

"*Gracias, gracias.*" The man in the bed smiled. But Franciscus had already moved on to the next bed. He seemed to me a man of immense strength and ability, yet without affection for the patients. He did not want to be touched by them. It was less kindness that he showed them than a reassurance that he would never give up, that he would bend every effort. If anyone could, he would solve the problems of their flesh.

Ward Rounds had disbanded and I was halfway down the corridor when I heard Dr. Franciscus' voice behind me.

"You speak Spanish." It seemed a command.

"I lived in Spain for two years," I told him.

"I'm taking a surgical team to Honduras next week to operate on the natives down there. I do it every year for three weeks, somewhere. This year, Honduras. I can arrange the time away from your duties here if you'd like to come along. You will act as interpreter. I'll show you how to use the clinical camera. What you'd see would make it worthwhile."

So it was that, a week later, the envy of my classmates, I joined the mobile surgical unit—surgeons, anesthetists, nurses and equipment— aboard a Military Air Transport plane to spend three weeks performing plastic surgery on people who had been previously selected by an advance team. Honduras. I don't suppose I shall ever see it again. Nor do I especially want to. From the plane it seemed a country made of clay—burnt umber, raw sienna, dry. It had a deadweight quality, as though the ground had no buoyancy, no air sacs through which a breeze might wander. Our destination was Comayagua, a town in the Central Highlands. The town itself was situated on the edge of one of the flatlands that were linked in a network between the granite mountains. Above, all was brown, with only an occasional Spanish cedar tree; below, patches of luxuriant tropical growth. It was a day's bus ride from the airport. For hours, the town kept appearing and disappearing with the convolutions of the road. At last, there it lay before us, panting and exhausted at the bottom of the mountain.

That was all I was to see of the countryside. From then on, there was only the derelict hospital of Comayagua, with the smell of spoiling bananas and the accumulated odors of everyone who had been sick there for the last hundred years. Of the two, I much preferred the frank smell of the sick. The heat of the place was incendiary. So hot that, as we stepped from the bus, our own words did not carry through the air, but hung limply at our lips and chins. Just in front of the hospital was a thirsty courtyard where mobs of waiting people squatted or lay in the meager shade, and where, on dry days, a fine dust rose through which untethered goats shouldered. Against the walls of this courtyard, gaunt, dejected men stood, their faces, like their country, preternaturally solemn, leaden. Here no one looked up at the sky. Every head was bent beneath a wide-brimmed straw hat. In the days that followed, from the doorway of the dispensary, I would watch the brown mountains sliding about, drinking the hospital into their shadow as the afternoon grew later and later, flattening us by their very altitude.

The people were mestizos, of mixed Spanish and Indian blood. They had flat, broad, dumb museum feet. At first they seemed to me indistinguishable the one from the other, without animation. All the vitality, the hidden sexuality, was in their black hair. Soon I was to know them by the fissures with which each face was graven. But, even so, compared to us, they were masked, shut away. My job was to follow Dr. Franciscus around, photograph the patients before and after surgery, interpret and generally act as aide-de-camp. It was exhilarating. Within days I had decided that I was not just useful, but essential. Despite that we spent all day in each other's company, there were no overtures of friendship from Dr. Franciscus. He knew my place, and I knew it, too. In the afternoon he examined the patients scheduled for the next day's surgery. I would call out a name from the doorway to the examining room. In the courtyard someone would rise. I would usher the patient in, and nudge him to the examining table where Franciscus stood, always, I thought, on the verge of irritability. I would read aloud the case history, then wait while he carried out his examination. While I took the "before" photographs, Dr. Franciscus would dictate into a tape recorder:

"Ulcerating basal cell carcinoma of the right orbit—six by eight centimeters—involving the right eye and extending into the floor of the orbit. Operative plan: wide excision with enucleation of the eye. Later, bone and skin grafting." The next morning we would be in the operating room where the procedure would be carried out.

We were more than two weeks into our tour of duty—a few days to go—when it happened. Earlier in the day I had caught sight of her through the window of the dispensary. A thin, dark Indian girl about fourteen years old. A figurine, orange-brown, terra-cotta, and still attached to the unshaped clay from which she had been carved. An older, sun-weathered woman stood behind and somewhat to the left of the girl. The mother was short and dumpy. She wore a broad-brimmed hat with a high crown, and a shapeless dress like a cassock. The girl had long, loose black hair. There were tiny gold hoops in her ears. The dress she wore could have been her mother's. Far too big, it hung from her thin shoulders at some risk of slipping down her arms. Even with her in it, the dress was empty, something hanging on the back of a door. Her breasts made only the smallest imprint in the cloth, her hips none at all. All the while, she pressed to her mouth a filthy, pink, balled-up rag as though to stanch a flow or buttress against pain. I knew that what she had come to show us, what we were there to see, was hidden beneath that pink cloth. As I watched, the woman handed down to her a gourd from which the girl drank, lapping like a dog. She was the last patient of the day. They had been waiting in the courtyard for hours.

"Imelda Valdez," I called out. Slowly she rose to her feet, the cloth never leaving her mouth, and followed her mother to the examining-room door. I shooed them in.

"You sit up there on the table," I told her. "Mother, you stand over there, please." I read from the chart:

"This is a fourteen-year-old girl with a complete, unilateral, left-sided cleft lip and cleft palate. No other diseases or congenital defects. Laboratory tests, chest X ray—negative."

"Tell her to take the rag away," said Dr. Franciscus. I did, and the girl shrank back, pressing the cloth all the more firmly.

"Listen, this is silly," said Franciscus. "Tell her I've got to see it. Either she behaves, or send her away."

"Please give me the cloth," I said to the girl as gently as possible. She did not. She could not. Just then, Franciscus reached up and, taking the hand that held the rag, pulled it away with a hard jerk.

For an instant the girl's head followed the cloth as it left her face, one arm still upflung against showing. Against all hope, she would hide herself. A moment later, she relaxed and sat still. She seemed to me then like an animal that looks outward at the infinite, at death, without fear, with recognition only.

Set as it was in the center of the girl's face, the defect was utterly hideous—a nude rubbery insect that had fastened there. The upper lip was widely split all the way to the nose. One white tooth perched upon the protruding upper jaw projected through the hole. Some of the bone seemed to have been gnawed away as well. Above the thing, clear almond eyes and long black hair reflected the light. Below, a slender neck where the pulse trilled visibly. Under our gaze the girl's eyes fell to her lap where her hands lay palms upward, half open. She was a beautiful bird with a crushed beak. And tense with the expectation of more shame.

"Open your mouth," said the surgeon. I translated. She did so, and the surgeon tipped back her head to see inside.

"The palate, too. Complete," he said. There was a long silence. At last he spoke.

"What is your name?" The margins of the wound melted until she herself was being sucked into it.

"Imelda." The syllables leaked through the hole with a slosh and a whistle.

"Tomorrow," said the surgeon, "I will fix your lip. *Mañana*."

It seemed to me that Hugh Franciscus, in spite of his years of experience, in spite of all the dreadful things he had seen, must have been awed by the sight of this girl. I could see it flit across his face for an instant. Perhaps it was her small act of concealment, that he had had to demand that she show him the lip, that he had had to force her to show it to him. Perhaps it was her resistance that intensified the disfigurement. Had she brought her mouth to him willingly, without shame, she would have been for him neither more nor less than any other patient.

He measured the defect with calipers, studied it from different angles, turning her head with a finger at her chin.

"How can it ever be put back together?" I asked.

"Take her picture," he said. And to her, "Look straight ahead." Through the eye of the camera she seemed more pitiful than ever, her humiliation more complete.

"Wait!" The surgeon stopped me. I lowered the camera. A strand of her hair had fallen across her face and found its way to her mouth, becoming stuck there by saliva. He removed the hair and secured it behind her ear.

"Go ahead," he ordered. There was the click of the camera. The girl winced.

"Take three more, just in case."

When the girl and her mother had left, he took paper and pen and with a few lines drew a remarkable likeness of the girl's face.

"Look," he said. "If this dot is A, and this one B, this, C and this, D, the incisions are made A to B, then C to D. CD must equal AB. It is all equilateral triangles." All well and good, but then came X and Y and rotation flaps and the rest.

"Do you see?" he asked.

"It is confusing," I told him.

"It is simply a matter of dropping the upper lip into a normal position, then crossing the gap with two triangular flaps. It is geometry," he said.

"Yes," I said. "Geometry." And relinquished all hope of becoming a plastic surgeon.

In the operating room the next morning the anesthesia had already been administered when we arrived from Ward Rounds. The tube emerging from the girl's mouth was pressed against her lower lip to be kept out of the field of surgery. Already, a nurse was scrubbing the face which swam in a reddish-brown lather. The tiny gold earrings were included in the scrub. Now and then, one of them gave a brave flash. The face was washed for the last time, and dried. Green towels were placed over the face to hide everything but the mouth and nose. The drapes were applied.

"Calipers!" The surgeon measured, locating the peak of the distorted Cupid's bow.

"Marking pen!" He placed the first blue dot at the apex of the bow. The nasal sills were dotted; next, the inferior philtral dimple, the vermilion line. The A flap and the B flap were outlined. On he worked, peppering the lip and nose, making sense out of chaos, realizing the lip that lay waiting in that deep essential pink, that only he could see. The last dot and line were placed. He was ready.

"Scalpel!" He held the knife above the girl's mouth.

"O.K. to go ahead?" he asked the anesthetist.

"Yes."

He lowered the knife.

"No! Wait!" The anesthetist's voice was tense, staccato. "Hold it!"

The surgeon's hand was motionless.

"What's the matter?"

"Something's wrong. I'm not sure. God, she's hot as a pistol. Blood pressure is way up. Pulse one eighty. Get a rectal temperature." A nurse fumbled beneath the drapes. We waited. The nurse retrieved the thermometer.

"One hundred seven . . . no . . . eight." There was disbelief in her voice.

"Malignant hyperthermia," said the anesthetist. "Ice! Ice! Get lots of ice!" I raced out the door, accosted the first nurse I saw.

"Ice!" I shouted. "*Hielo!* Quickly! *Hielo!*" The woman's expression was blank. I ran to another. "*Hielo! Hielo!* For the love of God, ice."

"*Hielo?*" She shrugged. "*Nada.*" I ran back to the operating room.

"There isn't any ice," I reported. Dr. Franciscus had ripped off his rubber gloves and was feeling the skin of the girl's abdomen. Above the mask his eyes were the eyes of a horse in battle.

"The EKG is wild . . ."

"I can't get a pulse . . ."

"What the hell . . ."

The surgeon reached for the girl's groin. No femoral pulse.

"EKG flat. My God! She's dead!"

"She can't be."

"She is."

The surgeon's fingers pressed the groin where there was no pulse to be felt, only his own pulse hammering at the girl's flesh to be let in.

It was noon, four hours later, when we left the operating room. It was a day so hot and humid I felt steamed open like an envelope. The woman was sitting on a bench in the courtyard in her dress like a cassock. In one hand she held the piece of cloth the girl had used to conceal her mouth. As we watched, she folded it once neatly, and then again, smoothing it, cleaning the cloth which might have been the head of the girl in her lap that she stroked and consoled.

"I'll do the talking here," he said. He would tell her himself, in whatever Spanish he could find. Only if she did not understand was I to speak for him. I watched him brace himself, set his shoulders. How could he tell her? I wondered. What? But I knew he would tell her everything, exactly as it had happened. As much for himself as for her, he needed to explain. But suppose she screamed, fell to the ground, attacked him, even? All that hope of love . . . gone. Even in his discomfort I knew that he was teaching me. The way to do it was professionally. Now he was standing above her. When the woman saw that he did not speak, she lifted her eyes and saw what he held crammed in his mouth to tell her. She knew, and rose to her feet.

"*Señora*," he began, "I am sorry." All at once he seemed to me shorter than he was, scarcely taller than she. There was a place at the crown of his head where the hair had grown thin. His lips were stones. He could hardly move them. The voice dry, dusty.

"No one could have known. Some bad reaction to the medicine for sleeping. It poisoned her. High fever. She did not wake up." The last, a whisper. The woman studied his lips as though she were deaf. He tried, but could not control a twitching at the corner of his mouth. He raised a thumb and forefinger to press something back into his eyes.

"*Muerte*," the woman announced to herself. Her eyes were human, deadly.

"*Si, muerte.*" At that moment he was like someone cast, still alive, as an effigy for his own tomb. He closed his eyes. Nor did he open them until he felt the touch of the woman's hand on his arm, a touch from which he did not withdraw. Then he looked and saw the grief corroding her face, breaking it down, melting the features so that eyes, nose, mouth ran together in a distortion, like the girl's. For a long time they stood in silence. It seemed to me that minutes passed. At last her face cleared, the features rearranged themselves. She spoke, the words coming slowly to make certain that he understood her. She would go home now. The next day her sons would come for the girl, to take her home for burial. The doctor must not be sad. God has decided. And she was happy now that the harelip had been fixed so that her daughter might go to Heaven without it. Her bare feet retreating were the felted pads of a great bereft animal.

The next morning I did not go to the wards, but stood at the gate leading from the courtyard to the road outside. Two young men in striped ponchos lifted the girl's body wrapped in a straw mat onto the back of a wooden cart. A donkey waited. I had been drawn to this place as one is drawn, inexplicably, to certain scenes of desolation—executions, battlefields. All at once, the woman looked up and saw me. She had taken off her hat. The heavy-hanging coil of her hair made her head seem larger, darker, noble. I pressed some money into her hand.

"For flowers," I said. "A priest." Her cheeks shook as though minutes ago a stone had been dropped into her navel and the ripples were just now reaching her head. I regretted having come to that place.

"*Si, si,*" the woman said. Her own face was stitched with flies. "The doctor is one of the angels. He has finished the work of God. My daughter is beautiful."

What could she mean! The lip had not been fixed. The girl had died before he would have done it.

"Only a fine line that God will erase in time," she said.

I reached into the cart and lifted a corner of the mat in which the girl had been rolled. Where the cleft had been there was now a fresh line of tiny sutures. The Cupid's bow was delicately shaped, the vermilion border aligned. The flattened nostril had now the same rounded shape as the other one. I let the mat fall over the face of the dead girl, but not before I had seen the touching place where the finest black hairs sprang from the temple.

"*Adiós, adiós . . .*" And the cart creaked away to the sound of hooves, a tinkling bell.

There are events in a doctor's life that seem to mark the boundary between youth and age, seeing and perceiving. Like certain dreams, they illuminate a whole lifetime of past behavior. After such an event, a doctor is not the same as he was before. It had seemed to me then to have been the act of someone demented, or at least insanely arrogant. An attempt to reorder events. Her death had come to him out of order. It should have come after the lip had been repaired, not before. He could have told the mother that, no, the lip had not been fixed. But he did not. He said nothing. It had been an act of omission, one of those strange lapses to which all of us are subject and which we live to regret. It must have been then, at that moment, that the knowledge of what he would do appeared to him. The words of the mother had not consoled him; they had hunted him down. He had not done it for her.

147

The dire necessity was his. He would not accept that Imelda had died before he could repair her lip. People who do such things break free from society. They follow their own lonely path. They have a secret which they can never reveal. I must never let on that I knew.

How often I have imagined it. Ten o'clock at night. The hospital of Comayagua is all but dark. Here and there lanterns tilt and skitter up and down the corridors. One of these lamps breaks free from the others and descends the stone steps to the underground room that is the morgue of the hospital. This room wears the expression as if it had waited all night for someone to come. No silence so deep as this place with its cargo of newly dead. Only the slow drip of water over stone. The door closes gassily and clicks shut. The lock is turned. There are four tables, each with a body encased in a paper shroud. There is no mistaking her. She is the smallest. The surgeon takes a knife from his pocket and slits open the paper shroud, that part in which the girl's head is enclosed. The wound seems to be living on long after she has died. Waves of heat emanate from it, blurring his vision. All at once, he turns to peer over his shoulder. He sees nothing, only a wooden crucifix on the wall.

He removes a package of instruments from a satchel and arranges them on a tray. Scalpel, scissors, forceps, needle holder. Sutures and gauze sponges are produced. Stealthy, hunched, engaged, he begins. The dots of blue dye are still there upon her mouth. He raises the scalpel, pauses. A second glance into the darkness. From the wall a small lizard watches and accepts. The first cut is made. A sluggish flow of dark blood appears. He wipes it away with a sponge. No new blood comes to take its place. Again and again he cuts, connecting each of the blue dots until the whole of the zigzag slice is made, first on one side of the cleft, then on the other. Now the edges of the cleft are lined with fresh tissue. He sets down the scalpel and takes up scissors and forceps, undermining the little flaps until each triangle is attached only at one side. He rotates each flap into its new position. He must be certain that they can be swung without tension. They can. He is ready to suture. He fits the tiny curved needle into the jaws of the needle holder. Each suture is placed precisely the same number of millimeters from the cut edge, and the same distance apart. He ties each knot down until the edges are apposed. Not too tightly. These are the most meticulous sutures of his life. He cuts each thread close to the knot. It goes well. The vermilion border with its white skin roll is exactly aligned. One more stitch and the Cupid's bow appears as if by magic. The man's face shines with moisture. Now the nostril is incised around the margin, released, and sutured into a round shape to match its mate. He wipes the blood from the face of the girl with gauze that he has dipped in water. Crumbs of light are scattered on the girl's face. The shroud is folded once more about her. The instruments are handed into the satchel. In a moment the morgue is dark and a lone lantern ascends the stairs and is extinguished.

Six weeks later I was in the darkened amphitheater of the Medical School. Tiers of seats rose in a semicircle above the small stage where Hugh Franciscus stood presenting the case material he had encountered in Honduras. It was the highlight of the year. The hall was filled. The night before he had arranged the slides in the order in which they were to be shown. I was at the controls of the slide projector.

"Next slide!" he would order from time to time in that military voice which had called forth blind obedience from generations of medical students, interns, residents and patients.

"This is a fifty-seven-year-old man with a severe burn contracture of the neck. You will notice the rigid webbing that has fused the chin to the presternal tissues. No motion of the head on the torso is possible. . . . Next slide!"

"Click," went the projector.

"Here he is after the excision of the scar tissue and with the head in full extension for the first time. The defect was then covered. . . . Next slide!"

"Click."

". . . with full-thickness drums of skin taken from the abdomen with the Padgett dermatome. Next slide!"

"Click."

And suddenly there she was, extracted from the shadows, suspended above and beyond all of us like a resurrection. There was the oval face, the long black hair unbraided, the tiny gold hoops in her ears. And that luminous gnawed mouth. The whole of her life seemed to have been summed up in this photograph. A long silence followed that was the surgeon's alone to break. Almost at once, like the anesthetist in the operating room in Comayagua, I knew that something was wrong.

It was not that the man would not speak as that he could not. The audience of doctors, nurses and students seemed to have been infected by the black, limitless silence. My own pulse doubled. It was hard to breathe. Why did he not call out for the next slide? Why did he not save himself? Why had he not removed this slide from the ones to be shown? All at once I knew that he had used his camera on her again. I could see the long black shadows of her hair flowing into the darker shadows of the morgue. The sudden blinding flash . . . The next slide would be the one taken in the morgue. He would be exposed.

In the dim light reflected from the slide, I saw him gazing up at her, seeing not the colored photograph, I thought, but the negative of it where the ghost of the girl was. For me, the amphitheater had become Honduras. I saw again that courtyard littered with patients. I could see the dust in the beam of light from the projector. It was then that I knew that she was his measure of perfection and pain—the one lost, the other gained. He, too, had heard the click of the camera, had seen her wince and felt his mercy enlarge. At last he spoke.

"Imelda." It was the one word he had heard her say. At the sound of his voice I removed the next slide from the projector. "Click" . . . and she was gone. "Click" again, and in her place the man with the orbital cancer. For a long moment Franciscus looked up in my direction, on his face an expression that I have given up trying to interpret. Gratitude? Sorrow? It made me think of the gaze of the girl when at last she understood that she must hand over to him the evidence of her body.

"This is a sixty-two-year-old man with a basal cell carcinoma of the temple eroding into the bony orbit . . ." he began as though nothing had happened.

At the end of the hour, even before the lights went on, there was loud applause. I hurried to find him among the departing crowd. I could not. Some weeks went by before I caught sight of him. He seemed vaguely convalescent, as though a fever had taken its toll before burning out.

Hugh Franciscus continued to teach for fifteen years, although he operated a good deal less, then gave it up entirely. It was as though he had grown tired of blood, of always having to be involved with blood, of having to draw it, spill it, wipe it away, stanch it. He was a quieter, softer man, I heard, the ferocity diminished. There were no more expeditions to Honduras or anywhere else.

I, too, have not been entirely free of her. Now and then, in the years that have passed, I see that donkey-cart cortège, or his face bent over hers in the morgue. I would like to have told him what I now know, that his unrealistic act was one of goodness, one of those small, persevering acts done, perhaps, to ward off madness. Like lighting a lamp, boiling water for tea, washing a shirt. But, of course, it's too late now.

Thought

1. "He seemed to be a man of immense strength and ability, yet without affection for the patients." Choose five sentences from the essay that are in keeping with Selzer's observations of Franciscus' character.

2. In what ways have both Selzer and Franciscus been changed by their experience with Imelda?

Style and Structure

3. Why do you think the author begins with the announcement of Franciscus' death?

4. a) Isolate and identify the different sections of this essay.
   b) What does each section contribute to the whole?

5. Consider Selzer's use of figurative language in his depiction of Imelda, her mother, and of the Honduras town and its inhabitants. Do you detect any bias in these descriptions? Explain.

6. a) What process, or processes, does Selzer analyze in this essay?
   b) Show how Selzer uses narrative techniques to enhance his analysis.

Response and Extension

7. In small groups or as a class, explore all the factors that went into the doctor's decision to operate on Imelda. Cite quotations from the essay to support your points. Do you agree with all of the author's suppositions about the doctor? What are your own conclusions regarding Franciscus' actions?

Unit Synthesis

1. Research a process that interests you. Write an essay that analyzes the causal relationships within that process, for example, a tennis serve, a hurricane, fibre optics, a car engine, a bee sting, jealousy, or the Internet.

2. a) Have your group report to the class on the effectiveness of a "bureaucratic" process linked to the functioning of your school, for example, lates; truancies; school dances.
   b) Draft a brief with recommendations for improvements and send it to the appropriate school authorities.

3. Write an introspective piece in which you explain a process such as grief, depression, failure, loss, success, joy, or love.

4. Write an essay about the way you interact with some natural event that has a profound effect on your interior life, for example, the return of spring, a shooting star, a blossoming magnolia, an ice storm, a January thaw, sun dogs, a salmon run, or sunrise in the mountains.

5. Imagine meeting an older relative, such as your mother, father, aunt, or grandparent, when that person was your age. Write a dialogue between yourself and that person.

6. Research a specific case in which the practice of medicine has appeared to run counter to community ethics.

Suggested Readings

Ackerman, Diane *A Natural History of Love*
Laurence, Margaret *The Stone Angel*
Peck, M. Scott *The Road Less Travelled*
Selzer, Richard *Mortal Lessons; Letters to a Young Surgeon; Resurrection*
Thomas, Lewis *The Youngest Science*

Writing to Persuade

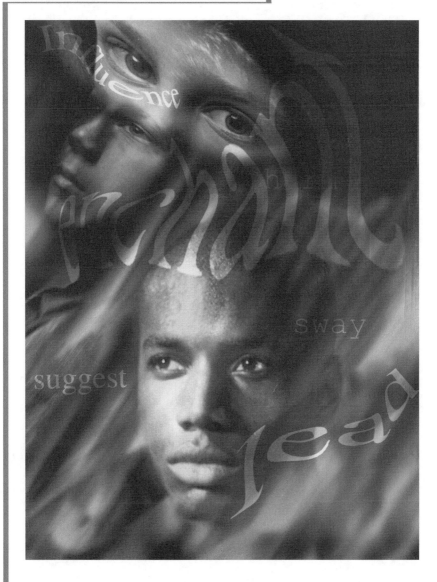

To be nobody-but-yourself—in a world which is doing its best, night and day, to make you everybody else—means to fight the hardest battle which any human being can fight; and never stop fighting.

e.e. cummings

A Poet's Advice to Students

e.e. cummings

A poet is somebody who feels, and who expresses his feeling through words.

This may sound easy. It isn't.

A lot of people think or believe or know they feel—but that's thinking or believing or knowing; not feeling. And poetry is feeling—not knowing or believing or thinking.

Almost anybody can learn to think or believe or know, but not a single human being can be taught to feel. Why? Because whenever you think or you believe or you know, you're a lot of other people; but the moment you feel, you're nobody-but-yourself.

To be nobody-but-yourself—in a world which is doing its best, night and day, to make you everybody else—means to fight the hardest battle which any human being can fight; and never stop fighting.

As for expressing nobody-but-yourself in words, that means working just a little harder than anybody who isn't a poet can possibly imagine. Why? Because nothing is quite as easy as using words like somebody else. We all of us do exactly this nearly all the time—and whenever we do it, we're not poets.

If, at the end of your first ten or fifteen years of fighting and working and feeling, you find you've written one line of one poem; you'll be very lucky indeed.

And so my advice to all young people who wish to become poets is: do something easy, like learning how to blow up the world—unless you're not only willing, but glad, to feel and work and fight till you die.

Does this sound dismal? It isn't.
It's the most wonderful life on earth.
Or so I feel.

Thought

1. In small groups, distinguish among thinking, believing, and feeling. Use examples from your own experience to help you define the differences between these terms.

2. Identify the three classes of people perceived by the writer. To which class do you belong? Explain.

3. Paraphrase cummings' definition of a poet.

4. What advice does cummings give to young, aspiring poets? Do you agree or disagree with this advice?

Style and Structure

5. What rhetorical devices does cummings use to make his point? Scrutinize this brief piece for stylistic techniques that enhance the force of his argument. Citing quotes from the essay, explain their persuasive effect.

6. Label the parts of the argument using the following terms: thesis, support, development, commentary, clarification, conclusion.

7. Show that the last word is the perfect conclusion to this piece.

Response and Extension

8. What sort of influences do you think cummings had in mind when he wrote, "in a world which is doing its best, night and day, to make you everybody else"? Write a series of brief expositions on each of these forces, persuading your reader of their power to make you conform.

9. "Whenever you think or you believe or you know, you're a lot of other people." Do you agree with cummings' assertion? Why or why not?

10. Read Bronwen Wallace's essay, "Shyly Slipping a Poem from the Purse" (p. 30).

    a) Are there legitimate grounds for comparison between Wallace's and cummings' approach to poetry? If so, what are they?

    b) Which essay do you find more inspiring or interesting on the subject? Explain.

Pandora Was a Feminist

Mary Meigs

Secrets. The origin of secrets—a great puzzle that I'm trying to solve, for it seems to me that there is an urgent need to decide which, if any, are necessary and which spring from the ego's need to protect its truths and its lies, hence, the idea that every self is a sacred place and that all secrets have the same sacred character. Other people's secrets, as we know, beg to be told, make up the fabric of gossip and innuendo even if severe penalties are attached to telling them. As for our own, they are raided, so to speak, by others with their conjectures, their analyses that we so fiercely reject (like ours of them). One's secret self is guarded as closely as spies guard secrets in wartime, not because of a real penalty for telling (unlike the spies), but an imaginary one, because of the feeling that it belongs to oneself, like one's brain, one's heart, and the illusion that it is invisible to others. But, in fact, those others are nibbling away, like fishes around bait, so that it might be better to give them an authentic whole to nibble on. Better still, perhaps, to sit in one of those cages in which one is completely visible but protected from over-eager sharks, the cage of indifference to what other people think. I often wonder if the secret of oneself is worth keeping, if it shouldn't be released like the contents of Pandora's box. That story is a wonderful example of patriarchal ingenuity, which has invented yet another mythical explanation for the woes of *man*kind, i.e. the unbridled curiosity of womankind. Personally, I think of Pandora not as irresponsible and foolish but as a radical feminist, sister of Eve and Bluebeard's wives, of all women who *want to know*. We are all Pandoras, each with her box complete with instructions not to open it, the box of the secret self.

Pandora, according to Zimmerman's *Dictionary of Classical Mythology*, was made with clay by Hephaestus at the request of Zeus, who desired to punish Prometheus for stealing fire from heaven by giving him a wife. "All the gods and goddesses of Olympus vied in giving her gifts:" beauty, eloquence, the art of singing, beautiful clothes, a gold crown, etc., not to mention the famous box, a gift from Zeus himself. But Prometheus saw through Zeus, and Pandora ended by marrying his brother Epimetheus (which means Afterthought). "Don't open the box," said Zeus. Naturally, Pandora opened it. So do I open things: Christmas presents before Christmas, the last page of a book to see how it's going to end (I have to know whether it will have a happy ending, or whether so-and-so will still be alive at the end. I hate suspense, cannot read detective stories, cannot look at movies full of suspense without intolerable anxiety.) But to get back to Pandora. "When the box was opened, a host of plagues escaped to harass hapless man; only Hope remained in the box." Why? It seems to me it would have been much better to let Hope out, too. "Women's curiosity is always punished," I remarked to Paul, a male friend. "Pandora's, Eve's, Bluebeard's wives." "Of course," he says. "Evil is woman's fault. That's part of history." He's making fun of me, of course. I say I think people should be less possessive of their secrets, that Pandora was right to open the box. And then he tells me a fascinating story about himself. He used to dream, he says, to remember his dreams and write them down, until one day a dream told him something about himself that he didn't want to know. So he pushed it back into his subconscious. "And I never remembered another dream!" Pandora couldn't possibly have been more curious about the contents of her box than I am about this dream-truth that he doesn't want to think about. I say to him that nothing in my dreams makes me want to censure them, that there is nothing they tell me that I don't want to think about, that they have helped me to think about the things I don't want to think about. And far from wanting to turn them off, I want to stimulate them, I want them to tell me the worst!

Curiosity, how it can be thought of as either a virtue or a vice, how it is a virtue for men in men's eyes and a vice for women which must be punished, and how the punishment becomes dogma until women, too, feel impatient with Eve, Pandora and Bluebeard's wives for being so foolish, for wanting to know. God or Zeus or Bluebeard loves to tempt them by inventing rules that as high-spirited women, they are bound to break. Don't eat of the fruit of the tree! Don't open that box! Don't look in the closet! Sometimes God, just for good measure, tests a man. Don't ask me *why*, he says to Job. But much more often, men's curiosity is rewarded and women's is punished. And yet when it comes to opening the Pandora's box which is in each of us, men and women are alike. Paul's self-censorship—the Pandora's box of his dreams—he seemed to think it was wrong to know *too much* about himself and called on the Zeus in himself to close the box forever. I wondered how often he had told this story, whether each telling wasn't to reinforce the lock, whether the thing he wanted to shut away didn't manage to reach out a paw under the lid like an angry kitten in a basket. He told it smiling, with a kind of excitement, triumph, ha! it almost got out! It seemed to me that it was amazingly discreet; it could be talked about without betraying what it was even to Paul. Perhaps it had become so tame that it was ready to be let out of the box; perhaps he told it as a way of taming it?

I think about *it*, the beast, silenced but still there in the dreams that are not allowed over the threshold of consciousness, and want to say, "Let it out. It won't hurt you," want to say that secrets, once released, often sheath their claws, stretch, rub against other people's ankles and finally curl up in a comfortable chair and go to sleep. Interestingly, Pandora was not punished (note that the plagues "escaped to harass hapless *man*"). Long after the affair of the box, Zeus sent a deluge to destroy mankind and Pandora's daughter, Pyrrha, and her husband, Deucalion (Prometheus' son), were the only survivors. They had the foresight to replace "the loss of mankind by throwing stones behind their backs; those Deucalion threw became men; those Pyrrha threw became women." So the sexes, each reproduced by a kind of parthenogenesis (another case of patriarchal wish-fulfillment), were equal for a while, and Pandora was the grandmother of all the women in the world. True, the "host of plagues" was still at large, but Zeus himself had invented them and put them in the box, a cover-up, so to speak, and Pandora had the courage to show everybody what Zeus was up to. It was a tremendous victory over Zeus, just as Eve had won a victory over God by disobeying his senseless edict about eating the fruit of the tree. Confronted by boxes that are not supposed to be opened, we contemporary Pandoras say to ourselves, "Where did this rule come from? Was it Zeus who told me not to open the box, and is he impersonating me so skillfully that I think his commands come from myself?"

Thought

1. What is the author's thesis? Summarize her central point in one or two sentences.
2. Paraphrase and explain the "great puzzle" that Meigs is trying to solve.
3. What does the author mean by "the secret of oneself"?
4. Analyze the relationship between the "secret of oneself" and "Pandora's Box" for a) Paul, b) the author.
5. Why, in the author's view, was Pandora a feminist? Do you agree? Explain.
6. In what sense did Pandora score a victory over Zeus?

Style and Structure

7. Analyzing the first paragraph, explain how Meigs makes a graceful shift from the general to the particular.
8. How does the author involve herself in the relationship among Eve, Pandora, and Bluebeard's wives?
9. Describe how, why, and to what effect Meigs plays with the use of the generic "man." How does this contribute to the overall tone of the essay?
10. To what purpose does Meigs make reference to her friend Paul?

Response and Extension

11. Write a critical essay that analyzes a fairy tale from a feminist perspective, for example "Cinderella," "Sleeping Beauty," "Little Red Riding Hood," or "Beauty and the Beast."
12. Consider some of your most important secrets. You may wish to decide whether or not they *need* to be secrets—and what might happen if they were to be told.

13. In a dictionary of classical mythology, look up the stories of Antigone, Aphrodite, Demeter, or other women who in one way or another avenge themselves. Write a humorous, impassioned, or coolly logical interpretive essay on one or more of these stories, providing your own imaginative, persuasive commentary.

The Character of Hamlet's Mother

Carolyn G. Heilbrun

The character of Hamlet's mother has not received the specific critical attention it deserves. Moreover, the traditional account of her personality as rendered by the critics will not stand up under close scrutiny of Shakespeare's play.

None of the critics of course has failed to see Gertrude as vital to the action of the play; not only is she the mother of the hero, the widow of the Ghost, and the wife of the current King of Denmark, but the fact of her hasty and, to the Elizabethans, incestuous marriage, the whole question of her "falling off," occupies a position of barely secondary importance in the mind of her son, and of the Ghost. Indeed, Freud and Jones see her, the object of Hamlet's Oedipus complex, as central to the motivation of the play.[1] But the critics, with no exception that I have been able to find, have accepted Hamlet's word "frailty" as applying to her whole personality, and have seen in her not one weakness, or passion in the Elizabethan sense, but a character of which weakness and lack of depth and vigorous intelligence are the entire explanation. Of her can it truly be said that carrying the "stamp of one defect," she did "in the general censure take corruption from that particular fault" (I.iv.35-36).

The critics are agreed that Gertrude was not a party to the late King's murder and indeed knew nothing of it, a point which, on the clear evidence of the play, is indisputable. They have also discussed whether or not Gertrude, guilty of more than an "o'er-hasty marriage," had committed adultery with Claudius before her husband's death. I will return to this point later on. Beyond discussing these two points, those critics who have dealt specifically with the Queen have traditionally seen her as well-meaning but shallow and feminine, in the pejorative sense of the word: incapable of any sustained rational process, superficial and flighty. It is this tradition which a closer reading of the play will show to be erroneous.

Professor Bradley describes the traditional Gertrude thus:

> The Queen was not a bad-hearted woman, not at all the woman to think little of murder. But she had a soft animal nature and was very dull and very shallow. She loved to be happy, like a sheep in the sun, and to do her justice, it pleased her to see others happy, like more sheep in the sun. . . . It was pleasant to sit upon her throne and see smiling faces around her, and foolish and unkind in Hamlet to persist in grieving for his father instead of marrying Ophelia and making everything comfortable. . . . The belief at the bottom of her heart was that the world is a place constructed simply that people may be happy in it in a good-humored sensual fashion.[2]

Later on, Bradley says of her that when affliction comes to her "the good in her nature struggles to the surface through the heavy mass of sloth."

Granville-Barker is not quite so extreme. Shakespeare, he says,

> gives us in Gertrude the woman who does not mature, who clings to her youth and all that belongs to it, whose charm will not change but at last fade and wither; a pretty creature, as we see her, desperately refusing to grow old. . . . She is drawn for us with unemphatic strokes, and she has but a passive part in the play's action. She moves throughout in Claudius' shadow; he holds her as he won her, by the witch-craft of his wit.[3]

Elsewhere Granville-Barker says "Gertrude, who will certainly never see forty-five again, might better be 'old.' [That is, portrayed by an older, mature actress.] But that would make her relations with Claudius—and *their* likelihood is vital to the play—quite incredible" (p. 226). Granville-Barker is saying here that a woman about forty-five years of age cannot feel any sexual passion nor arouse it. This is one of the mistakes which lie at the heart of the misunderstanding about Gertrude.

Professor Dover Wilson sees Gertrude as more forceful than either of these two critics will admit, but even he finds the Ghost's unwillingness to shock her with knowledge of his murder to be one of the basic motivations of the play, and he says of her, "Gertrude is always hoping for the best."[4]

Now whether Claudius won Gertrude before or after her husband's death, it was certainly not, as Granville-Barker implies, with "the witchcraft of his wit" alone. Granville-Barker would have us believe that Claudius won her simply by the force of his persuasive tongue. "It is plain," he writes, that the Queen "does little except echo his [Claudius'] wishes; sometimes—as in the welcome to Rosencrantz and Guildenstern—she repeats his very words" (p. 227), though Wilson must admit later that Gertrude does not tell Claudius everything. Without dwelling here on the psychology of the Ghost, or the greater burden borne by the Elizabethan words "witchcraft" and "wit," we can plainly see, for the Ghost tells us, how Claudius won the Queen: the Ghost considers his brother to be garbage, and "lust," the Ghost says, "will sate itself in a celestial bed and prey on garbage" (I.v.54-55). "Lust"—in a woman of forty-five or more—is the key word here. Bradley, Granville-Barker, and to a lesser extent Professor Dover Wilson, misunderstand Gertrude largely because they are unable to see lust, the desire for sexual relations, as the passion, in the Elizabethan sense of the word, the flaw, the weakness which drives Gertrude to an incestuous marriage, appalls her son, and keeps him from the throne. Unable to explain her marriage to Claudius as the act of any but a weak-minded vacillating woman, they fail to see Gertrude for the strong-minded, intelligent, succinct, and, apart from this passion, sensible woman that she is.

To understand Gertrude properly, it is only necessary to examine the lines Shakespeare has chosen for her to say. She is, except for her description of Ophelia's death, concise and pithy in speech, with a talent for seeing the essence of every situation presented before her eyes. If she is not profound, she is certainly never silly. We first hear her asking Hamlet to stop wearing black, to stop walking about with his eyes downcast, and to realize that death is an inevitable part of life. She is, in short, asking him not to give way to the passion of grief, a passion of whose force and dangers the Elizabethans are aware, as Miss Campbell has shown.[5] Claudius echoes her with a well-reasoned argument against grief which was, in its philosophy if not in its language, a piece of commonplace Elizabethan lore. After Claudius' speech, Gertrude asks Hamlet to remain in Denmark, where he is rightly loved. Her speeches have been short, however warm and loving, and conciseness of statement is not the mark of a dull and shallow woman.

We next hear her, as Queen and gracious hostess, welcoming Rosencrantz and Guildenstern to the court, hoping, with the King, that they may cheer Hamlet and discover what is depressing him. Claudius then tells Gertrude, when they are alone, that Polonius believes he knows what is upsetting Hamlet. The Queen answers:

> I doubt it is no other than the main,
> His father's death and our o'er-hasty marriage. (II.ii.56-57)

This statement is concise, remarkably to the point, and not a little courageous. It is not the statement of a dull, slothful woman who can only echo her husband's words. Next, Polonius enters with his most unbrief apotheosis to brevity. The Queen interrupts him with five words: "More matter with less art" (II.ii.95). It would be difficult to find a phrase more applicable to Polonius. When this gentleman, in no way deterred from his loquacity, after purveying the startling news that he has a daughter, begins to read a letter, the Queen asks pointedly "Came this from Hamlet to her?" (II.ii.114).

We see Gertrude next in Act III, asking Rosencrantz and Guildenstern, with her usual directness, if Hamlet received them well, and if they were able to tempt him to any pastime. But before leaving the room, she stops for a word of kindness to Ophelia. It is a humane gesture, for she is unwilling to leave Ophelia, the unhappy tool of the King and Polonius, without some kindly and intelligent appreciation of her help:

> And for your part, Ophelia, I do wish
> That your good beauties be the happy cause
> Of Hamlet's wildness. So shall I hope your virtues
> Will bring him to his wonted way again,
> To both your honors. (III.i.38-42)

It is difficult to see in this speech, as Bradley apparently does, the gushing shallow wish of a sentimental woman that class distinctions shall not stand in the way of true love.

At the play, the Queen asks Hamlet to sit near her. She is clearly try-ing to make him feel he has a place in the court of Denmark. She does not speak again until Hamlet asks her how she likes the play. "The lady doth protest too much, methinks" (III.ii.240) is her im-mortal comment on the player queen. The scene gives her four more words: when Claudius leaps to his feet, she asks "How fares my Lord?" (III.ii.278).

I will for the moment pass over the scene in the Queen's closet, to follow her quickly through the remainder of the play. After the closet scene, the Queen comes to speak to Claudius. She tells him, as Hamlet has asked her to, that he, Hamlet, is mad, and has killed Polonius. She adds, however, that he now weeps for what he has done. She does not wish Claudius to know what she now knows, how wild and fear-some Hamlet has become. Later, she does not wish to see Ophelia, but hearing how distracted she is, consents. When Laertes bursts in ready to attack Claudius, she immediately steps between Claudius and Laertes to protect the King, and tells Laertes it is not Claudius who has killed his father. Laertes will of course soon learn this, but it is Gertrude who manages to tell him before he can do any meaningless damage. She leaves Laertes and the King together, and then returns to tell Laertes that his sister is drowned. She gives her news directly, realizing that suspense will increase the pain of it, but this is the one time in the play when her usual pointed conciseness would be the mark neither of intelligence nor kindness, and so, gently, and at some length, she tells Laertes of his sister's death, giving him time to re-cover from the shock of grief, and to absorb the meaning of her words. At Ophelia's funeral the Queen scatters flowers over the grave:

> Sweets to the sweet; farewell!
> I hop'd thou shouldst have been my Hamlet's wife.
> I thought thy bride-bed to have deck'd, sweet maid,
> And not t'have strew'd thy grave. (V.i.266-269)

She is the only one present decently mourning the death of some-one young, and not heated in the fire of some personal passion.

At the match between Hamlet and Laertes, the Queen believes that Hamlet is out of training, but glad to see him at some sport, she gives him her handkerchief to wipe his brow, and drinks to his success. The drink is poisoned and she dies. But before she dies she does not waste time on vituperation; she warns Hamlet that the drink is poisoned to prevent his drinking it. They are her last words. Those critics who have thought her stupid admire her death; they call it uncharacteristic.

In Act III, when Hamlet goes to his mother in her closet his nerves are pitched at the very height of tension; he is on the edge of hysteria. The possibility of murdering his mother has in fact entered his mind, and he has just met and refused an opportunity to kill Claudius. His mother, meanwhile, waiting for him, has told Polonius not to fear for her, but she knows when she sees Hamlet that he may be violently mad. Hamlet quips with her, insults her, tells her he wishes she were not his mother, and when she, still retaining dignity, attempts to end the interview, Hamlet seizes her and she cries for help. The important thing to note is that the Queen's cry "Thou wilt not murder me" (III.iv.21) is not foolish. She has seen from Hamlet's demeanor that he is capable of murder, as indeed in the next instant he proves himself to be.

We next learn from the Queen's startled "As kill a king" (III.iv.30) that she has no knowledge of the murder, though of course this is only confirmation here of what we already know. Then the Queen asks Hamlet why he is so hysterical:

> What have I done, that thou dar'st wag thy tongue
> In noise so rude against me? (III.iv.39-40)

Hamlet tells her: it is her lust, the need of sexual passion, which has driven her from the arms and memory of her husband to the incomparably cruder charms of his brother. He cries out that she has not even the excuse of youth for her lust:

> O Shame! where is thy blush? Rebellious hell,
> If thou canst mutine in a matron's bones,
> To flaming youth let virtue be as wax
> And melt in her own fire. Proclaim no shame
> When the compulsive ardor gives the charge,
> Since frost itself as actively doth burn,
> And reason panders will. (III.iv.82-87)

This is not only a lust, but a lust which throws out of joint all the structure of human mortality and relationships. And the Queen admits it. If there is one quality that has characterized, and will characterize, every speech of Gertrude's in the play, it is the ability to see reality clearly, and to express it. This talent is not lost when turned upon herself:

> O Hamlet, speak no more!
> Thou turn'st mine eyes into my very soul,
> And there I see such black and grained spots
> As will not leave their tinct. (III.iv.88-91)

She knows that lust has driven her, that this is her sin, and she admits it. Not that she wishes to linger in the contemplation of her sin. No more, she cries, no more. And then the Ghost appears to Hamlet. The Queen thinks him mad again—as well she might—but she promises Hamlet that she will not betray him—and she does not.

Where, in all that we have seen of Gertrude, is there the picture of "a soft animal nature, very dull and very shallow"? She may indeed be "animal" in the sense of "lustful." But it does not follow that because she wishes to continue a life of sexual experience, her brain is soft or her wit unperceptive.

Some critics, having accepted Gertrude as a weak and vacillating woman, see no reason to suppose that she did not fall victim to Claudius' charms before the death of her husband and commit adultery with him. These critics, Professor Bradley among them (p. 166), claim that the elder Hamlet clearly tells his son that Gertrude has committed adultery with Claudius in the speech beginning "Ay that incestuous, that adulterate beast" (I.v.41ff). Professor Dover Wilson presents the argument:

> Is the Ghost speaking here of the o'er-hasty marriage of Claudius and Gertrude? Assuredly not. His "certain term" is drawing rapidly to an end, and he is already beginning to "scent the morning air." Hamlet knew of the marriage, and his whole soul was filled with nausea at the thought of the speedy hasting to "incestuous sheets." Why then should the Ghost waste precious moments in telling Hamlet what he was fully cognizant of before? . . . Moreover, though the word "incestuous" was applicable to the marriage, the rest of the passage is entirely inapplicable to it. Expressions like "witchcraft", "traitorous gifts", "seduce", "shameful lust", and "seeming virtuous" may be noted in passing. But the rest of the quotation leaves no doubt upon the matter. (p. 293)

Professor Dover Wilson and other critics have accepted the Ghost's word "adulterate" in its modern meaning. The Elizabethan word "adultery," however, was not restricted to its modern meaning, but was used to define any sexual relationship which could be called unchaste, including of course an incestuous one.[6] Certainly the elder Hamlet considered the marriage of Claudius and Gertrude to be unchaste and unseemly, and while his use of the word "adulterate" indicates his very strong feelings about the marriage, it would not to an Elizabethan audience necessarily mean that he believed Gertrude to have been false to him before his death. It is important to notice, too, that the Ghost does not apply the term "adulterate" to Gertrude, and he may well have considered the term a just description of Claudius' entire sexual life.

But even if the Ghost used the word "adulterate" in full awareness of its modern restricted meaning, it is not necessary to assume on the basis of this single speech (and it is the only shadow of evidence we have for such a conclusion) that Gertrude was unfaithful to him while he lived. It is quite probable that the elder Hamlet still considered himself married to Gertrude, and he is moreover revolted that her lust for him ("why she would hang on him as if increase of appetite had grown by what it fed on") should have so easily transferred itself to another. This is why he uses the expressions "seduce," "shameful lust," and others. Professor Dover Wilson has himself said "Hamlet knew of the marriage, and his whole soul was filled with nausea at the thought of the speedy hasting to incestuous sheets"; the soul of the elder Hamlet was undoubtedly filled with nausea too, and this could well explain his using such strong language, as well as his taking the time to mention the matter at all. It is not necessary to consider Gertrude an adulteress to account for the speech of the Ghost.

Gertrude's lust was, of course, more important to the plot than we may at first perceive. Charlton Lewis, among others, has shown how Shakespeare kept many of the facts of the plots from which he borrowed without maintaining the structures which explained them. In the original Belleforest story, Gertrude (substituting Shakespeare's more familiar names) was daughter of the king; to become king, it was necessary to marry her. The elder Hamlet, in marrying Gertrude, ousted Claudius from the throne.[7] Shakespeare retained the shell of this in his play. When she no longer has a husband, the form of election would be followed to declare the next king, in this case undoubtedly her son Hamlet. By marrying Gertrude, Claudius "popp'd in between th' election and my hopes" (V.ii.65), that is, kept young Hamlet from the throne. Gertrude's flaw of lust made Claudius' ambition possible, for without taking advantage of the Queen's desire still to be married, he could not have been king.

But Gertrude, if she is lustful, is also intelligent, penetrating, and gifted with a remarkable talent for concise and pithy speech. In all the play, the person whose language hers most closely resembles is Horatio. "Sweets to the sweet," she has said at Ophelia's grave. "Good night sweet prince," Horatio says at the end. They are neither of them dull, or shallow, or slothful, though one of them is passion's slave.

Endnotes

1. William Shakespeare, *Hamlet*, with a psychoanalytical study by Ernest Jones, M.D. (London: Vision Press, 1947), pp. 7-42.
2. A.C. Bradley, *Shakespearean Tragedy* (New York: Macmillan, 1949), p. 167.
3. Harley Granville-Barker, *Prefaces to Shakespeare* (Princeton: Princeton University Press, 1946), 1:227.
4. J. Dover Wilson, *What Happens in Hamlet* (Cambridge: Cambridge University Press, 1951), p. 125.
5. Lily B. Campbell, *Shakespeare's Tragic Heroes* (New York: Barnes & Noble, 1952), pp. 112-113.
6. See Bertram Joseph, *Conscience and the King* (London: Chatto & Windus, 1953), pp. 16-19.
7. Charlton M. Lewis, *The Genesis of Hamlet* (New York: Henry Holt, 1907), p. 36.

Thought

1. a) Compose a point-form character sketch of Gertrude according to "the traditional account of her personality as rendered by the critics." Be sure to support your sketch with evidence from the essay.

   b) Again referring to the essay, write a character sketch of Gertrude according to Heilbrun's analysis.

c) Which of these two views is more consistent with your own thinking about Gertrude? Explain.

2. In what ways does Heilbrun's analysis of Gertrude reflect changes in the "traditional" view of women in contemporary society?

3. Has Heilbrun convinced you of her position? Explain.

Style and Structure

4. Describe the tone of this essay. How does it contribute to the persuasiveness of Heilbrun's argument?

5. Heilbrun treats Gertrude's speeches in chronological order, except for the scene in the Queen's closet, which she skips over and returns to at the end. Explain why.

6. Divide the essay into its logical components. Using a graphic flow chart, show the contribution to Heilbrun's argument made by each component.

7. Show how Heilbrun systematically attacks the various aspects of the "traditional" view.

8. How does Heilbrun's interpretation of the words "lust," "adulterate," and "incestuous" contribute to her understanding of Gertrude?

9. In what ways has Heilbrun made strategic use of direct quotations to support her argument?

Response and Extension

10. How might Heilbrun's non-traditional assessment of Gertrude affect traditional interpretations of the other major characters in the play, i.e. Hamlet and Hamlet senior, Claudius, Laertes, and Ophelia?

11. Consider three female literary heroines (e.g. Lady MacBeth, Catherine Earnshaw, Juliet, Daisy Buchanan) and re-evaluate them in light of Heilbrun's "non-traditional" analysis.

My Home Is Not Broken, It Works

Carol Kleiman

One summer day, my son Robert, then five years old, took me by the hand and asked me to go outside with him.

Holding on tightly, he carefully walked around the house with me, looking at doors and windows and shaking his head. There was something he didn't understand.

"Mommy," he finally asked, pressing my hand with his warm, chubby fingers, "is our home broken?"

His words shot through my body, alerting every protective instinct, activating my private defense system, the one I hold in reserve to ward off attacks against women and children.

"Oh, Robbie," I answered, hugging him, "did someone tell you that we have a broken home?"

"Yes," he said sweetly. "But it doesn't *look* broken!"

"It's not," I assured him. "Our house is not broken and neither are we."

I explained that "broken" is some people's way of describing a home with only one parent, usually the mother. Sometimes there was only one parent because of divorce, like us. "There are still lots of homes like ours. And they're still homes."

Robbie looked relieved and went to play with his friends. I stood there, shaking with anger.

What a way to put down a little kid and me, too, I thought. I supported my three children, fed and clothed them. I was there for them emotionally and physically. I managed to keep up payments on the house. Although we struggled financially, we were happy and loving. What was "broken" about us?

That was in 1970. The expression is as prevalent today as it was then. We've made some headway in raising the issue of sexist expressions, including such formerly popular ones as calling women "girls," "gals," or "broads." We've even sensitized a few headline writers to their unhealthy habit of describing women as "grandmothers" and "mothers" while the stories about them are totally unrelated to their biological roles. Such as: "Grandmother Elected Prime Minister."

But a household headed by a woman is still a "broken home," despite the fact that more than 5 million women raise their families alone. A residence in which a man is not in residence, the phrase implies, is not a home. Two decades into the second wave of the Women's Movement, the phrase is often used as an explanation for a terrible crime, as if a woman alone were disreputable and can only raise a vicious miscreant who will naturally prey upon society: "The alleged murderer is a loner and comes from a broken home."

Over the years, similar buzzwords have sent me buzzing. Even though I work for a newspaper and understand how journalists are misunderstood, I am constantly writing letters of protest to publications that deprecate me and all women with frequent use of expressions such as "divorcée," "unwed" mother, and "illegitimate" children. They have something offensively in common: they tell us that if no husband/father exists, neither do women and children.

It's true that society does not help single or divorced women raise their children or keep their families intact. The scorn felt for so-called broken homes is expressed in the lack of support systems for heads of those households, in the withholding of federally funded quality child care, job training and equal pay, and in the meanness with which aid to dependent children is doled out.

The expression "broken home" suggests that my children never had a chance in life because their father was not present, and what I did doesn't count. I *know* that's not true, and it's not true for millions of other Americans also stigmatized by the term.

On a recent Thanksgiving, my trio—Catharine, then 21; Raymond, Jr., 19; and Robert, 18—gathered in Chicago for the holiday. After they left, I found a note on my desk that they had written and signed before dispersing to their various colleges from coast to coast.

It begins: "Yet another Thanksgiving holiday has drawn our family together for a few meaningful days. It's just enough time to touch base, strengthen our bond, and reaffirm how important we are to one another."

As I read on, I remembered Robbie's question a dozen years ago and how much it hurt. Here was the real answer to the question: Is our home broken? The note ended: "We thank you for making us what we are."

Thought

1. Why was Kleiman so angry over the incident involving her son?

2. Explain the connotations of the words that Kleiman perceives as deprecating to women. What, in your opinion, is the status of these words today?

Style and Structure

3. Describe the tone of this essay. How does it contribute to the effectiveness of Kleiman's argument?

4. a) Identify the different approaches Kleiman uses to build her argument.
   b) Analyze how together these make for such a persuasive essay.

Response and Extension

5. For discussion: What is your definition of a family?

6. Over a set period of time maintain a running check on newspapers and magazines—including ads—for any sexist language or images. Collect the pieces, compile your findings, and present your analysis to the class. Or, write letters of protest to the editor as Kleiman did. Try to make your objections as succinct and persuasive as you can.

7. Prepare a report on the legal process involved in the dissolution of marriage. Your report should take into consideration the latest developments in family law, both in federal and provincial legislation.

8. For discussion: Kleiman asserts that "society does not help single or divorced women raise their children or keep their families intact." This essay was written in the early eighties. In what ways do you think things have improved for single mothers since then? In what ways are they the same, and how might they be worse?

9. Write a letter to one of your parents, expressing your feelings about your family.

Individual Liberty and Public Control

Bertrand Russell

Society cannot exist without law and order, and cannot advance except through the initiative of vigorous innovators. Yet law and order are always hostile to innovations, and innovators are almost always to some extent anarchists. Those whose minds are dominated by fear of a relapse toward barbarism will emphasize the importance of law and order, while those who are inspired by the hope of an advance toward civilization will usually be more conscious of the need of individual initiative. Both temperaments are necessary, and wisdom lies in allowing each to operate freely where it is beneficent. But those who are on the side of law and order, since they are reinforced by custom and the instinct for upholding the *status quo*, have no need of a reasoned defense. It is the innovators who have difficulty in being allowed to exist and work. Each generation believes that this difficulty is a thing of the past, but each generation is tolerant only of past innovations. Those of its own day are met with the same persecution as if the principle of toleration had never been heard of.

On any matter of general interest, there is usually in any given community, at any given time, a received opinion, which is accepted as a matter of course by all who give no special thought to the matter. Any questioning of the received opinion arouses hostility, for a number of reasons.

The most important of these is the instinct of conventionality, which exists in all gregarious animals, and often leads them to put to death any markedly peculiar member of the herd. The next most important is the feeling of insecurity aroused by doubt as to the beliefs by which we are in the habit of regulating our lives. Whoever has tried to explain the philosophy of Berkeley to a plain man will have seen in its unadulterated form the anger aroused by this feeling. What the plain man derives from Berkeley's philosophy at a first hearing is an uncomfortable suspicion that nothing is solid, so that it is rash to sit on a chair or to expect the floor to sustain us. Because this suspicion is uncomfortable it is irritating, except to those who regard the whole argument as merely nonsense. And in a more or less analogous way any questioning of what has been taken for granted destroys the feeling of standing on solid ground, and produces a condition of bewildered fear.

A third reason which makes men dislike novel opinions is, that vested interests are bound up with old beliefs. The long fight of the Church against science, from Giordano Bruno to Darwin, is attributable to this motive, among others. The horror of socialism which existed in the remote past was entirely attributable to this case. But it would be a mistake to assume, as is done by those who seek economic motives everywhere, that vested interests are the principal source of anger against novelties in thought. If this were the case, intellectual progress would be much more rapid than it is. The instinct of conventionality, horror of uncertainty, and vested interests, all militate against the acceptance of a new idea. And it is even harder to think of a new idea than to get it accepted: most people might spend a lifetime in reflection without ever making a genuinely original discovery.

In view of all these obstacles, it is not likely that any society at any time will suffer from a plethora of heretical opinions. Least of all is this likely in a modern civilized society, where the conditions of life are in constant rapid change, and demand, for successful adaptation, an equally rapid change in intellectual outlook. There should, therefore, be an attempt to encourage rather than discourage the expression of new beliefs and the dissemination of knowledge tending to support them. But the very opposite is in fact the case. From childhood upwards, everything is done to make the minds of men and women conventional and sterile. And if, by misadventure, some spark of imagination remains, its unfortunate possessor is considered unsound and dangerous, worthy only of contempt in time of peace and of prison or a traitor's death in time of war. Yet such men are known to have been in the past the chief benefactors of mankind, and are the very men who receive most honor as soon as they are safely dead.

The whole realm of thought and opinion is utterly unsuited to public control: it ought to be as free, and as spontaneous, as is possible to those who know what others have believed. The state is justified in insisting that children shall be educated, but it is not justified in forcing their education to proceed on a uniform plan and to be directed to the production of a dead level of glib uniformity. Education, and the life of the mind generally, is a matter in which individual initiative is the chief thing needed; the function of the state should begin and end with insistence on *some* kind of education, and, if possible, a kind which promotes mental individualism, not a kind which happens to conform to the prejudices of government officials.

II

Questions of practical morals raise more difficult problems than questions of mere opinion. The Thugs of India honestly believe it their duty to commit murders, but the government does not acquiesce. Conscientious objectors honestly hold the opposite opinion, and again the government does not acquiesce. The punishment of conscientious objectors seems clearly a violation of individual liberty within its legitimate sphere.

It is generally assumed without question that the state has a right to punish certain kinds of sexual irregularity. No one doubts that the Mormons sincerely believed polygamy to be a desirable practice, yet the United States required them to abandon its legal recognition, and probably any other Christian country would have done likewise. Nevertheless, I do not think this prohibition was wise. Polygamy is legally permitted in many parts of the world, but is not much practiced except by chiefs and potentates. I think that in all such cases the law should intervene only when there is some injury inflicted without the consent of the injured person.

It is obvious that men and women would not tolerate having their wives or husbands selected by the state, whatever eugenists might have to say in favor of such a plan. In this, it seems clear that ordinary public opinion is in the right, not because people choose wisely, but because any choice of their own is better than a forced marriage. What applies to marriage ought also to apply to the choice of a trade or profession: although some men have no marked preferences, most men greatly prefer some occupations to others, and are far more likely to be useful citizens if they follow their preferences than if they are thwarted by a public authority.

III

We may now arrive at certain general principles in regard to individual liberty and public control.

The greater part of human impulses may be divided into two classes, those which are possessive and those which are constructive or creative. Property is the direct expression of possessiveness; science and art are among the most direct expressions of creativeness. Possessiveness is either defensive or aggressive; it seeks either to retain something against a robber, or to acquire something from a present holder. In either case, an attitude of hostility to others is of its essence.

The whole realm of the possessive impulses, and of the use of force to which they give rise, stands in need of control by a public neutral authority, in the interests of liberty no less than of justice. Within a nation, this public authority will naturally be the state; in relations between nations, if the present anarchy is to cease, it will have to be some international parliament. But the motive underlying the public control of men's possessive impulses should always be the increase of liberty, both by the prevention of private tyranny, and by the liberation of creative impulses. If public control is not to do more harm than good, it must be so exercised as to leave the utmost freedom of private initiative in all ways that do not involve the private use of force. In this respect, all governments have always failed egregiously, and there is no evidence that they are improving.

The creative impulses, unlike those that are possessive, are directed to ends in which one man's gain is not another man's loss. The man who makes a scientific discovery or writes a poem is enriching others at the same time as himself. Any increase in knowledge or good-will is a gain to all who are affected by it, not only to the actual possessor. Force cannot create such things, though it can destroy them; no principle of distributive justice applies to them, since the gain of each is the gain of all. For these reasons, the creative part of a man's activity ought to be as free as possible from all public control, in order that it may remain spontaneous and full of vigor. The only function of the state in regard to this part of the individual life should be to do everything possible toward providing outlets and opportunities.

Huge organizations, both political and economic, are one of the distinguishing characteristics of the modern world. These organizations have immense power, and often use their power to discourage originality in thought and action. They ought, on the contrary, to give the freest scope that is possible without producing anarchy or violent conflict.

The problem which faces the modern world is the combination of individual initiative with the increase in the scope and size of organizations. Unless it is solved, individuals will grow less and less full of life and vigor, more and more passively submissive to conditions imposed upon them. A society composed of such individuals cannot be progressive, or add much to the world's stock of mental and spiritual possessions.

Only personal liberty and the encouragement of initiative can secure these things. Those who resist authority when it encroaches upon the legitimate sphere of the individual are performing a service to society, however little society may value it. In regard to the past, this is universally acknowledged; but it is no less true in regard to the present and the future.

Thought

1. Do you share Russell's view of the difficulty of freedom of thought? Why or why not?

2. Explain the paradox contained in the first two sentences of the essay.

3. How does Russell account for the hostility that greets someone who questions "received opinion"? Discuss a contemporary figure whose reception supports Russell's argument.

4. Outline the differences, in Russell's view, between possessiveness and creativity. Do you think these differences are valid?

Style and Structure

5. Russell cites no statistics, states few facts, and appeals to no authority other than himself. How, then, does he make his essay so persuasive?

6. This essay is divided into three sections. Summarize the organizing idea for each section, and explain how each contributes to the development of Russell's argument.

Response and Extension

7. Russell writes of the feeling of insecurity that arises when you are led to question your own assumptions. In your journal recount a past experience that challenged a "received opinion" of your own. What did you learn in the process?

8. "I like to walk about amidst the beautiful things that adorn the world; but private wealth I should decline, or any sort of personal possessions, because they would take away my liberty." — George Santayana

Assess this statement in the context of what Russell says about the possessive impulse. What is your own response to Santayana's assertion?

9. Outline in your journal, or develop into a persuasive essay, a genuinely original idea of your own.

10. Debate the following statement: "From childhood upwards, everything is done to make the minds of men and women conventional and sterile."

11. Write a personal essay that examines the limits of your own choices, with reference to the types of obstacles that Russell discusses in his essay.

12. Consider an issue or an episode in your own school in which individual liberty comes up against public control. In groups or as a class, discuss the pros and cons of each side. In deciding on what principle you favour in this situation, make reference to points that Russell makes in his essay.

13. What kinds of "organizations" today have the effect of "discouraging originality in thought and action"? Write a short, persuasive piece on one of these societal influences.

Institutionalized Racism and Canadian History: Notes of a Black Canadian

Adrienne Shadd

It always amazes me when people express surprise that there might be a "race problem" in Canada, or when they attribute the "problem" to a minority of prejudiced individuals. Racism is, and always has been, one of the bedrock institutions of Canadian society, embedded in the very fabric of our thinking, our personality.

I am a fifth-generation black Canadian who was born and raised in a small black farming village called North Buxton, near Chatham, Ontario. North Buxton is a community comprised of the descendants of the famous Elgin Settlement of escaped slaves who travelled the Underground Railroad to freedom in Canada in the 1850s. As a young girl growing up in the fifties and sixties, I became aware of the overt hostility of whites in the area when we would visit nearby towns. Children would sometimes sneer at us and spit, or call us names. When we would go into the local ice cream parlour, the man behind the counter would serve us last, after all the whites had been served, even if they came into the shop after us. Southwestern Ontario may as well have been below the Mason-Dixon line in those days. Dresden, home of the historic Uncle Tom's Cabin, made national headlines in 1954 when blacks tested the local restaurants after the passage of the Fair Accommodation Practices Act and found that two openly refused to serve them. This came as no surprise, given that for years certain eateries, hotels, and recreation clubs were restricted to us, and at one time blacks could only sit in designated sections of movie theatres (usually the balcony), if admitted at all. Yet this particular incident sent shock waves through the nation, embarrassed about such evidence of racial "intolerance" going on in its own backyard.

Somehow, this kind of racism never bothered me. I always felt superior to people who were so blind that they could not see our basic humanity. Such overt prejudice, to my mind, revealed a fundamental weakness or fear. Although, instinctively, I knew that I was not inferior, there was not one positive role model outside our tiny community, and the image of blacks in the media was universally derogatory. Africans were portrayed as backward heathens in the Tarzan movies we saw, and black Americans were depicted through the characters of Step 'n Fetchit, Amos 'n Andy, Buckwheat of "Our Gang" fame, or the many maids who graced the television and movie screens in small bit parts. (Black Canadians were virtually nonexistent in Canadian media.) I used to wonder if it could really be true that black people the world over were so poor, downtrodden, inarticulate, and intellectually inferior, as the depictions seemed to suggest.

At the age of 10, we moved to Toronto. In the largely white neighbourhood where we lived, I was initially greeted by silent, nervous stares on the part of some children, who appeared afraid of me, or at least afraid to confront me openly. Later, as I began to develop an awareness of the Civil Rights and Black Power movements through my readings, certain friends would respond with a frozen silence if I brought up the name of Malcolm X, or, for that matter, the latest soul record on the charts. Looking back, I can see that things ran fairly smoothly as long as the question of race could be ignored, and as long as I did not transgress the bounds of artificial "colour blindness" under which I was constrained. This, apparently, was the Torontonian approach to race relations.

I share these reminiscences to illustrate the different forms which racism has taken over time, and in varying locales in Canada, whether in the form of overt hostility and social ostracism as in southwestern Ontario, or in the subtle, polite hypocrisy of race relations in Toronto in the sixties.

But how, you may ask, do these personal experiences represent examples of institutionalized racism? Do they not depend on the attitudes of people, which vary from individual to individual? Are not our Canadian laws and policies very clear about the fundamental rights of all people to equal treatment and opportunities?

The problem with this line of thinking is that it fails to recognize how powerfully attitudes and behaviours are shaped by the social climate and practices around us. If the only image you have of black women is derived from the one on your pancake box, then there is something wrong with the media portrayal of racial minorities. If there are no visible minorities in the boardrooms of the corporate world, and few in positions of influence and authority in the workforce, this sends a message far more potent than the human rights legislation set up to create a more equitable distribution of rewards and opportunities. When generation after generation of school children continue to be taught only about the accomplishments of white Europeans in Canada—mostly men—the myth that this is "traditionally a white country," as I heard a reporter say the other day, will persist, unchallenged.

The selective recording of some historical events and the deliberate omission of others have not been accidental, and they have had far-reaching consequences. Blacks and other people "of colour" are viewed as recent newcomers, or worse, "foreigners" who have no claim to a Canadian heritage except through the "generosity" of Canadian immigration officials, who "allow" a certain quota of us to enter each year.

But this myth that Canada is a white country is insidious because, on the one hand, it is so ingrained in the national consciousness, and on the other hand, so lacking in foundation. There is a tendency to forget that Native peoples were here first; blacks, first brought as slaves in the 1600 and 1700s, were among the earliest to settle on Canadian soil; the presence of the Chinese is traced to the 19th century. In fact, people from a wide variety of races and nationalities helped to build this country. Unfortunately, this really is not reflected in our school curricula.

The long black presence and contribution to Canada's development continues to go unacknowledged. People are surprised to learn, for example, that 10% of the Loyalists who migrated to British North America after the American Revolution were black. Their descendants, particularly in the Maritimes, have been living in quasi-segregated communities for over 20 years. Blacks were one of the largest groups to enter the country during the 19th century when 40-60 000 fugitive slaves and free people "of colour" sought refuge in Canada West (Ontario) between 1815-1860.

Standard textbooks never mention that, in 1734, part of the city of Montreal was burned down by Marie-Joseph Angelique, a black female slave, when she learned of her impending sale by her slave mistress. Most Canadians are not even aware that slavery existed in this country. Women's history courses fail to acknowledge that the first newspaper-woman in Canada was a black, Mary Ann Shadd, who edited a paper for fugitives between 1853-1859 in Toronto and later Chatham, Ontario. Heartwarming stories such as that of Joe Fortes—a Barbadian-born sailor who came to British Columbia in 1885 and subsequently, as the lifeguard of English Bay, taught three generations of young people to swim—are all but forgotten. Fortes is considered a true Canadian hero to those who are still around to remember him, but it seems that many younger British Columbians believe Fortes was a white man. And did any of you know that the term "the real McCoy" was coined after the inventions of a black man, Elijah McCoy, born in Harrow, Ontario, in 1840?

Today's students, black and white, look to the United States for information regarding the Civil Rights Movement, unaware that a gripping saga exists right here in Ontario. In the forties and fifties, organizations such as the Windsor Council on Group Relations, the National Unity Association of Chatham-Dresden-North Buxton, the Brotherhood of Sleeping Car Porters, and the Negro Citizens' Association of Toronto fought segregation in housing, accommodations, and employment, as well as racist immigration laws. Much of the antidiscrimination and human rights legislation that we now take for granted are a direct result of the struggles which these groups waged.

On a more personal level, even the most subtle and polite forms of racism can be detrimental, especially as they affect children. In my own case, when we moved to Toronto I was made to feel different, alien, even though no one specifically referred to my racial origin. It is a feeling which has never fully left me and perhaps explains why to this day I do not feel comfortable in the company of a group of white people. And when some whites think they are paying black people a compliment by saying, "We don't think of you as black," as my sister's friends have told her, this is not just a misplaced nicety; it is an insult. We are not seeking "honorary" white status.

Before we as a society can liberate ourselves from the grip of racism, we have to acknowledge that it exists, and that it is not something which has been blown out of proportion; neither is it the figment of some people's imaginations. If we can do this much, we will at least have moved out from under the heavy shroud of self-delusion and deceit. That in itself would be a refreshing step forward.

Thought

1. a) Cite three examples from Shadd's essay that lead her to state "Racism is and always has been one of the bedrock institutions of Canadian society."
   b) Suggest examples of racism from your own experience that concur with Shadd's allegations.

2. a) Explain what Shadd means by "institutionalized racism."
   b) Provide three examples of how racism has become institutionalized in our society.

3. Do you agree with Shadd's conclusions in the final paragraph? Explain.

Style and Structure

4. Shadd makes use of both anecdotal and historical evidence to support her thesis. Assess the effectiveness of both styles of presentation. Cite quotes from the essay to support your analysis.

5. a) By comparing Shadd's introduction and conclusion explain how she has built her argument, from opening statement to closing recommendation.
   b) Choose an essay in this anthology whose introduction and conclusion are less closely related than those of Shadd. Account for the difference by describing the structure of this second essay.

Response and Extension

6. Choose a current movie or TV show and, in the context of Shadd's arguments, analyze its representation of people who make up our society. Share your findings with the class.

7. In groups, discuss the ways in which society discriminates against adolescents.

8. Shadd restricts the discussion of racism primarily to black Canadians. What other groups in Canadian society have experienced institutionalized racism? Explain why you think so. If possible, support your opinion with examples of representation—or lack thereof—in the media, in school texts, or in positions of power.

9. As a class, discuss whether racism is an institution in your school and in your community.

10. Devise practical strategies to improve race relations in your school and community. Put these plans to work.

11. Devise a human rights code for your school and ensure that it is implemented.

Unit Synthesis

1. Compare cummings' essay on poetry with that of Bronwen Wallace ("Shyly Slipping a Poem from the Purse," p. 30) and of Pablo Neruda ("Shakespeare, Prince of Light," p. 238). Which of these approaches to poetry persuades you most? Explain why.

2. "The state is justified in insisting that children shall be educated, but it is not justified in forcing their education to proceed on a uniform plan and to be directed to the production of a dead level of glib uniformity." Write an essay that examines the degree to which the essays by cummings and Shadd support Russell's opinion.

3. "There should," writes Russell, "be an attempt to encourage rather than discourage the expression of new beliefs and the dissemination of knowledge tending to support them." Write an essay relating this statement to the ideas expressed by Meigs, Kleiman, and Heilbrun.

4. a) What is your definition of a feminist? Make reference to the essays by Meigs, Kleiman, and Heilbrun in your answer.
   b) Sometimes people will preface a statement with "I'm not a feminist, but . . ." Why do you think they feel the need to qualify their position in this way?

5. Research a prominent figure in the women's movement. Write an essay that presents information on her background, accomplishments, and beliefs. Be sure to incorporate your own evaluation of her ideas.

6. Write a persuasive essay that takes a stand on an important public issue. For example: freedom of expression and access versus censorship; free enterprise versus state regulation of the marketplace; the public's right to know versus the individual's right to privacy.

7. As a class, compose a series of monologues entitled "The Voices of the Oppressed." Perform your monologues for a school assembly.

8. Write your own definitions of the following words: poetry; secret; family; liberty. Be as original, precise, imaginative, and persuasive as you can.

9. For debate: Racism (or sexism) is an institution devised to preserve the status quo.

10. Write a persuasive essay for your school newspaper which addresses an injustice you have noticed in your school, for example, the abandonment of competitive inter-school sport in favour of intra-school sport.

Suggested Readings

Bolen, Jean *Goddesses in Every Woman*

Campbell, Maria *Half-Breed*

Dove, Rita *Thomas and Beulah*

Eiseler, Riane *The Chalice and the Sword*

Fromm, Erich *To Have or To Be*

Heilbrun, Carolyn *Hamlet's Mother*

Hooks, Bell *From Margin to Center; Black Looks; Race and Representation*

Kaufmann, Walter *From Shakespeare to Existentialism*

Lord, Audre *Sister Outsider; A Burst of Light*

Morrison, Toni *The Bluest Eye*

Paglia, Camille *Sex, Art and American Popular Culture*

Phelps, Ethel Johnston *The Maid of the North: Feminist Folk Tales from around the World*

Nelson, Maria Burton *The Stronger Women Get, the More Men Love Football; Are We Winning Yet?*

Pirsig, Robert M. *Zen and the Art of Motorcycle Maintenance*

Rich, Adrienne *Adrienne Rich's Poetry and Prose*

Sartre, Jean-Paul *Nausea*

Walker, Alice *In Search of Our Mothers' Gardens*

Writing to Reflect

Infinity is not terribly lively, not terribly emotional.... The more finite a thing is, the more it is charged with life, emotions, joy, fears, compassion.

Joseph Brodsky

In Selfish Pursuit

Anthony Brandt

I **want** to talk about the pursuit of happiness and the dilemmas it leads us into. But I should explain my own bias, my old habit of contempt for this pursuit, before I begin. Until I looked up the history of the phrase not too long ago, I believed that happiness was an unworthy goal and couldn't understand why Jefferson gave it such weight when he wrote the Declaration of Independence. Life and liberty were inalienable rights clearly enough, but why the pursuit of happiness? Why not something more substantial, like greatness or knowledge?

As it turns out, Jefferson did not mean by happiness what we mean by it; we tend to think of happiness as a feeling, an entirely subjective delight, the inner grin that appears when life seems free of problems and disappears when they return. The pursuit of happiness so defined inevitably becomes a matter of managing one's internal state, one's moods. And my moods are characteristically, even genetically, somewhat dour. My father was a Swede by descent and as phlegmatic as that race is supposed to be. My mother was a fierce woman who more often inspired fear in me than delight. One day, I remember, I pulled a muscle so badly she had to take me to the doctor. Walking to the car, I started to groan from the pain; "Keep it to yourself," she snapped. I've hardly allowed myself to groan since. She was a stoic, and her stoicism became the model for my own. Over the years I developed a certain indifference to how I feel. I've lived with minor ailments for years and done nothing about them. I've come to believe that I should ignore my internal emotional state as well.

My whole disposition, in short, led me to this contempt for the pursuit of happiness. I am a quiet, occasionally grim, somewhat ascetic man, willing, I've always thought, to leave happiness to those lucky people who are born cheerful. I am of the type that has trouble letting go and having fun. I can't remember jokes when I've heard them. And life has always seemed to me a testing ground; like a fox crossing the ice or a soldier in a minefield, you proceed with great caution, take nothing for granted, and count yourself blessed just to have made it to the other side.

But I am a living contradiction; I am in fact—beneath the moods, the stoicism, the seriousness—a happy man. How so? It comes from the conditions of my life. My two children have grown up healthy, bright, and decent; I live in one of the loveliest villages in America. My wife loves and delights me, and I her. Most important of all, I believe to the center of my being that the work I am doing is the work I was meant to do. So this dour man, who can't dance, who worries that he drinks too much, is secretly pleased with himself and is free not to believe in the pursuit of happiness because he has already caught up with it.

I don't, however, feel entirely comfortable with this outcome. You will detect the note of self-congratulation in my account of myself. I am aware of it, but I'm not sure what to do about it. Should I deny my feelings? A friend of mine on the West Coast recently wrote me that after two years of trying to adjust to having diabetes and to establish himself in his career at the same time, he had come out whole and modestly successful, and he was greatly pleased. Those who love the man can only be pleased for him. He earned it, didn't he? We turn guilty too quickly, I think, when we consider our circumstances and our successes and pronounce them good. I know I react this way; some part of me is sure I'm ripe for tragedy, that whatever success I have and whatever pleasure I take in it will be taken away. I don't really deserve it, I tell myself.

It becomes practically a fixed sequence: you arrive at a goal and that makes you happy, but then you notice that the happiness is composed half of relief, half of self-satisfaction; the latter half makes you distinctly nervous, and you fall to chewing on your achievements, discounting them. This then becomes the spur to more achievements, more happiness, more guilt. How much better, I sometimes think, to have no goals, just to live day by day. Would I be happy then? No, my mother's ghost wouldn't allow it. Life is hard, she told me; life is a struggle. So I struggle happily on, running through the sequence again and again, fighting off the impulse to pat myself on the back but remaining, like my friend, fundamentally pleased. That's the American way, isn't it? My contempt for the pursuit of happiness is a joke. I'm playing this game as hard as the next fellow.

But I have doubts. There are plenty of ways besides the American way. We Americans identify the pursuit of happiness with the pursuit of success, money, achievement; we think we'll be happy when we make it, although we love to believe that those who do make it are actually quite miserable. But I think of my father, who seemed to have no ambition, perfectly content, as far as I could tell, to work in the same job for the same company for thirty-five years, to come home to his wife and children every single night, read the paper, eat dinner, never go anywhere but to our cottage at the shore for two weeks and weekends during the summer. My father was intelligent and talented; he had a beautiful singing voice, he could draw with great accuracy, but he made no effort to develop any of his talents. An assistant manager for twenty years, he had no desire to become manager. It used to drive my mother crazy; she was ambitious for him, she wanted him to push. He was immovable. When he retired, he spent the next ten years puttering around in his garden, which he never finished, and doing crossword puzzles. Still driving my mother crazy. I used to think he had wasted his life. Arrogant of me. I remember visiting him in his office and always finding him having a good time, chatting with his fellow workers, the very image of a happy man. Was this wasteful?

My brother and I are both driven workaholics; my father lived in an entirely different framework. I think of the Greeks in connection with him; their idea of a happy life was a life led outside history, a quiet life like his. Their archetypal illustration was the story Herodotus tells about the lawgiver Solon's conversation with the Lydian king Croesus, who was legendary for his wealth. Solon, who was legendary for his wisdom, was on a ten-year tour of the known world when he met Croesus, who showed him his treasury and then asked him who he thought was the happiest of all the men he had met. Croesus believed, of course, that being the richest he would certainly have to be the happiest. Solon rapidly set him straight. Who is a happy man? He who "is whole of limb," Solon replied, "a stranger to disease, free from misfortune, happy in his children, and comely to look upon." No more is necessary, except that he die well.

All of this was true of my father. He had enough money; he was whole of limb; he was almost never sick; he loved his children; he was even relatively good-looking. And he died well. The only time he ever spent in a hospital was the last four days of his life; he had a heart attack, spent four days in intensive care, and then, as quietly as he had lived, died. Here was happiness, not pursued but possessed anyhow.

Then there's the price those of us like his two sons pay, and force others to, for our obsession with this will-o'-the-wisp, happiness. A woman I hoped to marry wanted me to give up free-lance writing and get a job in public relations. I was making about six thousand dollars a year at the time and living on my dreams and my MasterCard. We had nothing. It was clear to both of us that we could hardly make a decent life together if my prospects didn't rapidly improve. And I might have made forty thousand dollars a year in PR. I flirted with the idea, saw some people, but nothing came of it. No one will hire me, I told her. You didn't really try, she replied. What do you mean? I said, indignant; of course I did. Of course I didn't. The truth I didn't want to admit to her, or to myself, was that I loved the work I was doing more than I loved her. She left eventually, and I was glad to see her go. I wanted the guilt she represented out of my life.

We can be selfish and ruthless in the pursuit of happiness, make choices other people have to live and suffer with, and there's no guarantee that it's going to work out. The odds are, in fact, that we won't make it, whatever "it" is, that the losses will outweigh the gains. The odds are what's keeping my friend Paul, who desperately wants to change his life, from doing it. Paul is thirty-five, married, and has an eleven-year-old son. He works as an advertising copywriter and does well, but what he really wants is to go back to graduate school, get his Ph.D. in English literature, then get a teaching job and write fiction on the side. But to do all this would mean selling his house, asking his wife to go to work, and using the savings he has accumulated for his son's education for his own. He tells me that he sometimes spends hours figuring out exactly what he would need, how much the house would bring, how much his wife might make if she got a job, and what his chances are of getting a job in the overcrowded market for Ph.D.s. But no matter how carefully he draws up this budget—the figures, he says, are a simulacrum of his loyalties—there's never enough money.

The risks involved in such a choice are enormous, and Paul is at heart not ruthless or selfish enough to take them. If he were alone, he says, sure. And he says his wife is willing to stand behind him whatever he decides. But he can't do it, and this seems in most respects admirable; it was apparently my father's choice, it is the Greek choice, the choice to be content with one's lot and not ask too many sacrifices from other people in the service of something so insubstantial, so vague, as a possibility of happiness beyond what one already has. And yet Paul is not a happy man. He is not ruthless or selfish, no, but he sees this as a lack of courage, a failure to believe in his own talent; he calls himself a coward.

I understand Paul and I know what he's going through. I made my choice a long time ago, but it took me a long time to make it. And when I did, it cost me everything I owned, and it cost my ex-wife and my two kids and later my fiancée, not to mention assorted friends and relatives, one hell of a lot of pain. And for what? I am proud of the work I've done, proud of staying with it when the reward was only six thousand dollars a year and my hair was already starting to turn gray; but I'm not proud of my own ruthlessness and selfishness and I wish I had had it in me to be more like my father.

The pursuit of happiness was serious business to Jefferson, but his idea of happiness, as I mentioned at the beginning, was quite different from ours. Happiness at the time of the Declaration was not a state of mind that one pursued in and for oneself but a version of the common good, an idea of general human felicity that one pursued both for oneself and for all. Jefferson was trying to establish the idea that government has no right to stand in the way of our pursuit of felicity so conceived. The form that felicity took for Jefferson was a society composed very much along the Greek model, with lots of farmers living quiet lives, practicing quiet virtues, making money but not too much, and reading Herodotus by candlelight.

It hasn't turned out that way. We have identified happiness with success and we are stuck with it now, so that people like my father seem like washouts to people like my mother and the only happiness I can find is in the struggle to succeed. I suppose it couldn't have happened otherwise. But I am tempted to cry, Enough! To rest easy with what I have, finish reading Herodotus and then move on to Plutarch, perhaps take up crossword puzzles, leave pursuits to others. A gentleman farmer. It was wise of my father not to finish his garden, for he would only have had to start another. Now he's gone, I missed the message of his life, I have condemned myself to this pursuit. Oh, I love it, make no mistake, but the pursuit of happiness feels to me sometimes like a dog chasing its tail and half of me thinks that we have made a giant mistake, that the American way is little more than the exaltation of greed.

Thought

1. The author outlines the "fixed sequence" of the pursuit of happiness. In your opinion, to what extent is he describing our shared human nature, and to what extent his own inclinations? Explain.

2. a) How does the author's understanding of happiness differ from his father's?
   b) Which of these views of happiness is closer to your own? Explain.

3. Do you agree that one can be "selfish and ruthless in the pursuit of happiness"? Justify your opinion.

4. a) Is Brandt justified in asserting that "the American way is little more than the exaltation of greed"?
   b) Is this the Canadian view also?

5. Analyze how Brandt depicts the relations between particular men and women. What conflicts, and what roles, do these relationships have in common? What historical context informs these situations?

Style and Structure

6. Describe the tone of this essay, and explain how it influences your understanding of its thesis.

7. Consider several of Brandt's anecdotes. Which of these are illustrative, and which are developmental? Explain.

8. Brandt makes two separate references to the American Declaration of Independence. Explain how the placement of these references serves to develop his main point.

9. "The exaltation of greed": Analyze and explain the rhetorical effect of this concluding phrase.

Response and Extension

10. For discussion: To what extent are selfishness and the pursuit of happiness synonymous?

11. Interview someone whom you consider to be happy, and write an essay in which you reflect upon why this is so.

12. In your journal, reflect upon what makes you happy.

Listening to Boredom

Joseph Brodsky

A **substantial** part of what lies ahead of you is going to be claimed by boredom. The reason I'd like to talk to you about it today, on this lofty occasion, is that I believe no liberal arts college prepares you for that eventuality. Neither the humanities nor science offers courses in boredom. At best, they may acquaint you with the sensation by incurring it. But what is a casual contact to an incurable malaise? The worst monotonous drone coming from a lectern or the most eye-splitting textbook written in turgid English is nothing in comparison to the psychological Sahara that starts right in your bedroom and spurns the horizon.

Known under several aliases—anguish, ennui, tedium, the doldrums, humdrum, the blahs, apathy, listlessness, stolidity, lethargy, languor, etc.—boredom is a complex phenomenon and by and large a product of repetition. It would seem, then, that the best remedy against it would be constant inventiveness and originality. That is what you, young and new-fangled, would hope for. Alas, life won't supply you with the option, for life's main medium is precisely repetition.

One may argue, of course, that repeated attempts at originality and inventiveness are the vehicle of progress and, in the same breath, civilization. As benefits of hindsight go, however, this one is not the most valuable. For if we divide the history of our species by scientific discoveries, not to mention new ethical concepts, the result will not be very impressive. We'll get, technically speaking, centuries of boredom. The very notion of originality or innovation spells out the monotony of standard reality, of life.

The other trouble with originality and inventiveness is that they literally pay off. Provided that you are capable of either, you will become well-off rather fast. Desirable as that may be, most of you know firsthand that nobody is as bored as the rich, for money buys time, and time is repetitive. Assuming that you are not heading for poverty, one can expect your being hit by boredom as soon as the first tools of self-gratification become available to you. Thanks to modern technology, those tools are as numerous as boredom's symptoms. In light of their function—to render you oblivious to the redundancy of time—their abundance is revealing.

As for poverty, boredom is the most brutal part of its misery, and escape from it takes more radical forms: violent rebellion or drug addiction. Both are temporary, for the misery of poverty is infinite; both, because of that infinity, are costly. In general, a man shooting heroin into his vein does so largely for the same reason you rent a video: to dodge the redundancy of time. The difference, though, is that he spends more than he's got, and that his means of escaping become as redundant as what he is escaping from faster than yours. On the whole, the difference in tactility between a syringe's needle and a stereo's push button roughly corresponds to the difference between the acuteness of time's impact upon the have-nots and the dullness of its impact on the haves. But, whether rich or poor, you will inevitably be afflicted by monotony. Potential haves, you'll be bored with your work, your friends, your spouses, your lovers, the view from your window, the furniture or wallpaper in your room, your thoughts, yourselves. Accordingly, you'll try to devise ways of escape. Apart from the self-gratifying gadgets I mentioned before, you may take up changing your job, residence, company, climate; you may take up promiscuity, alcohol, travel, cooking lessons, drugs, psychoanalysis.

In fact, you may lump all these together, and for a while that may work. Until the day, of course, when you wake up in your bedroom amidst a new family and a different wallpaper, in a different state and climate, with a heap of bills from your travel agent and your shrink, yet with the same stale feeling toward the light of day pouring through your window. You'll put on your loafers only to discover that they're lacking bootstraps by which to lift yourself up from what you recognize. Depending on your temperament and your age, you will either panic or resign yourself to the familiarity of the sensation, or else you'll go through the rigmarole of change once more. Neurosis and depression will enter your lexicon; pills, your medicine cabinet.

Basically, there is nothing wrong with turning life into the constant quest for alternatives, into leapfrogging jobs, spouses, and surroundings, provided that you can afford the alimony and jumbled memories. This predicament, after all, has been sufficiently glamorized on-screen and in Romantic poetry. The rub, however, is that before long this quest turns into a full-time occupation, with your need for an alternative coming to match a drug addict's daily fix.

There is yet another way out of boredom, however. Not a better one, perhaps, from your point of view, and not necessarily secure, but straight and inexpensive. When hit by boredom, let yourself be crushed by it; submerge, hit bottom. In general, with things unpleasant, the rule is: The sooner you hit bottom, the faster you surface. The idea here is to exact a full look at the worst. The reason boredom deserves such scrutiny is that it represents pure, undiluted time in all its repetitive, redundant, monotonous splendor.

Boredom is your window on the properties of time that one tends to ignore to the likely peril of one's mental equilibrium. It is your window on time's infinity. Once this window opens, don't try to shut it; on the contrary, throw it wide open. For boredom speaks the language of time, and it teaches you the most valuable lesson of your life: the lesson of your utter insignificance. It is valuable to you, as well as to those you are to rub shoulders with. "You are finite," time tells you in the voice of boredom, "and whatever you do is, from my point of view, futile." As music to your ears, this, of course, may not count; yet the sense of futility, of the limited significance of even your best, most ardent actions, is better than the illusion of their consequences and the attendant self-aggrandizement.

For boredom is an invasion of time into your set of values. It puts your existence into its proper perspective, the net result of which is precision and humility. The former, it must be noted, breeds the latter. The more you learn about your own size, the more humble and the more compassionate you become to your likes, to the dust aswirl in a sunbeam or already immobile atop your table.

If it takes will-paralyzing boredom to bring your insignificance home, then hail the boredom. You are insignificant because you are finite. Yet infinity is not terribly lively, not terribly emotional. Your boredom, at least, tells you that much. And the more finite a thing is, the more it is charged with life, emotions, joy, fears, compassion.

What's good about boredom, about anguish and the sense of meaninglessness of your own, of everything else's existence, is that it is not a deception. Try to embrace, or let yourself be embraced by, boredom and anguish, which are larger than you anyhow. No doubt you'll find that bosom smothering, yet try to endure it as long as you can, and then some more. Above all, don't think you've goofed somewhere along the line, don't try to retrace your steps to correct the error. No, as W. H. Auden said, "Believe your pain." This awful bear hug is no mistake. Nothing that disturbs you ever is.

Thought

1. According to Brodsky, what is the relationship between boredom and monotony?

2. Do you agree with Brodsky that boredom is inevitable? Explain.

3. How is boredom different for the rich as opposed to the poor? Explain.

4. This piece, in a slightly different form, was originally delivered as a commencement address with the title "In Praise of Boredom." What does Brodsky find praiseworthy about this state?

5. Assess Brodsky's advice about how to escape boredom.

6. Describe how Brodsky makes the unexpected link between joy and the awareness of one's insignificance.

Style and Structure

7. **a)** Identify and explain the metaphors Brodsky uses for boredom. **b)** Which one do you think is most appropriate? Explain.

8. Brodsky writes: "In general, a man shooting heroin into his vein does so largely for the same reason you rent a video: to dodge the redundancy of time." Explain whether or not you think this is an appropriate comparison.

9. Does Brodsky appeal more to logic or to emotion? Explain.

Response and Extension

10. "Boredom speaks the language of time." In your groups discuss the implications of this statement.

11. **a)** What bores you?
    b) What "shape" does your boredom take?
    c) Would you change your boredom for someone else's?

12. Write a reflective essay about how one can lead a productive life without experiencing boredom.

13. Compare the author's view of time with Marjorie Kelly's in her essay, "You Can't Always Get Done What You Want" (p. 10). List the similarities and differences between these essays, analyzing which you think is, for example, more practical, interesting, helpful, or profound.

On Hating Piano Lessons

Phyllis Theroux

When I was growing up, I conceived of children as being of two kinds: those who took lessons and those who did not. I was the second kind, although I sometimes accompanied my horseback-riding, accordion-playing, baton-twirling friends to their classes and, by osmosis, learned a few things that enabled me to fake an expertise in a crowd. But with one exception I was self-taught, flinging my arms and legs around the living room doing badly executed *tours jetés* to Gilbert and Sullivan records, which allowed me to assume all the parts and, on one occasion, to break my ankle. I did, however, take piano lessons.

Once I discovered the sound that three fingers simultaneously placed on the right keys could produce, I longed so loudly and consistently for piano lessons that my mother began to think maybe I was a genius and she did not want to go to her grave thinking I had become a short-order cook for want of an option. Options, in the long run, are what lessons are all about.

Now I am a parent. I think about giving my children options and lessons, although children don't understand that their once-a-week session with Madame Faustini at the keyboard cancels out their mother's once-a-month visit to "The Magic Scissors." But hair-cuts play second fiddle to Beethoven if I am financially solvent, and this year my ten-year-old daughter is taking piano lessons—under duress.

My daughter does not like piano lessons. They are too hard. Her teacher, a wild and dedicated woman who drives around in a yellow convertible and annually volunteers to sit on the "Dunk-'Em" chair at the school bazaar, understands about ten-year-old girls who would rather be talking on the telephone, and she always tries to give her pieces to learn that are on the jazzy side. But my daughter, though dutiful, has not been won over by this enlightened approach. Furthermore, she claims, her heart lies with gymnastics, a message I bought last year, along with a leotard which now lies neglected in her bottom bureau drawer.

When she was halfway through gymnastics, her heart began to rove down the hall toward a tap-dancing class that sounded a lot better to her ears. I canceled gymnastics and enrolled her in tap, wanting to stake this small developing plant, my daughter, with the kinds of support that would strengthen and develop her soul.

Unfortunately, her soul turned out to be a shifting, shiftless creature, and her interest in tap dancing waned after the sixth lesson. Suddenly, she saw pottery (which happened to have a class in the same building) as the wave of her future. But tiring of always chasing cultural advantages that were in another room, I decided that what my daughter wanted was immaterial. I wanted her to take piano lessons.

At the beginning, all was well. But when she had gone through the honeymoon period of her first few lessons and realized there was more to it than pasting gold stars in new music books, gymnastics began to appeal to her anew. This time, however, I looked her straight in the eye and said, unflinchingly, "This year it's piano lessons. In fact, next year it's piano lessons, too, unless I can't afford them." It seemed important to let her know that there was no way out.

My daughter thinks I am cruel, that I don't understand her, that I am trying to force her to be something she is not. My daughter is right. I want her, when she is thirty-five or sixty and feeling temporarily low on being, to be able to converse with Mozart, call up Clementi, or have a romp with Rodgers and Hammerstein at *will*, which is what lessons of any kind develop the capacity to use.

This is a difficult wish to communicate to a child who looks at me with "don't make me do it" eyes when I drop her off for a lesson where she must spend another hour forcing her mind and fingers up and down the G and treble clefs. But I have hardened myself to her accusatory looks, and while my daughter has her reasons for complaint, my old heart has its reasons for making her suffer which her heart, being young, cannot fully understand.

There will come a time, I think, as I watch you trudge up the steps to your teacher's house, when your heart will be empty. There will come a time when words, no matter how many or how eloquent, will do you no good at all. There will come a time when no one thing or person can adequately express the soul inside you that needs to be articulated. And then, my gymnastic, tap-dancing daughter, if I have been sufficiently "cruel" to you, you will have music.

But Time divides us at this moment. There are some things one cannot explain to a ten-year-old girl who is only in Book One of piano and life. I must adjust myself to being the mean parent who doesn't understand, and perhaps I don't. Perhaps my daughter is a gymnast, or a tap dancer, or the world's number one potter who, when she is grown, will rightly accuse me of having thrown her on the wrong wheel. But in the meantime, in-between time, she is taking piano lessons.

Thought

1. Identify the thesis of this essay.

2. According to the writer, what purpose do lessons serve? Do you agree with her?

3. Consider the contexts in which the author uses the word "soul." What can you infer from these about how she conceptualizes a person's soul?

4. Why does Theroux decide that "What my daughter wanted was immaterial"? Is she justified in this decision?

Style and Structure

5. Indicate the shifts in focus that Theroux uses to structure her essay. What purposes are served by these shifts?

6. Demonstrate that Theroux uses humour effectively to emphasize her thesis.

7. What effect does the author achieve by the series of sentences beginning with "There will come a time when . . ."?

Response and Extension

8. Write an essay reflecting upon a sport or activity that you were forced to participate in as a child. Be sure to include your feelings about the situation then and your feelings about it now.

9. Write a letter to your parent or guardian explaining why you will not do something he or she wants you to do.

10. What lessons would you like your own children to take? Explain why.

Welfare was a Life Raft, but Now We Can Swim

Barbara Hager

I remember how we used to count down to welfare-cheque day. I was 12; my brothers were 10 and 5. The cheque would arrive in the mailbox on the first or second of the month. My mother would try to pretend she wasn't anxious, but she would look out the window every five minutes to see if the mailman was on our block.

When it finally arrived, my mother would cash the cheque within the hour, and go directly to Safeway to buy a cart full of food. When we lived in Edmonton, the store was a mile from our house, so we would take a cab home. But in Calgary we lived in subsidized town-houses directly across from the store, so we saved two or three dollars a month in cab fare just living there.

After shopping for food, she would go to the landlord's apartment to pay the rent, which included utilities, in cash. The only other bill we had, since we didn't have a car or credit cards, was for the telephone. She would buy a money order and take the bus downtown to pay the bill at the head office.

We weren't on welfare intentionally. My father stopped living with us full-time when I was 4 or 5, and from that time on my mother alternated between welfare and low-paying jobs. She tried school a few times—a year of classes that were supposed to lead up to a degree in social work, a course in restaurant management. She worked off and on, too: arranging flowers, waiting tables, painting airplanes, and working on an assembly line at a vegetable cannery. But the money wasn't much more than welfare paid, and she had to worry about who was looking after us, and if we were getting into trouble.

So we grew up on federal assistance, though at the time I wasn't aware of who actually sent the cheque. I did know, however, how people could avoid welfare: by finding good jobs or by having fathers who lived with them who had good jobs.

I started working when I was 12. By 14, I had a dozen babysitting clients, a job at the local library, and a weekly house-cleaning job. I always had my own money. I didn't expect my mother to buy my clothes, gifts or movie tickets. Sometimes I lent her money that she didn't pay back. When I turned 15, I started paying $50 a month rent to my mother, who told me that every other kid who had a job did the same.

The neighbourhood where we lived was middle-class—the low-income housing complex seemed almost to have been built there by mistake. My friends lived nearby in split-level houses with two-car garages. They went on trips to Hawaii with their parents, and their older brothers and sisters attended universities down east. They had matching furniture in their houses, and fridges that were always full.

Once or twice my mother got behind in her bills. We probably had to spend the rent money on a gift, or a trip to see my older sister in Edmonton, or something. I just remember the calls from the bill collectors at all hours of the day and night. Someone in the family would finally lend her a few hundred dollars, but until then, I can remember the way she avoided answering the phone for months, didn't open her mail, just stopped dealing with money for a while.

It must have really gotten her down, the money problem, because somehow she scraped up enough money to buy a late-model car, and we gave away most of our furniture and moved to another province. She got a job at a restaurant in the small town where we moved, and for a while we got off welfare.

When my mother decided to move again to look for work in another town, I chose to stay alone in the town to finish high school. I was declared emancipated at 16, and the province sent my "assistance" check directly to the family I lived with. I continued to work, sometimes 20 or 25 hours a week, while playing basketball and finishing high school.

My mother resorted to welfare on and off for the next 10 years, until she launched a career as a nanny, which was a way to solve the rent problem, since she lived rent-free with the families, and got a salary too.

Looking back, I realize that my mother tried numerous ways to get off welfare. It was clearly a place she did not want to be. Sometimes it was through a job (usually short-lived), sometimes through a training program that the authorities paid her to take (somewhat successful, if you count the sporadic career in the restaurant business), and sometimes she would enter into a relationship with a man who could support her and her children (rarer yet).

I'm in my 30s now, with two small children. My husband and I have been blessed with a long, steady relationship. We have not, however, avoided living below the national poverty level at times over the past 15 years. We spent three years in a small southern American city where my husband worked for close to minimum wage for his uncle, and I worked for the city at half the wages that I had earned at a government job in a large northern city. When I left my job to work as an arts consultant, there were months when none of my clients paid my invoices, our bills did not get paid, the bill collectors began to call, and I stopped opening the mail.

Once we thought about applying for food stamps, but someone paid an invoice, and we didn't have to act on it. It was harder on my husband to consider social assistance, having grown up in a two-working-parent household. When middle-class people find themselves on welfare, the fall is much greater than for those of us who grew up on it.

What I learned most about growing up on welfare is that without it my brothers and I might not be where we are today—educated, hard-working and employed. Though we have never discussed it, I can see a pattern that we have all developed to avoid welfare. We work hard at our marriages because poverty strikes single parents first. We've found ways to learn the skills we need to get jobs that pay more than $8 an hour. My youngest brother is a forester, the other a pilot, and I've worked in professional positions for government for most of the past decade.

Strangely enough, the three of us have all been involved in hiring and training welfare recipients to work for us. Last month I found money to hire one of my summer employees as a part-time arts administrator. She has two young children, and her new part-time salary pays slightly more than her previous net on social assistance. I accidentally overheard her talking to her social worker on the phone after I offered her the job. She proudly informed her that she would be working now, and would probably only need child-care support until the job went full time. When she finished the call, she hung up the phone and let out a sigh that I could hear down the hallway.

We went out for coffee that day to celebrate. She insisted on paying the bill.

Thought

1. Interpret what you think were the author's feelings about living on welfare, from childhood on up to adulthood.

2. In your own words, describe everything the author has learned from her experiences.

3. Show how Hager's behaviour is consistent with the title of the essay.

4. What is the thesis of this essay? In one succinct sentence, express what you think is the essence of the author's message.

5. Citing quotes from the essay, describe your impressions of the author's character.

Style and Structure

6. Consider the first three paragraphs. Why do you think Hager chose to begin her essay in this way?

7. Describe the tone of this essay. How does the author's voice contribute to the power of her message?

8. Why does Hager conclude with the anecdote about her summer employee?

Response and Extension

9. How do you think the government should respond to people who are out of work? Write your own official statement of principles.

10. Recount your own work experiences in an essay that reflects on what meaning and value they have had for you.

The Suit

Norman Doidge

This is a true story about a suit. The suit has lived in my Uncle Henry's closet for thirty-three years. It is my dead father's suit.

Though never on display, its exact whereabouts is never in doubt. Whenever weather changes, or soldiers are imagined, it is always his brother's suit that comes first to Uncle Henry's mind. It has to do with refusing to give up. The suit has been there since my father went to get an elevator, waited for the door to open, and stepped into an elevator shaft that turned out to be empty and fell to the bottom. He lay there unconscious for a day until he was discovered. His head was smashed and his brain stem injured. My father, a Holocaust survivor, died in Toronto two days later at the age of thirty-three. Uncle Henry was visiting from New York at the time, looking into setting up a furniture business with my father. I was seventeen months then, my brother two months. Now, in my thirties myself, I think of the empty suit.

Perhaps I saw the awe-inspiring but silent suit on its hanger six or seven times. I can't remember my father wearing it, and I don't think I can remember my father. But I remember the suit.

Where there are no readily retrievable memories, substitutes must suffice. I knew him as one knows the numbness of the phantom limb which out of nowhere speaks out to say "I am here, but I am missing"; I had the indelible knowledge that a number was tattooed on his arm but didn't know the number; I knew stories of him telling stories to survive and his life-giving gift of the gab; heard others hum the songs he was always singing; I remembered standing as a child of four or five with my mother and brother, staring at his tombstone, and I knew that the name on the stone was not his real name,

Leon Greenspan, but the alias that he used to escape and that he became saddled with after the war. And yes, I knew of his suit.

But Henry had lots of solid memories of him, and the suit was just the beginning. "There are no brothers now like there were then," Henry said in his thick Polish accent, which was either lilting or severe, his eyebrows quivering as he turned to the closet every third or fourth of my almost yearly visits to New York. In Toronto, I heard only stories of him after the war, his brief happy years after the Holocaust. Such stories were always told in the strained voices of adults looking at a child who has lost his parent.

Arriving in Ontario from Europe, a wandering polyglot who had become accustomed in concentration camps to physical labour, Leon took the first job he was offered, as a lumberjack in the north. With his earnings he soon made his way to Toronto. He was a "greener," emerging from a line of immigrants, when my mother met him and soon fell in love. When she herself died in her mid-forties, I had nowhere near mined her memory of him.

But in New York there was Uncle Henry who knew him during the war and before. Hence many trips. Always the discussion turned to the suit. "I would not trade this suit for anything of any kind, and I would not trade this suit for my life," said Henry each time he pulled it out. And he meant it.

First Henry had two brothers, then only one, then only a suit. When the Nazis invaded Poland, my father attempted to smuggle his ten-year-old brother, Arthur, out of the city of Cracow, and then out of the country, by paying a Polish woman to hide Arthur until he got him Hungarian papers and a passport. For more money, she turned the Jewish child over to the Gestapo. They murdered him. Such baggage Leon carried with him when he was arrested in 1939 and sent to Heinrich Himmler Prison in Lublin, because he had the same last name, Greenspan, as the man who had assassinated Ernst vom Rath, a German embassy worker, in Paris. Snippets of the story of the two surviving brothers, and my father's experiences in the Plaszów camp, then Auschwitz from the middle of 1942 to 1944, emerged. Then Mauthausen and Gusen and Melk. Uncle Henry asked him, "How did you survive in Auschwitz for two years, when people frequently didn't last there for two weeks?" "Luck, and people liked me," said Leon. Stories that could be told were buried in stories that could not be. Then the unspeakable stories came out, in spurts of agonizing pain, in these visits to New York. Every third or fourth time Henry would go to the closet where the suit was.

Stories of disappearance, and stories of escape. Sitting quietly at the table on each visit was Grandma Golda, her sad, beautiful face finely lined and swirled, stamped with the fingerprint of her fate. Occasionally she would have a flashback to the camps, and the family would remind her that this was New York, 1980. At the age of sixteen Grandma Golda travelled alone from Poland to Italy to buy corals for the family business, reciting Dante's *Divine Comedy* in Italian on the train. As she recounted the story, she would begin singing the Italian and her face would light up, as though the musical verses were enough of a cue to transport her back to the adventures of her youth.

In her mid-fifties, Golda, her youngest son already murdered and her husband's whereabouts unknown, was forced onto another train and when she got off she found herself standing face to face with Dr. Josef Mengele in Auschwitz. In that fateful moment she was able to overcome vain hopes, and ascertain what the Nazis really had planned for those in the line to the left which was filled with the old, the grey, and the weak. She reasoned that, no matter what Mengele told her, she would go into the line to the right where the younger Jews were being directed. Despite his instructions, she moved quietly to the right. In this way she escaped the crematoria the first time. She quickly reckoned that further survival would require that she convey the impression of eternal youth. Her Italian came in handy when she realized that one of the camp's doctors, an Italian (also a Jewish prisoner), had access in the infirmary to purple cleaning crystals with which she concocted a black hair dye that she used herself, shared with inmates, or exchanged for food. Grandma Golda died at the age of ninety-six, with a full head of white hair.

In Austria, towards the end of the war, my father chanced upon and seized his ex-commandant who was in disguise, trying to escape at the train station. The man, who had killed thousands of Jews, offered him money not to turn him in. "But your father said that won't be necessary and he forced the man's head onto the track and broke his neck with his foot like that." Henry slammed down his foot. Silence. The suit.

Today when I was visiting, Uncle Henry was proud because he had recently lost twenty pounds. But all topics still led to my father. "Your father became heavy." I thought of the dashing pictures of him several years after the liberation. "Oh yes, he put on a lot of weight in the year after he married your mother," said Henry as he turned to the back room, "a lot of weight."

I followed, under the usual spell. He pulled out the suit and held it out like a newborn baby. "He always went to the finest tailor." "Exactly how tall was he?" I asked, with respect to the suit. "Your height, about," said Henry.

An idea was forming in my head which seemed, after all these years of awe and fear, not sacrilegious. It seemed just the thing to do. With the possible exception of his broken watch and his tefillin, I had, at that point in my conscious memory, never touched an article of my father's, let alone his clothing. The broken watch seemed outside of time, the tefillin a binding to another world. Each time I had touched them they had seemed to disappear into a hole in the valley of memory. But somehow the suit that had enveloped him seemed different: it was a menacing presence. Until today. The uncanny sense that Uncle Henry had been showing me something forbidden to me faded. Here was a man's brother, showing his nephew who couldn't remember his father, his father's rather expensive, rather unworn suit. He was conducting the ceremony quite beautifully, linking me to my rightful inheritance, sewing together generations torn asunder.

"Should I try it on?"

The question that for years I would have thought obscene came out loud and clear. "Why not?" said Henry. "Have you . . . ever . . ." I began. "Of course," he said as he unbuttoned it and slipped it off the hanger, "many times."

I put it on and was immediately amazed by the length of the sleeves, which were almost perfect—just a quarter of an inch too long on the palm. I fingered the edges, my fingers filled with yearning. Years of being unable to sense his bulk, his corporeal worth, faded. I am his size in the shoulders, I thought. Therefore, he is my father. QED. And the familiar girth. I too bloat up like this if I don't watch myself. Another proof for the existence. I am his son. I *am* a Greenspan. Surely, given the chance, he would have lost the weight, had the suit taken in. My God he must have been a forty-four, no, six, no, eight! In deep dark brown. My colour. Did we have the same colouring? I had always assumed he was fair, like my brother. I was tugged by a force to the mirror to see myself in the dazzling suit, hoping that Henry would not for a moment think this avarice, that I wanted the suit for myself, but would realize, as one who loved the suit, that this was beyond a great privilege. It was a necessary rite, even a responsibility.

And as I began thinking that this could last forever, me locked in the suit, as I began to look towards the corner in the closet, and thought of drawing its sleeves sleepily off my arms, I half heard Henry say, "I had to have that suit cleaned three times." But I was not listening until he said, "Your father died in that suit."

It seemed all over. Now I was dazed. Marked for death. Henry in the background talking about how the bloodstains wouldn't come out at first washing, while I was realizing my worst fear about the cracked face of his watch, my eyes racing from the broken two buttons on the sleeve to the collar near where his limp head had lain, Leon, me, someone in this suit at the bottom of the elevator shaft groaning over Tisha B'av, July 29, 1955, until he was found, comatose . . . but by now I was dizzy—what had I joined? for forever? having so recklessly put my hands through the holes of the sleeves! Strangling in the grip of the perfect fit my heart pounded. "His heart was very strong," said Henry. "His brain was dead but his heart wouldn't die for two days." O God, I thought, Henry was terrifying the life out of me! Why? I had only wanted a moment to make up for a lifetime without the weight of his hand on my shoulder. (In an age that belittles its patrimony, trust the fatherless to seek out and cherish the weight of a man.)

But as I looked up, I did not see in Henry's eyes the ambush I had feared, so much as I realized, as my heart began to slow, that this peculiar, uncanny ceremony conveyed weight. Henry seemed off in the corner of the room mumbling, but actually he was, as he was typically, about three inches from my dissociated face. Henry was saying something that would seem ghoulish, but which was, if one knew what he knew, an attempt at reassurance: giving himself through me a speech which said that my father's heart lasted, long after his brain had died. With tears in his eyes he was saying, "For several whole days, though his brain had been destroyed, his heart refused to die."

Torn from the man we both loved, torn after all those losses, something in us could last. It had to do with not giving up. I saw all this written on his tormented avuncular face. I lowered my head, and wept. This too was a story of survival. This was not a story of lightness, absence, or that which cannot be. This was a story about a suit.

Thought

1. Why does Henry keep his dead brother's suit?
2. a) What do all the family stories have in common?
   b) What purpose do these stories serve?
3. a) Trace the author's thoughts and feelings as he puts on his father's suit.
   b) Explain what Doidge means when he asks himself, "What had I gained?"
4. How does the author employ the concept of weight in the last two paragraphs of his essay?
5. Explain why you think his father's suit had been for so long a "menacing presence" for the author.

Style and Structure

6. Describe the tone of the opening two paragraphs and how they relate to the theme of the essay.
7. Although he is reflecting on events in the past, how does the author keep his reflections active in the present?
8. The author alludes twice to the refusal to give up: first in the second paragraph, and again in the last paragraph. Consider the context of these references and compare the meaning that each evokes. What effects does the author achieve by repeating this phrase?

Response and Extension

9. Bring to class an object or photograph that is charged with memories for you. Present to your group, or the class, the stories associated with the object.

10. In groups, discuss how you and your family keep alive the memories of a deceased relative.

11. For discussion: Why does the author refer to our time as an "age that belittles its patriarchy"?

12. In your journal, reflect upon the characteristics of your parents that you perceive in yourself.

Are There Any Questions?

Robert Fulghum

"Are there any questions?" An offer that comes at the end of college lectures and long meetings. Said when an audience is not only overdosed with information, but when there is no time left anyhow. At times like that you sure do have questions. Like, "Can we leave now?" and "What the hell was this meeting for?" and "Where can I get a drink?"

The gesture is supposed to indicate openness on the part of the speaker, I suppose, but if in fact you do ask a question, both the speaker and the audience will give you drop-dead looks. And some fool—some earnest idiot—always asks. And the speaker always answers. By repeating most of what he has already said.

But if there is a little time left and there is a little silence in response to the invitation, I usually ask the most important question of all: "What is the Meaning of Life?"

You never know, somebody may have the answer, and I'd really hate to miss it because I was too socially inhibited to ask. But when I ask, it's usually taken as a kind of absurdist move—people laugh and nod and gather up their stuff and the meeting is dismissed on that ridiculous note.

Once, and only once, I asked that question and got a serious answer. One that is with me still.

First, I must tell you where this happened, because the place has a power of its own. In Greece again.

Near the village of Gonia on a rocky bay of the island of Crete, sits a Greek Orthodox monastery. Alongside it, on land donated by the monastery, is an institute dedicated to human understanding and peace, and especially to rapprochement between Germans and Cretans. An improbable task, given the bitter residue of wartime.

This site is important, because it overlooks the small airstrip at Maleme where Nazi paratroopers invaded Crete and were attacked by peasants wielding kitchen knives and hay scythes. The retribution was terrible. The populations of whole villages were lined up and shot for assaulting Hitler's finest troops. High above the institute is a cemetery with a single cross marking the mass grave of Cretan partisans. And across the bay on yet another hill is the regimented burial ground of the Nazi paratroopers. The memorials are so placed that all might see and never forget. Hate was the only weapon the Cretans had at the end, and it was a weapon many vowed never to give up. Never ever.

Against this heavy curtain of history, in this place where the stone of hatred is hard and thick, the existence of an institute devoted to healing the wounds of war is a fragile paradox. How has it come to be here? The answer is a man. Alexander Papaderos.

A doctor of philosophy, teacher, politician, resident of Athens but a son of this soil. At war's end he came to believe that the Germans and the Cretans had much to give one another—much to learn from one another. That they had an example to set. For if they could forgive each other and construct a creative relationship, then any people could.

To make a lovely story short, Papaderos succeeded. The institute became a reality—a conference ground on the site of horror—and it was in fact a source of productive interaction between the two countries. Books have been written on the dreams that were realized by what people gave to people in this place.

By the time I came to the institute for a summer session, Alexander Papaderos had become a living legend. One look at him and you saw his strength and intensity—energy, physical power, courage, intelligence, passion, and vivacity radiated from his person. And to speak to him, to shake his hand, to be in a room with him when he spoke, was to experience his extraordinary electric humanity. Few men live up to their reputations when you get close. Alexander Papaderos was an exception.

At the last session on the last morning of a two-week seminar on Greek culture, led by intellectuals and experts in their fields who were recruited by Papaderos from across Greece, Papaderos rose from his chair at the back of the room and walked to the front, where he stood in the bright Greek sunlight of an open window and looked out. We followed his gaze across the bay to the iron cross marking the German cemetery.

He turned. And made the ritual gesture: "Are there any questions?"

Quiet quilted the room. These two weeks had generated enough questions for a lifetime, but for now there was only silence.

"No questions?" Papaderos swept the room with his eyes.

So. I asked.

"Dr. Papaderos, what is the meaning of life?"

The usual laughter followed, and people stirred to go.

Papaderos held up his hand and stilled the room and looked at me for a long time, asking with his eyes if I was serious and seeing from my eyes that I was.

"I will answer your question."

Taking his wallet out of his hip pocket, he fished into a leather billfold and brought out a very small round mirror, about the size of a quarter.

And what he said went like this:

"When I was a small child, during the war, we were very poor and we lived in a remote village. One day, on the road, I found the broken pieces of a mirror. A German motorcycle had been wrecked in that place.

"I tried to find all the pieces and put them together, but it was not possible, so I kept only the largest piece. This one. And by scratching it on a stone I made it round. I began to play with it as a toy and became fascinated by the fact that I could reflect light into dark places where the sun would never shine—in deep holes and crevices and dark closets. It became a game for me to get light into the most inaccessible places I could find.

"I kept the little mirror, and as I went about my growing up, I would take it out in idle moments and continue the challenge of the game. As I became a man, I grew to understand that this was not just a child's game but a metaphor for what I might do with my life. I came to understand that I am not the light or the source of light. But light—truth, understanding, knowledge—is there, and it will only shine in many dark places if I reflect it.

"I am a fragment of a mirror whose whole design and shape I do not know. Nevertheless, with what I have I can reflect light into the dark places of this world—into the black places in the hearts of men—and change some things in some people. Perhaps others may see and do likewise. This is what I am about. This is the meaning of my life."

And then he took his small mirror and, holding it carefully, caught the bright rays of daylight streaming through the window and reflected them onto my face and onto my hands folded on the desk.

Much of what I experienced in the way of information about Greek culture and history that summer is gone from memory. But in the wallet of my mind I carry a small round mirror still.

Are there any questions?

Thought

1. What motivates the author to ask, "What is the meaning of life"?

2. Enumerate the ways in which Alexander Papaderos is "an exception."

3. Why does Papaderos reflect "the bright rays of daylight" onto the author's face and hands?

4. In response to the author's question Papaderos describes the meaning of his life. Has he answered Fulghum's question? Explain.

Style and Structure

5. Fulghum observes that "the place has a power of its own." Show how he incorporates the power of place into his reflections.

6. What effect is achieved by allowing Papaderos to tell his own story?

7. Is the metaphor of the mirror overstated? Explain.

Response and Extension

8. What incidents from your own life do you reflect upon most? Why?

9. Recount to your group the story you most frequently tell about yourself. In your journal, reflect on what this story reveals about you.

10. In groups, compile a list of serious questions for which you would like serious answers. Compare these with questions raised by the other groups, and compile a class list.

11. Choose an everyday object that could represent a person's particular talent, gift, or aptitude. Compose a fictional narrative recounting how the object came to be a symbol of your character's significance.

Unit Synthesis

1. Write a short play (five to ten minutes in duration) in which several characters—the different sides of your personality—converse. You may wish to include some of the characters who populate your dreams.

2. Write an essay in which you reflect upon one of the most significant times—whether it be a moment, an episode, a relationship—from your past.

3. Consider the depiction of mothers in the essays by Theroux and Hager, and of fathers in the essays of Brandt and Doidge. Analyze the similarities in the roles of the two mothers and two fathers, respectively. Do any of these depictions have bearing on your own relationship to either of your parents? In a reflective essay explore these various links.

4. Have a serious conversation with an older relative and ask that person to reflect upon your past and your life.

5. Analyze the role of pride and humility in the essays by Brandt, Brodsky, Kleiman, and Hager. Write a reflective essay on what you think might constitute pride for these writers, and for yourself.

6. Write an essay in which you reflect upon a social and economic issue, for example, unemployment; society's responsibility to youth; education.

7. How do you think two or three of the other essayists in this unit would answer Fulghum's question, "What is the meaning of [your] life"? Try to extrapolate in creative ways from their essays.

8. Describe the way in which a particular piece of music helps you to reflect.

Suggested Readings

Buber, Martin *I and Thou*
Dillard, Annie *An American Childhood*
Findley, Timothy *Inside Memory*
Flanner, Janet *Paris Was Yesterday*
Fulghum, Robert *It Was On Fire When I Lay Down On It*
Hubbell, Sue *A Country Year*
Kitchen, Fred *Brother to the Ox*
Kittredge, William *Owning It All*
Merton, Thomas *The Seven Storey Mountain*
Montaigne, Michel de *Essays*
Neruda, Pablo *Passions and Impressions*
Pascal, Blaise *Pensées*
Saint Augustine *Confessions*
Sarton, May *At Seventy*
Shostakovich, Dimitri *Testimony*
Smart, Elizabeth *Necessary Secrets*

Writing to Inspire

One thin boy walked out in front of a column of tanks, and he stood there, just stood there.... The tank moved to the side and he moved quietly with it.... Finally some people took him away. It was like a sort of dance.

Maggie Helwig

Reply to the U.S. Government

Chief Seattle

Yonder sky that has wept tears of compassion upon my people for centuries untold, and which to us appears changeless and eternal, may change. Today is fair. Tomorrow may be overcast with clouds. My words are like the stars that never change. Whatever Seattle says the great chief at Washington can rely upon with as much certainty as he can upon the return of the sun or the seasons. The White Chief says that Big Chief at Washington sends us greetings of friendship and goodwill. That is kind of him for we know he has little need of our friendship in return. His people are many. They are like the grass that covers vast prairies. My people are few. They resemble the scattering trees of a storm-swept plain. The great, and—I presume—good, White Chief sends us word that he wishes to buy our lands but is willing to allow us enough to live comfortably. This indeed appears just, even generous, for the Red Man no longer has rights that he need respect, and the offer may be wise also, as we are no longer in need of an extensive country. . . . I will not dwell on, nor mourn over, our untimely decay, nor reproach our paleface brothers with hastening it, as we too may have been somewhat to blame.

Youth is impulsive. When our young men grow angry at some real or imaginary wrong, and disfigure their faces with black paint, it denotes that their hearts are black, and then they are often cruel and relentless, and our old men and old women are unable to restrain them. Thus it has ever been. Thus it was when the white men first began to push our forefathers further westward. But let us hope that the hostilities between us may never return. We would have everything to lose and nothing to gain. Revenge by young men is considered gain, even at the cost of their own lives, but old men who stay at home in times of war, and mothers who have sons to lose, know better.

Our good father at Washington—for I presume he is now our father as well as yours, since King George has moved his boundaries further north—our great good father, I say, sends us word that if we do as he desires he will protect us. His brave warriors will be to us a bristling wall of strength, and his wonderful ships of war will fill our harbors so that our ancient enemies far to the northward—the Hydas and Tsimpsians—will cease to frighten our women, children, and old men. Then in reality will he be our father and we his children. But can that ever be? Your God is not our God! Your God loves your people and hates mine. He folds his strong and protecting arms lovingly about the paleface and leads him by the hand as a father leads his infant son—but He has forsaken His red children—if they really are his. Our God, the Great Spirit, seems also to have forsaken us. Your God makes your people wax strong every day. Soon they will fill the land. Our people are ebbing away like a rapidly receding tide that will never return. The white man's God cannot love our people or He would protect them. They seem to be orphans who can look nowhere for help. How then can we be brothers? How can your God become our God and renew our prosperity and awaken in us dreams of returning greatness? If we have a common heavenly father He must be partial—for He came to his paleface children. We never saw Him. He gave you laws but He had no word for His red children whose teeming multitudes once filled this vast continent as stars fill the firmament. No; we are two distinct races with separate origins and separate destinies. There is little common between us.

To us the ashes of our ancestors are sacred and their resting place is hallowed ground. You wander far from the graves of your ancestors and seemingly without regret. Your religion was written upon tables of stone by the iron finger of your God so that you could not forget. The Red Man could never comprehend nor remember it. Our religion is the traditions of our ancestors—the dreams of our old men, given them in solemn hours of night by the Great Spirit; and the visions of our sachems; and it is written in the hearts of our people.

Your dead cease to love you and the land of their nativity as soon as they pass the portals of the tomb and wander way beyond the stars.

They are soon forgotten and never return. Our dead never forget the beautiful world that gave them being.

Day and night cannot dwell together. The Red Man has ever fled the approach of the White Man, as the morning mist flees before the morning sun. However, your proposition seems fair and I think that my people will accept it and will retire to the reservation you offer them. Then we will dwell apart in peace, for the words of the Great White Chief seem to be the words of nature speaking to my people out of dense darkness.

It matters little where we pass the remnant of our days. They will not be many. A few more moons; a few more winters—and not one of the descendants of the mighty hosts that once moved over this broad land or lived in happy homes, protected by the Great Spirit, will remain to mourn over the graves of a people once more powerful and hopeful than yours. But why should I mourn at the untimely fate of my people? Tribe follows tribe, and nation follows nation, like the waves of the sea. It is the order of nature, and regret is useless. Your time of decay may be distant, but it will surely come, for even the White Man whose God walked and talked with him as friend with friend, cannot be exempt from the common destiny. We may be brothers after all. We will see.

We will ponder your proposition, and when we decide we will let you know. But should we accept it, I here and now make this condition that we will not be denied the privilege without molestation of visiting at any time the tombs of our ancestors, friends and children. Every part of this soil is sacred in the estimation of my people. Every hillside, every valley, every plain and grove, has been hallowed by some sad or happy event in days long vanished. . . . The very dust upon which you now stand responds more lovingly to their footsteps than to yours, because it is rich with the blood of our ancestors and our bare feet are conscious of the sympathetic touch. . . . Even the little children who lived here and rejoiced here for a brief season will love these somber solitudes and at eventide they greet shadowy returning spirits. And when the last Red Man shall have perished, and the memory of my tribe shall have become a myth among the White Men, these shores will swarm with the invisible dead of my tribe, and when your children's children think themselves alone in the field, the store, the shop, upon the highway, or in the silence of the pathless woods, they will not be alone. . . . At night when the streets of your cities and villages are silent and you think them deserted, they will throng with the returning hosts that once filled and still love this beautiful land. The White Man will never be alone.

Let him be just and deal kindly with my people, for the dead are not powerless. Dead, did I say? There is no death, only a change of worlds.

Thought

1. Identify the issue to which Chief Seattle is replying

2. According to Chief Seattle, how are his people different from those of the "White Chief"?

3. **a)** What future does Chief Seattle envision for his people? **b)** Has history borne out his vision? Explain.

4. List all the reasons why you think reverence for the dead is so important to Chief Seattle and his people.

5. What does Chief Seattle's reply imply about his people's relationship to the land? How does this differ from non-aboriginal views?

Style and Structure

6. For what purposes does Chief Seattle make extensive references to nature?

7. Show how the imagery and figurative language in this speech are integral to its message.

8. Write an analysis of how both voice and context contribute to such a strong feeling of dignity and pathos in this essay.

Response and Extension

9. Research the historical context of Chief Seattle's reply, and write a brief essay outlining the forces that led up to this poignant moment.

10. This piece was intended to serve a practical purpose, to make an important spiritual and political statement. Compose a "reply" of your own. Address it to a particular person or organization and state your beliefs in response to an injustice.

11. "Every hillside, every valley, every plain and grove, has been hallowed by some sad or happy event in days long vanished …" Describe a place that has been "hallowed" by an event in your own life. Evoke the particular significance of this place through the use of distinctive voice, imagery, and figurative language.

12. Make a tape or present directly to the class an enactment of this speech. Chief Seattle shifts his viewpoint several times throughout his address, and these shifts can be expressed through the use of deliberate pauses, and changes in tone and inflection. Try to make your rendition of this speech as dramatic and compelling as you can.

Naked to Laughter when Leaves Fall

(Written in knowledge of Government change in 1971)

Ray Guy

The sun also rises. It already has. Is the light so bright that we are blinded and do not recognize the dawn?

What the day's weather will be remains to be seen but let's get up and get cracking. We have a busy time ahead of us. There's enough light now to see what our real work is. We're beginning to see what we have to do. We can see what sacrifices we'll have to make while we try to repair the great damage committed. Would you be afraid to set potatoes again? Would you be ashamed of driving a three-year-old car?

Yes? Then read no more. Toronto is waiting for you. Go with our blessing. We must see what our own Country can give us without being perennial parasites on someone else. If that doesn't suit you'll have to move on.

The work will require more energy and will become more urgent as time passes.

The goal of the work is a simple one: Newfoundland will live and we will live in Newfoundland. We are only 500 000—the population of a medium-sized city of North America.

How much would it take to force us all out of Newfoundland? How much did it take to force people off smaller islands?

The same tears but more of them. The same heartbreak but more of it. The same pain deeper than words but multiplied. To go away and not even have a place to come back to on holidays. Not the comfort of the hope of someday being able to come back. Not even that.

It is a strange, illogical and perhaps primitive feeling to feel at home here and only here. But it is a real feeling. If it is not, then where does the pain come from?

We will work to avoid this pain because for us it is a pain too hard to bear. This work will require all our energy. Now that it is coming light and the fog of twenty-two years is lifting, we can see what our job is.

There is no time to lose and we must get busy. It will take more heads than one. We have learned that, if nothing else. We will all have to think deeper than we have thought and work harder than we have worked. It will take more than one day and it will take us all.

We have to ask questions and try to find the answers. What right has Newfoundland to exist at all? What economic basis? Are we destined to live forever off the taxes of Hamilton steel workers? Can anyone put into plain words the difference between "able-bodied relief" and "regional disparity payments?"

How could we live forever like that and still retain even a shred of dignity to our backs? Hasn't it been proven that "great new industries" will never raise us to the level of even a watered-down version of southern Ontario?

And with the price of a one-way air ticket to Toronto so low why settle for a watered-down version? Standard of living? But what about quality of living? Isn't that a point to be looked at also?

Could it be made more painful to stay than to leave? What if we can never support more than 500 000? Will the surplus always have to go? Is there really a parallel between internal centralization, the traditional exodus, and the thought that Newfoundland may be deserted altogether?

Or is it that in the first case those who moved were still in Newfoundland, and in the second case there was the hope, until death, of being able to come back one day? But what of exile without hope?

Is Newfoundland an orphan in the storm? Were we not a burden on Britain so that she was glad to unload us unto Canada? And are not the Hamilton taxpayers beginning to resent the same burden so that we get from them Newfie jokes?

If we are no longer useful to the United States even for military purposes are we then of interest only to carpetbaggers who suck the blood from us—as in earlier days?

In the light that is now rising we will struggle no longer against shadows but with substance. If there is an octopus we must see the extent of its tentacles.

In the struggles before now we were told that we were fighting for country and home. What if we sit back and fail to join in now? If, as we were told, country and home were saved in blood, are we now going to drown it in beer?

It is dawning, and what the day's weather will be like remains to be seen. But we can take a stiff breeze or two.

And one morning early, sometime soon, the sun will rise in a cloudless and deep blue sky on grass so green it seems to be afire; its heat will soon bring out the smell of the earth, there'll be hardly a breeze on the water and all the long day until nearly ten o'clock in the evening the sun will shine and it will be fresh and warm and clear.

And we will have our soul back.

What a remarkable Country is Newfoundland! A person might live to the end of his days and never cease to marvel and wonder, one way or another. There is no place else.

Thought

1. Compare the various views about Newfoundland expressed in the essay, and analyze their contexts.

2. This essay is clearly addressed to Newfoundlanders who were familiar with the specific political context of the author's views. Nonetheless, Guy's message transcends the particulars. Explain in your own words the essence of what Guy is trying to impart to his readers.

3. In groups, discuss the nature of the economic imbalance that Guy refers to throughout his essay.

Style and Structure

4. The author's opening sentence, "The sun also rises," is the title of a novel by Ernest Hemingway, taken in turn from the Bible. How does Guy go on to use the metaphor of light throughout the essay?

5. **a)** Explain the author's use of the metaphors of fog and dawn.
   b) What other metaphors and images are found in this essay? Analyze their effectiveness in the context of Guy's thesis.

6. This essay is a call to action. What rhetorical techniques does Guy use to provoke the reader? Explain how you think elements of his writing style serve to strengthen—or weaken—his argument.

Response and Extension

7. Research the particular historical and political context of Guy's essay. What is the significance of his capitalizing the word "country"?

8. Compare Guy's evocation of Newfoundland with Laurence's evocation of a prairie town in her essay, "Where the World Began" (p. 23).

9. Consider a place to which you have developed a strong sense of belonging and from which you have been forced to leave. Write a composition explaining your thoughts and feelings about having to leave that place.

10. For discussion: How is Guy's essay relevant to today's Newfoundland?

Shakespeare, Prince of Light

Pablo Neruda

Goneril, Regan, Hamlet, Angus, Duncan, Glansdale, Mortimer, Ariel, Leontes . . .

These names from Shakespeare were part of our childhood; they crystallized and became the substance of our dreams. Even when we could scarcely read, we knew that behind the names lay a continent with rivers and kings, clans and castles and archipelagos, that some-day we would explore. The names of these somber, or radiant, pro-tagonists revealed to us the texture of poetry, the first peal of a great bell. Later, much later, come the days and years when we discover the lines and lives of these names. We discover suffering and remorse, martyrdom and cruelty, beings of blood, creatures of air, voices illu-minated for a magic feast, banquets attended by bloodstained ghosts. All that action, all those souls, all those passions—all that life.

In every epoch, one bard assumes responsibility for the dreams and the wisdom of the age: he expresses the growth, the expansion, of that world. His name is Alighieri, Victor Hugo, Lope de Vega, Walt Whitman.

Above all, his name is Shakespeare.

These bards amass leaves, and among the leaves one hears birdcalls; beneath these leaves roots grow. They are the leaves of great trees.

They are leaves, and eyes. They multiply and gaze down on us, insignificant men, through all the passing ages, they gaze on us and help us discover ourselves: they reveal to us our labyrinths.

In the case of Shakespeare, there is a third revelation, as there will be others: that of the sorcery of his distilled poetry. Few poets are so compact and secret, so secure in the heart of their diamond.

The sonnets were carved from the opal of tears, from the ruby of love, from the emerald of jealousy, from the amethyst of mourning.

They were carved from fire, made from air, sculpted from crystal.

The sonnets were uprooted from nature so whole that, from first to last, one hears how water flows, how the wind dances, and how, golden or flowering, the cycles of the seasons and fruits follow one after the other.

The sonnets hold an infinity of keys, of magic formulas: static majesty, speeding arrows.

The sonnets are banners that one by one rise to flutter from the castle tower. And though exposed to weather and to time, they conserve the magenta of their stars, the turquoise of their half-moons, the splendor of their blazing hearts.

I have read Shakespeare's poetry for many years; the poems, unlike the plays, do not tell of lives, of battles, of derring-do.

There is the stark whiteness of the page, the purity of the road of poetry. Along that road glide endless rows of images, like tiny ships laden with honey.

Amid this excess of riches in which the driving power of creativity moves in time with intelligence, we see, we can almost feel, an unwavering and flourishing Shakespeare, and note that the most striking aspect of his poems is not their abundant power but their exacting form.

My name is written in my copy of the *Sonnets*, along with the day and the month in 1930 when I bought the book on the island of Java.

It has been with me, then, for thirty-four years.

There, on that far-off island, it was my model, the purest of fountains, deep forests, a fabulous multitude of hitherto unknown myths; it was crystalline law. Because Shakespeare's poetry, like that of Góngora and Mallarmé, plays with the light of reason, imposes a strict, if secret, code. In a word, during those lost years of my life, Shakespeare's poetry kept open a line of communication with Western culture. By Western, naturally, I mean Pushkin and Karl Marx, Bach and Hölderlin, Lord Tennyson and Mayakovsky.

Of course, poetry recurs throughout the plays as well, in the towers of Elsinore, in the castle of Macbeth, on Prospero's ship, among the perfume of pomegranates in Verona.

A phantasmagorical wind blows through the tunnel of each play. The oldest sound in the world, the sound of the human heart, is the matter from which these unforgettable words are formed. Fantasy and humanity appear in all the plays, along with the parlance of the common man, the signs of the marketplace, the vulgar voices of parasites and buffoons, all accompanied by the steely ring of suits of armor locked in crazed combat.

But what I like best is to follow the extravagant flow of Shakespeare's poetry, a harmony painted on the wall of time in blue, enamel, and magic seafoam, an amalgam imprinted on our eternity.

As an example, in the pastoral idyll *Venus and Adonis*, published in 1593, there is the flickering of cool shadows on flowing waters, the insinuating green of singing groves, cascades of rippling poetry, and myth fleeing into the greenery.

Then suddenly a steed appears, dissipating fantasy with its pounding hoofs, as "His eye, which scornfully glisters like fire, shows his hot courage and his high desire."

Yes, if a painter were to paint that horse: "His art with nature's workmanship at strife, as if the dead the living should exceed." There is no description that can equal that of this amorous, furious horse galloping with real hoofs through marvelous sextets.

And I mention it, though Shakespeare's bestiary contained traces of many beasts, and his herbarium retains the color and scent of many flowers, because that pawing steed is the theme of his ode, the generative force of nature captured by a great synthesizer of dreams.

This autumn I was given the task of translating *Romeo and Juliet*.

I accepted the request with humility. With humility, and with a sense of duty, because in fact I did not feel capable of decanting that passionate love story into Spanish. But I had to do it, since this is the anniversary of Shakespeare's birth, the year of universal veneration of the poet who opened new universes to man.

Translating with pleasure, and with honor, the tragedy of those star-crossed lovers, I made a discovery.

I realized that underlying the plot of undying love and inescapable death there was a second drama, a second subject, a second principal theme.

Romeo and Juliet is a great plea for peace among men. It is a condemnation of pointless hatred, a denunciation of the barbarity of war, and the solemn consecration of peace.

When Prince Escalus, in moving and exemplary language, reproaches the feudal clans who are staining the streets of Verona with blood, we realize that the Prince is the incarnation of enlightenment, of dignity, and of peace.

When Benvolio reproaches Tybalt for his warlike temperament, saying: "I do but keep the peace; put up thy sword," the fierce swordsman replies: "What! drawn, and talk of peace? I hate the word . . ."

So, peace was despised by some in Elizabethan Europe. Centuries later, Gabriela Mistral—persecuted and insulted for her defense of peace, dismissed from the Chilean newspaper that had published her articles for thirty years—wrote her famous phrase: "Peace, that accursed word." One sees that the world and the press continued to be governed by Tybalts, by swordsmen.

One reason more, then, to love William Shakespeare, the greatest of all human beings. There will always be time and space to explore in Shakespeare, to lose ourselves, or begin the long journey around his statue, like the Lilliputians around Gulliver. And though we may go a long way without reaching the end, we always return with hands filled with fragrance and blood, with flowers and sorrows, with mortal treasures.

At this solemn moment, it is my pleasure to open the door of tributes, raising the curtain so the dazzling, pensive figure of the Bard may appear. And across four centuries I would say to him: "Greetings, Prince of Light! Good health, sir itinerant actor! We are the heirs to your great dreams; we dream them still. Your words do honor to the entire world."

And, more quietly, I would whisper into his ear: "My friend, I thank you."

Thought

1. This essay is a tribute, a paean, a song of praise. Does it inspire *you* to read Shakespeare? Why or why not?

2. According to Neruda, in what does the greatness of Shakespeare lie?

3. In your own words, describe why you think Neruda prefers Shakespeare's poetry to his plays.

4. Describe the visual sensation produced by Neruda's description of *Venus and Adonis*.

5. What discovery has Neruda made about *Romeo and Juliet*? Do you agree with him?

Style and Structure

6. To whom does Neruda refer in his use of the words "our" and "we" in the second paragraph? What is your response to this usage?

7. What meanings are evoked by Neruda's use of the jewel metaphors to describe Shakespeare's poetry?

8. Select three examples of each of Neruda's a) poetic diction, b) figurative language, c) unusual syntax. Show how these elements contribute to the lyrical nature of the essay.

Response and Extension

9. "The most striking aspect of his poems is not their abundant power but their exacting form."
   a) What is the form of a sonnet?
   b) From a collection of Shakespeare's sonnets choose one you particularly like. How does it exemplify the sonnet form?
   c) Write your own appreciation of this sonnet.

10. The great "bards," Neruda observes, "help us discover ourselves: they reveal to us our labyrinths." Using Neruda's essay as your model, write a lyrical essay praising the artistic and human qualities of the artist you most admire. How does he or she help you to discover yourself?

Tiananmen

Maggie Helwig

The shattered children lie in a chaos of blood and bicycles, and the soldiers are firing into the crowd. They are firing into the unarmed crowd. The survivors try to drag their wounded through the blood, out of the square, and the tanks run over living bodies, and they keep coming back, back into the square, the unarmed children, the terrible children, the girls in flowered dresses and the spectacled boys, they keep coming back and they are all dying and buses are burning all over the night.

This is not politics any more. This has not been politics for a long time now. We know what this is. This is the dream against the world, we all know what this is, this is the beautiful end of all things, *oh God*.

Tiananmen, Tiananmen, apocalypse.

They sit in the square in the rain, around their little fires, the perfect ones, the purified. They have fasted and prayed. They have been cold and become perfect, and they want the dream. They want the world. They want *everything* and they want it *now*.

We will make the dream become real. We will drag God down to earth and make him stay. In the shadow of the Forbidden City we will make the great good place, the holy place, the living place.

The words do not matter. Democracy is a word as good as any. They are on the top of a high hill, they are alone, they are utterly free and utterly terrible and utterly doomed.

The cycle-cabs race through the streets with the dying, to hospitals where the floors run with rivers of blood. We are all weeping. No-one knows what has happened. The soldiers are firing again into the crowd, with AK-47s and machine-guns, tanks rolling down the Avenue of Eternal Peace, the children lie dead at the foot of Mao's tomb. And they are coming back, again they are coming back into the square, they are ready to die, they are already dead. The soldiers are moving through the streets, spraying bullets at random, killing, killing, they will have to keep shooting until there is no-one left to kill.

Fire. Buses burning, personnel carriers, red and white flares, the night all strafed with fire, when the children fight back it is with fire, they burn the tanks and their men. Silhouettes run against the fire, out of the square, into the square, into the fire.

We are all weeping. We cannot stop weeping. We are at the edge of it all. This is not a thing there are words for. This is the ultimate thing.

Tiananmen, Tiananmen, apocalypse.

We want the world. We want the world. We want *everything*. We want to live. *We want it now.*

There will be no compromise. We will make the great good place, the living place, or we will all die. You will have to keep shooting until there is no-one left to kill.

The purified ones are on the top of a high hill. They are ready to die. They are so alive. There will be no compromise.

Across the world is a man whose black fire eyes are a thousand years old, and once the children were in the streets for him and for one little time he held God in his hurt hands. He dies. All things become old and are not good anymore, and pull back from the edge.

In Tiananmen Square they will not pull back. All the little children are dying.

And dawn came, and night came, and dawn, and it has not ended yet. How many people will they have to kill? How many until there is no-one left? How many people until the world ends? Tiananmen, Tiananmen.

They wear bright colours, the pure ones, the living, dying ones. They wear bright colours, and they dragged God down into that square where they camped, squatting in the scraps with little fires, bits of food, the terrible intensity of the dream. For three weeks they made the holy place by the Forbidden City, by the tomb of a man who also died.

Oh the sweet bodies crushed under the tanks, torn into pieces by machine guns, by AK-47 assault rifles, the sweet flesh ground into pulp in Tiananmen Square, and they say survivors hacked off chunks of the sweet flesh and took it to the soldiers, crying: see what you have done. See what you have done.

Today they have not killed. We are waiting to see what comes now. There are stories that the army is turning on itself, but nobody knows. There is no news. There is no word. It is very silent and unsure.

Yesterday one radio announcer dared to say one sentence of what has happened. We do not think he is still alive.

They were so ordinary, these boys and girls, so like the rest of us, and now they are so pure and awful and dead. Three thousand are dead in two days. Three thousand. Shot to death in Tiananmen Square.

Late in the murder, as it was ending, one thin boy walked out in front of a column of tanks, and he stood there, just stood there, his arms loose, seeming a bit confused but very calm. The tank moved to the side and he moved quietly with it. The tank moved forward. He grabbed the gun barrel and climbed onto it, climbed over the tank for a minute, down, stood in front again. Finally some people took him away. It was like a sort of dance.

We are very still. We are waiting. We are waiting for the world to end. For they have done this for us, these pure ones. We believe now in the end of all things. Tiananmen, apocalypse.

Can this world be saved? *Can this world be saved?*

Thought

1. a) Research the etymology of the word "apocalypse."
   b) In what sense are the events in Tiananmen Square an "apocalypse"?

2. Explain what the author means by saying, "This is not politics any more."

Style and Structure

3. From what point of view is this piece written? Explain.

4. How has the writer conveyed the "chaos" of this incident?

5. **a)** What effects are achieved by the refrain "Tiananmen, Tiananmen"?

   b) What effects are achieved by the repetition of the final question?

6. List some examples of Helwig's use of hyperbole. Describe why you think she has chosen to use these images, and their rhetorical effects.

7. What are for you the most striking images in the essay? Explain why.

Response and Extension

8. **a)** Research and report to the class on the events in Tiananmen Square.

   b) How do newspaper and magazine accounts of the episode differ in style from Helwig's piece?

   c) In your view, which style of writing is more effective? Explain.

9. What aspect of this piece disturbed you the most? In your journal write about your reactions to that most disturbing aspect.

10. For discussion: If the author had not referred to it by name, would you have known where these events occurred? Where else in the world might these events have taken place? Why?

The Almond Trees

Albert Camus

"**D**o you know," Napoleon once said to Fontanes, "what astounds me most about the world? The impotence of force to establish anything. There are only two powers in the world: the sword and the mind. In the end, the sword is always conquered by the mind."

Conquerors, you see, are sometimes melancholy. They have to pay some price for so much vainglory. But what a hundred years ago was true of the sword is no longer true today of the tank. Conquerors have made progress, and the dismal silence of places without intelligence has been established for years at a time in a lacerated Europe. At the time of the hideous wars of Flanders, Dutch painters could still perhaps paint the cockerels in their farmyards. The Hundred Years War has likewise been forgotten, and yet the prayers of Silesian mystics still linger in some hearts. But today, things have changed; the painter and the monk have been drafted—we are one with the world. The mind has lost that regal certainty which a conqueror could acknowledge; it exhausts itself now in cursing force, for want of knowing how to master it.

Some noble souls keep on deploring this, saying it is evil. We do not know if it is evil, but we know it is a fact. The conclusion is that we must come to terms with it. All we need know, then, is what we want. And what we want precisely is never again to bow beneath the sword, never again to count force as being in the right unless it is serving the mind.

The task is endless, it's true. But we are here to pursue it. I do not have enough faith in reason to subscribe to a belief in progress or to any philosophy of history. I do believe at least that man's awareness of his destiny has never ceased to advance. We have not overcome our condition, and yet we know it better. We know that we live in contradiction, but we also know that we must refuse this contradiction and do what is needed to reduce it. Our task as men is to find the few principles that will calm the infinite anguish of free souls. We must mend what has been torn apart, make justice imaginable again in a world so obviously unjust, give happiness a meaning once more to peoples poisoned by the misery of the century. Naturally, it is a superhuman task. But superhuman is the term for tasks men take a long time to accomplish, that's all.

Let us know our aims then, holding fast to the mind, even if force puts on a thoughtful or a comfortable face in order to seduce us. The first thing is not to despair. Let us not listen too much to those who proclaim that the world is at an end. Civilizations do not die so easily, and even if our world were to collapse, it would not have been the first. It is indeed true that we live in tragic times. But too many people confuse tragedy with despair. "Tragedy," Lawrence said, "ought to be a great kick at misery." This is a healthy and immediately applicable thought. There are many things today deserving such a kick.

When I lived in Algiers, I would wait patiently all winter because I knew that in the course of one night, one cold, pure February night, the almond trees of the Vallée des Consuls would be covered with white flowers. I would marvel then at the sight of this fragile snow resisting the rains and the wind from the sea. Yet every year it lasted just long enough to prepare the fruit.

There is no symbol here. We will not win our happiness with symbols. We'll need something more solid. I mean only that sometimes, when life weighs too heavily today in a Europe still full of misery, I turn toward those shining lands where so much strength is still intact. I know them too well not to realize that they are the chosen land where courage and contemplation can live in harmony. Thinking of them teaches me that if we are to save the mind we must ignore its gloomy virtues and celebrate its strength and wonder. Our world is poisoned by its misery, and seems to wallow in it. It has utterly surrendered to that evil which Nietzsche called the spirit of heaviness. Let us not add to this. It is futile to weep over the mind, it is enough to labor for it.

But where are the conquering virtues of the mind? The same Nietzsche listed them as mortal enemies to heaviness of the spirit.

For him, they are strength of character, taste, the "world," classical happiness, severe pride, the cold frugality of the wise. More than ever, these virtues are necessary today, and each of us can choose the one that suits him best. Before the vastness of the undertaking, let no one forget strength of character. I don't mean the theatrical kind on political platforms, complete with frowns and threatening gestures. But the kind that through the virtue of its purity and its sap, stands up to all the winds that blow in from the sea. Such is the strength of character that in the winter of the world will prepare the fruit.

Thought

1. According to Camus, what major change has occurred to the mind since Napoleon's time?

2. In the author's view, what is the task of humanity? Do you agree?

3. What place do the almond trees occupy in Camus' thought?

4. Which of the "conquering virtues of the mind" do you think is the most necessary to the world today?

5. In your own words, elaborate on the point Camus makes with his reference to the painter and the monk.

6. "Tragedy ought to be a great kick at misery." Explain what you think is meant by this quote from D. H. Lawrence.

Style and Structure

7. What rhetorical use does Camus make of the quotations from Napoleon and Lawrence?

8. What effect do you think Camus intended by his statement, "There is no symbol here"?

9. What figurative language does Camus employ in this essay? Describe how these images work to heighten the impact of his message.

Response and Extension

10. Camus describes the kind of strength of character that "stands up to all the winds that blow in from the sea." List as many images and metaphors as you can that evoke your own definition of "strength of character."

11. Choose an image from the natural world that could represent a particular idea of yours. Develop this idea into a lyrical essay and, in the manner of Camus, use the image to form the climax of your argument.

12. a) What are the issues that engender a "spirit of heaviness" in people today?

    b) In what ways are we now, more than ever, "at one with the world"?

Unit Synthesis

1. By referring to each of the writers in this unit, write a lyrical essay that celebrates the human spirit.

2. Write an essay comparing Ray Guy's attitude to Newfoundland to that of Chief Seattle's to the land of his ancestors.

3. In one way or another, each of these essays addresses questions of force, conflict, and power. Analyze the thematic links between these essays.

Suggested Readings

Brown, Dee *Bury My Heart at Wounded Knee*
Camus, Albert *The Outsider; The Plague; The Fall*
Carr, Emily *Klee Wyck*
Carter, Forrest *The Education of Little Tree*
Craven, Margaret *I Heard the Owl Call my Name*
Hillerman, Tony *The Hall of the Dancing God*
Hubert, Cam *Dreamspeaker*
Kinsella, W.P. *The Moccasin Telegraph*
Momaday, N. Scott *House Made of Dawn*
Neruda, Pablo *Memoirs; Residence on Earth; The Captain's Verses; Twenty Love Songs and a Song of Despair*
Proulx, E. Annie *The Shipping News*

On Writing an Essay

What defines an essay? An essay may explore a thought, analyze an idea, express a feeling, or establish the parameters of a debate. But whatever its form or its intent, an essay always builds an argument. It seeks to convince the reader of its main point: its thesis.

This thesis is, essentially, an opinion. The thesis asks you to re-think some aspect of a world you thought you knew. The writer believes that we don't understand as well as we should something that's going on around us. Stop, the essay says, and reconsider the last day of summer, the true meaning of boredom, a single mother, a political revolt. The essayist wants us to look again at something we may have thought we already understood.

If you've been asked to write on a subject that's familiar to you and that you already have an opinion about, it will be relatively easy to state your opinion and give reasons to support it. But if the topic or issue is new to you your opinion will be harder to determine. It could be only after researching the topic, only after scratching out all your ideas on the page, that your thoughts on the matter will begin to come into focus. When you've located good resource material and unearthed interesting points, when you've written down your thoughts and they all seem to lead in a particular direction, then it's time to start honing in on a clearly worded expression of your position.

Your thesis statement must express your opinion, and this opinion must be relevant to the assigned topic. Make sure that you can provide a strong support for your thesis. The effectiveness of your essay depends on how well you are able to persuade the reader of your position. Finally, the more concise and focused your thesis statement, the better. Broad statements and easy generalizations do not make for compelling arguments.

After you've decided on a working thesis, and after you've jotted down as many ideas as you can, it is wise to make a point-form outline of your essay. This outline enables you to see the whole all at once; to assess the shape and flow of your thoughts. When composing your outline, first decide which of your ideas will form the main points of your essay. Order these so that they form a logical progression and lead to a resounding conclusion. Then consider how you will organize the ideas that support each main point. Set up categories and sub-categories of ideas: this will help you to think about how each thought will lead logically to the next. Finally, scrutinize the structure you've created and make sure it all flows together. You might have to do some reorganizing.

Once you think you have a workable outline, begin to write. And write again. If you're like some writers, you'll revise your initial outline almost beyond recognition by the time you've written two or three drafts of your essay.

When you read a clearly argued, well-structured essay it's easy to think that the writer had all her ideas already in her head when she sat down at her computer; that she had only to spin out her thoughts in perfect form and style. But who can know how many confused, half-formed opinions, how many drafts, how many fruitless tangents this writer followed before she arrived at her concise, cohesive, well-wrought whole?

The process of writing an essay is, *at its best*, an exploratory one. You may well begin by composing an outline that itemizes your introduction, builds the body, carves out your conclusion. But to write your entire essay adhering strictly to this same outline could be a sterile exercise. For as you begin to write you may find—and it's better if you do—that other aspects of the issue occur to you, that your perspective shifts, unexpected connections surface, that your thoughts have moved beyond the sketchy outlines with which they begun.

Your essay might not develop in a smooth line. You might want to focus on one particular idea, write a few paragraphs about it, develop and refine your thought and style—all before you even have the whole of your argument worked out. You may want to do this simply because you're inspired and compelled to follow this particular idea, because it's a fruitful one and worth developing right then and there.

It's often wise to write the second paragraph before the first; the body of the essay before its introduction and conclusion. This makes sense, for you can more effectively lead into and sum up your argument if you've already got one in place.

In the face of all this creative confusion it's important to keep your thesis in mind. Make sure that all your ideas contribute to it in a significant way. For it is your thesis that ultimately influences the essay's overall shape and structure: everything else follows from it.

As your argument develops, revise your thesis if necessary, and shape your ideas into a new cohesive whole. Keep reworking your outline to keep yourself on track. Think of it as a continual balancing act between the flow of ideas and the shape in which to house them.

Once you've written your essay it's a really good idea to leave it for a little while, even for one day. When you read it again with a fresh perspective you're much more likely to notice gaps in reasoning, inconsistencies, repetitions, awkward writing, etc. You may wish to revise whole paragraphs, or move a few around. Have you put enough emphasis on the strongest point of your argument? You may want to devote more space to it, or use a memorable image to help convey it. As well, look for opportunities to improve your writing technique: to incorporate some stylistic fluorish, to smooth rough transitions, to correct grammar and spelling.

Finally, learn to listen to the voices in the back of your mind. Something significant could well be whispering there, and the good writer is the person who knows how to still the clamour in the foreground and calmly consider the humble noises in the far reaches. There's nothing like the act of writing, of stringing ideas together on the page, to help bring these thoughts forward. Carol Shields in her essay "The Same Ticking Clock" quotes another writer who said, "When I write I am free" (p. 88). Indeed, the most rewarding approach to essay writing is to follow your thought where it leads you.

Elements of the Well-Written Essay

In order to write good essays it's important to be able to recognize one when you read it. It's a cliché but it's true: the more good writing you read, the better your chances are of becoming a good writer. Gloria Steinem's essay "The Time Factor," featured in the following pages, offers a good model for an essay. All the structural elements are present here in a concise form: introduction, statement of thesis, development of supporting argument, conclusion. To be able to recognize these elements, and to appreciate how good writers make their words flow easily and pleasurably through them, is a crucial step in developing your own skill as a writer.

Thesis

Although the manner in which the thesis is conveyed varies from essay to essay, this thesis is always present, and informs everything else. An essay without a thesis is, in short, not an essay at all.

This thesis may or may not be stated explicitly, in one sentence. The thesis statement often appears near the beginning of the essay—it may in fact appear in the very first sentence. Consider Gloria Steinem's first line and thesis statement: "Planning ahead is a measure of class." This is a powerful opener: a provocative assertion that confronts the reader squarely. (Indeed, the paragraph as a whole is a good example of an effective introduction: it commands the reader's attention, sets a clear direction, and does not linger long. The author puts herself out on a limb, and the reader reads on to find out how she got there.)

Or, the writer may choose to lead up to his or her statement, and so it may not appear until towards the middle of the essay. Moreover, the statement may not necessarily take the form of one key sentence that you can pick out and quote as being the essay's central argument. It may be a point that requires two or three sentences to express.

Or—it may not be stated at all. But there is still a thesis: in these cases it is implied rather than explicit. It should, nevertheless, be clear to the reader what the writer is saying. Essays with implied theses can be some of the most compelling essays to read. Like fiction, the meanings lie below the surface, and it falls to the reader to interpret the words on the page. A good example of an essay with an implied thesis is Barbara Hager's "Welfare was a Life Raft, but Now We Can Swim" (p. 209). Read this essay and consider what, in essence, the author is saying. Compose the statement that you think best captures the author's thesis. Consider how she is able to convey her message without ever actually stating it.

Now choose several essays in this anthology that appeal to you most. Identify the thesis statement in each of these essays. You may be able to simply quote a line or two from the essay. You may have to take a key phrase and turn it into a complete statement. Or, you may have to compose a sentence or two of your own in order to summarize the author's main point. But remember that whatever form it takes, this essential point can always be found. Look at how the author leads up to it, or states it baldly right off, or arrives at it so subtly you hardly know how it happened. Think about what persuasive effect was intended, and achieved, by each approach.

Development

Within the conventional form of the essay—introduction, body, conclusion—there are many approaches to developing an argument.

An argument can proceed along a more or less linear, satisfyingly straightforward path. A leads to B, B to C, and so on. Carolyn

Heilbrun's "The Character of Hamlet's Mother" (p. 163) is one of the more formal essays in this anthology. In this work of literary criticism Heilbrun looks at different aspects of the "traditional" interpretation of Hamlet's mother—and refutes them one by one. The task Heilbrun has set herself exerts a strong influence over the shape and direction of her argument. In a looser, more musing style, Neil McDonald considers his reactions to a poster about AIDS. His argument sets off on a particular path, catches itself, and turns back with a qualification. He asserts something, then questions his own assertion. In the process, the reader is drawn into the space the author has created by his own open-ended reflections.

Sometimes B and C can complicate or expand A in rather unexpected ways. The path of development in an essay can appear to meander. The author can engage us with anecdote, spin out a reflection, entertain us with another story, express an idea. But make no mistake: in a good essay, there is nothing here that doesn't pertain to the building of an argument. For example, after making her assertion about time and class in the first paragraph, Steinem devotes the next three paragraphs to personal anecdote. She is, actually, warming us up. We can just see that long-ago boy in high school making his bitter comment about Saturday night. We lean closer in as the author confides her own youthful, misbegotten ideas about "flexibility." We understand, we nod our heads—she's got us hooked.

Then Steinem opens her fifth paragraph with a marked shift of tone, from intimate friend to decisive authority. With calm assurance she begins: "Clearly there is more to this fear of the future . . . ." Her expansion of the idea of class to include gender and race follows logically from her anecdotes about herself, the husbands of friends, the successful black journalist. This is a pivotal moment, for it enables her to focus now on the role of women in particular.

(Carol Shields uses the same approach in her essay. She begins with a general idea and, midway through, zeroes in on one particular aspect of it. This movement from the general to the particular is one approach among many to developing a thesis. Many of the essays in this anthology, for example, work in quite the opposite direction.)

Steinem looks at the current thinking of the women's movement, and claims with approval in paragraph 7 that "we've begun to challenge . . . ." But just when her readers are accepting this (practically patting themselves on the back) Steinem raises the stakes again: just how effectively *are* we thinking about future planning? She has asked her readers to think, and now asks us to think again, more critically. She challenges us to consider the necessary, practical steps to get there from here. Then in paragraph 9 she clarifies her approach by warning us of the dangers of imitating the "culturally masculine" approach to time. This leads to her next paragraph, in which she arrives at a positive evaluation of both approaches, and a deeper look at our human experience of living in time.

In all of this Steinem has not cited any statistics, or quoted any authoritative sources. In order to support her argument she has relied on personal anecdote, informed observation, and her own critical evaluation of what she sees around her. Her readers have been called upon to empathize, accept, perceive, reconsider, think more profoundly, act. Steinem has travelled quite a distance from her opening statements. In a few short paragraphs she has expanded, complicated, clarified, and deepened the issue at hand.

It is useful to map out the structure of a good essay. We are not necessarily aware of "structure" when reading an essay that compels us: the effect is of an effortless flow of ideas forming a satisfying whole. To go back and analyze its structure is to unearth the blueprint, and so to understand better what the author did to make it all look so easy.

Construct an outline for each of the essays you have chosen. Note how the author builds his or her argument. Look for the different ways the thesis is supported, and how the level of thought develops. There are a number of approaches to stucturing one's ideas; the ones you will reveal for yourself here will give you an idea of some possibilities.

Conclusion

The conclusion of an essay should, of course, follow logically from the preceding argument. It should sum up, reiterate, even expand the view—or in a final flourish, offer a last twist on it. It should make judgments that carry weight and offer insights that reflect an original way of looking at things.

How closely should the conclusion correspond to the introduction? Look back at your chosen group of essays and compare their respective introductions and conclusions.

The conclusions of the more formal essays tend to reassert the introductions in an expanded context or at a deeper level. For example, consider the introduction and conclusion of Adrienne Shadd's essay, "Institutionalized Racism and Canadian History" (p. 183). Shadd states her thesis clearly, right at the beginning. She then goes on to support and develop it through an interweaving of personal experience and historical fact. Shadd's conclusion reiterates her original premise, but with all the force of persuasion she has accumulated through the course of building her argument. This classic structure is like a well-built house: strong and cohesive.

In other essays the conclusions echo the introductions in quite altered contexts. Here the author's path twists and turns and develops quite beyond the opening statement. For example, look at Annie Dillard's "Living Like Weasels" (p. 15). She begins her first paragraph with the deceptively obvious statement, "A weasel is wild," and goes on to describe the habits of the weasel. It's all quite straightforward. Now read the conclusion, and see to what reflective lengths this creature has taken the author. Although the seeds of the conclusion are contained in the introduction (see what Dillard does with the simple observation, "obedient to instinct"), the author's path is unexpected. The progress of her thought is seemingly loose and twisting, but it is logically coherent. She has travelled far afield, but she has kept the thread unbroken.

Now compare Steinem's introduction and conclusion. Let us consider her conclusion as comprising the last two paragraphs. How does she go from her first line (and thesis statement): "Planning ahead is a measure of class" to "And time is all there is"? By deepening her concerns: from the reasons why men and women approach time differently, she comes to reflect on how the extremes of both approaches "waste" time. She too has travelled far. She has surprised the reader by transforming a look at gender inequality into a reflection on our shared human approach to time. And all this in a logical, paragraph-by-paragraph progression.

The sense of surprise is essential to good writing, as long as it follows from the argument in question. It's the sensation we experience when we come upon a new insight, a new perception: something that, without realizing it, we somehow already knew—only now we're able to put it into words. This returns to the earlier point about essay writing as an exploratory activity. It is just these surprises that occur to us as we write; unexpected connections that bring pleasure to writer and reader alike.

The Time Factor

Gloria Steinem

Thesis Statement

Planning ahead is a measure of class. The rich and even the middle class plan for future generations, but the poor can plan ahead only a few weeks or days.

Elaboration of Thesis

I remember finding this calm insight in some sociological text and feeling instant recognition. Yes, of course, our sense of time was partly a function of power, or the lack of it. It rang true even in the entirely economic sense the writer had in mind.

Personal Reflection

"The guys who own the factories hand them down to their sons and great-grandsons" I remember a boy in my high school saying bitterly. "On this side of town, we just plan for Saturday night."

Thesis Supported by Direct Quotations

But it also seemed equally true of most of the women I knew—including myself—regardless of the class we supposedly belonged to. Though I had left my factory-working neighborhood, gone to college, become a journalist, and thus was middle class, I still felt that I couldn't plan ahead. I had to be flexible—first, so that I could be ready to get on a plane for any writing assignment (even though the male writers I knew launched into books and other long-term projects on their own), and then so that I could adapt to the career and priorities of an eventual husband and children (even though I was leading a rewarding life without either). Among the results of this uncertainty were a stunning lack of career planning and such smaller penalties as no savings, no insurance, and an apartment that lacked basic pieces of furniture.

Change of Focus; Thesis Extension

Examples from Personal Experience

On the other hand, I had friends who were married to men whose long-term career plans were compatible with their own, yet they still lived their lives in day-to-day response to any

Connective

Shift of Focus to Include Personal Experiences of Friends

possible needs of their husbands and children. Moreover, the one male colleague who shared or even understood this sense of powerlessness was a successful black journalist and literary critic who admitted that even after twenty years he planned only one assignment at a time. He couldn't forget his dependence on the approval of white editors.

Clearly there is more to this fear of the future than a conventional definition of class could explain. There is also caste: the unchangeable marks of sex and race that bring a whole constellation of cultural injunctions against power, even the limited power of controlling one's own life.

We haven't yet examined time-sense and future planning as functions of discrimination, but we have begun to struggle with them, consciously or not. As a movement, women have become painfully conscious of too much reaction and living from one emergency to the next, with too little initiative and planned action of our own; hence many of our losses to a much smaller but more entrenched and consistent right wing.

Though the cultural habit of living in the present and glazing over the future goes deep, we've begun to challenge the cultural punishment awaiting the "pushy" and "selfish" women (and the "uppity" minority men) who try to break through it and control their own lives.

Even so, feminist writers and theorists tend to avoid the future by lavishing all our analytical abilities on what's wrong with the present, or on revisions of history and critiques of the influential male thinkers of the past. The big, original, and certainly courageous books of this wave of feminism have been more diagnostic than prescriptive. We need pragmatic planners and visionary futurists, but can we think of even one

Transition to Thesis Development; Broadening of Definition of "Class"

Logical Development of Argument; Assessment of Current State of Struggle

Connectives

feminist five-year-plan? Perhaps the closest we have come is visionary architecture or feminist science fiction, but they generally avoid the practical steps of how to get from here to there.

Connective

Obviously, many of us need to extend our time-sense—to have the courage to plan for the future, even while most of us are struggling to keep our heads above water in the present. But this does not mean a flat-out imitation of the culturally masculine habit of planning ahead, living in the future, and thus living a deferred life. It doesn't mean the traditional sacrifice of spontaneous action, or a sensitive awareness of the present, that comes from long years of career education with little intrusion of reality, from corporate pressure to work now for the sake of a reward after retirement, or, least logical of all, from patriarchal religions that expect obedience now in return for a reward after death.

Call to Action; Clarification of Goal

In fact, the ability to live in the present, to tolerate uncertainty, and to remain open, spontaneous, and flexible are all culturally female qualities that many men need and have been denied. As usual, both halves of the polarized masculine-feminine division need to learn from each other's experiences. If men spent more time raising small children, for instance, they would be forced to develop more patience and flexibility. If women had more power in the planning of natural resources and other long-term processes—or even in the planning of our own careers and reproductive lives—we would have to develop more sense of the future and of cause and effect.

Summation of Argument; Balanced Recommendations

An obsession with reacting to the present, feminine-style, or on controlling and living in the future, masculine-style, are both wasteful of time.

Emphatic Conclusion

And time is all there is.

Intensifier of Conclusion

Contents by Theme

Conflict
The Almond Trees *(Albert Camus)*
Faces of the Enemy *(Sam Keen)*
The Leering That Has to Stop *(Ann Fuller)*
Marginal Men *(Barbara Ehrenreich)*
Tiananmen *(Maggie Helwig)*

Family
Deficits *(Michael Ignatieff)*
Life as We Know It *(Michael Bérubé)*
My Home Is Not Broken, It Works *(Carol Kleiman)*
On Hating Piano Lessons *(Phyllis Theroux)*
The Suit *(Norman Doidge)*
Welfare was a Life Raft, but Now We Can Swim *(Barbara Hager)*

Introspection
The Almond Trees *(Albert Camus)*
Blasting Music to Drown Out Reality *(Sydney J. Harris)*
Deficits *(Michael Ignatieff)*
In Bed *(Joan Didion)*
In Selfish Pursuit *(Anthony Brandt)*
Labour Day is a Dreaded Bell in the Schoolyard of the Mind *(Harry Bruce)*
Listening to Boredom *(Joseph Brodsky)*
Living Like Weasels *(Annie Dillard)*
Marginal Men *(Barbara Ehrenreich)*
"On a Field, Sable, The Letter A, Gules" *(Neil McDonald)*
The Same Ticking Clock *(Carol Shields)*
The Time Factor *(Gloria Steinem)*
Where the World Began *(Margaret Laurence)*
You Can't Always Get Done What You Want *(Marjorie Kelly)*

Language and Literature
The Character of Hamlet's Mother *(Carolyn Heilbrun)*
"On a Field, Sable, The Letter A, Gules" *(Neil McDonald)*
Pandora Was a Feminist *(Mary Meigs)*
A Poet's Advice to Students *(e.e. cummings)*
The Same Ticking Clock *(Carol Shields)*
Shakespeare, Prince of Light *(Pablo Neruda)*
Shyly Slipping a Poem from the Purse *(Bronwen Wallace)*

The Natural World
Arks Can't Save Aardvarks *(Stan Rowe)*
Living Like Weasels *(Annie Dillard)*
Reply to the U.S. Government *(Chief Seattle)*
Seven Wonders *(Lewis Thomas)*
Thunderstrokes and Firebolts *(Janice McEwan)*

Where the World Began *(Margaret Laurence)*
Why Leaves Turn Color in the Fall *(Diane Ackerman)*

Relationships

Are There Any Questions? *(Robert Fulghum)*
Faces of the Enemy *(Sam Keen)*
Living Like Weasels *(Annie Dillard)*
The Monster *(Deems Taylor)*
My Home Is Not Broken, It Works *(Carol Kleiman)*
On Hating Piano Lessons *(Phyllis Theroux)*
Pandora Was a Feminist *(Mary Meigs)*
The Suit *(Norman Doidge)*

Science and Technology

Arks Can't Save Aardvarks *(Stan Rowe)*
Seven Wonders *(Lewis Thomas)*
Thunderstrokes and Firebolts *(Janice McEwan)*
Unreasonable Facsimile *(Frederick Allen)*

Societal Issues

Faces of the Enemy *(Sam Keen)*
Imelda *(Richard Selzer)*
In Selfish Pursuit *(Anthony Brandt)*
Instititutionalized Racism and Canadian History *(Adrienne Shadd)*
The Leering That Has to Stop *(Ann Fuller)*
Life as We Know It *(Michael Bérubé)*
Marginal Men *(Barbara Ehrenreich)*
Naked to Laughter when Leaves Fall *(Ray Guy)*
Reply to the U.S. Government *(Chief Seattle)*
The Suit *(Norman Doidge)*
Tiananmen *(Maggie Helwig)*
The Time Factor *(Gloria Steinem)*
Welfare was a Life Raft, but Now We Can Swim *(Barbara Hager)*

Values

The Almond Trees *(Albert Camus)*
Are There Any Questions? *(Robert Fulghum)*
Blasting Music to Drown Out Reality *(Sydney J. Harris)*
Faces of the Enemy *(Sam Keen)*
Imelda *(Richard Selzer)*
In Selfish Pursuit *(Anthony Brandt)*
Individual Liberty and Public Control *(Bertrand Russell)*
Life As We Know It *(Michael Bérubé)*
Marginal Men *(Barbara Ehrenreich)*
The Monster *(Deems Taylor)*
My Home Is Not Broken, It Works *(Carol Kleiman)*
Pandora Was a Feminist *(Mary Meigs)*
Reply to the U.S. Government *(Chief Seattle)*
The Time Factor *(Gloria Steinem)*
Welfare was a Life Raft, b ut Now We Can Swim *(Barbara Hager)*

Credits

Blasting Music to Drown Out Reality from PIECES OF EIGHT by Sydney J. Harris. Copyright © 1975, 1976, 1977, 1979, 1980, 1981 by The Chicago Daily news, The Chicago Sun-Times, Field Newspaper Syndicate, and Sydney J. Harris. Copyright © 1982 by Houghton Mifflin Co. Reprinted by permission of Houghton Mifflin Co. All rights reserved. **Living Like Weasels** from *Teaching a Stone to Talk* by Annie Dillard. Copyright © 1988 by Annie Dillard. Reprinted by permission of HarperCollins Publishers, Inc. **Where the World Began** from HEART OF A STRANGER by Margaret Laurence. Used by permission of the Canadian publishers McClelland & Stewart, Toronto. **Shyly Slipping a Poem from the Purse** by Bronwen Wallace is reprinted from ARGUMENTS WITH THE WORLD: ESSAYS by Bronwen Wallace, edited by Joanne Page, by permission of Quarry Press Inc. **Seven Wonders** copyright © 1983 by Lewis Thomas, from LATE NIGHT THOUGHTS ON LISTENING TO MAHLER'S NINTH by Lewis Thomas. Used by permission of Viking Penguin, a division of Penguin Books USA Inc. **Arks Can't Save Aardvarks** from *Home Place: Essays on Ecology* by Stan Rowe, reprinted with permission of NeWest Publishers Ltd., Edmonton. **In Bed** from THE WHITE ALBUM by Joan Didion. Copyright © 1979 by Joan Didion. Reprinted by permission of Farrar, Straus & Giroux, Inc. **The Leering That Has to Stop** Article by Ann Fuller. Reprinted by permission of The Globe and Mail. **Unreasonable Facsimile** The Atlantic Monthly, August '94. Reprinted by permission of the author. **The Same Ticking Clock** by Carol Shields reprinted with permission of Bella Pomer Agency Inc./Toronto, Ont. **"On a Field, Sable, the Letter A, Gules": Signs, Symbols, and Possession of Thought** by Neil McDonald first published in GRAIN, Volume 22, #3, Winter 1995. Reprinted with permission of the author. **Why Leaves Turn Color in the Fall** from A NATURAL HISTORY OF THE SENSES by Diane Ackerman. Copyright © 1990 by Diane Ackerman. Reprinted by permission of Random House, Inc. **Life as We Know It** by Michael Bérubé copyright © 1994 by Harper's Magazine. All rights reserved. Reproduced from the December issue by special permission. **Imelda** from *Letters to a Young Doctor*. Copyright © 1982 by David Goldman and Janet Selzer, Trustees. Reprinted by permission of Georges Borchardt, Inc. for the author. **A Poet's Advice to Students** is reprinted from A MISCELLANY REVISED by E.E. Cummings, Ed. George James Firmage, by permission of Liveright Publishing Corp. © 1955 by E.E. Cummings. © 1965 by Marion Morehouse Cummings. **The Character of Hamlet's Mother** reprinted by permission of Carolyn G. Heilbrun. Copyright © 1990 by Carolyn G. Heilbrun. **My Home Is Not Broken, It Works** by Carol Kleiman, originally published in Ms., is reprinted by permission of the author. Copyright © by Carol Kleiman. **Institutionalized Racism and Canadian History** by Adrienne Shadd reprinted by permission of the author. **In Selfish Pursuit** by Anthony Brandt from Esquire Magazine, March '84. Reprinted by permission of the author. **Welfare was a Life Raft, but Now We Can Swim** reprinted with permission of Barbara Hager/Métis writer. The Suit taken from Saturday Night Magazine, June '94. Reprinted by permission of Norman Doidge. **Are There Any Questions?** from IT WAS ON FIRE WHEN I LAY DOWN ON IT by Robert Fulghum. Copyright © 1988, 1989 by Robert Fulghum. Reprinted by permission of Villard Books, a division of Random House, Inc. **Naked to Laughter when Leaves Fall** by Ray Guy published with the permission of Breakwater, St. John's, Nfld. Copyright by the author. **Tiananmen** by Maggie Helwig reprinted from *Apocalypse Jazz* by permission of Oberon Press. **The Almond Trees** from LYRICAL AND CRITICAL ESSAYS by Albert Camus, trans., P. Thody. Copyright © 1968 by Alfred A. Knopf Inc. © 1967 by Hamish Hamilton Ltd. and Alfred A. Knopf Inc. Reprinted with permission. **The Time Factor** © Gloria Steinem, Ms. Magazine, March 1980.